BLADE RUNNER 2019

TITAN COMICS
ALCON PUBLISHING

Also Available:
Blade Runner 2019
Volume 1 – *Los Angeles*

Coming soon:
Blade Runner 2019
Volume 3 – *Home Again, Home Again* (Feb 2021)

DEDICATED TO:

The memory of the visual futurist, SYD MEAD, the American industrial designer, concept artist, and visionary who died on December 30th, 2019.

Special thanks to: Roger Servick for your invaluable assistance. Thank you Philip K. Dick, Ridley Scott, Hampton Fancher, David Peoples and Michael Deeley for creating such an incredible world.

BLADE RUNNER 2019: OFF-WORLD

SENIOR CREATIVE EDITOR | David Leach

TITAN COMICS

Managing Editor | MARTIN EDEN
Editorial Assistant | PHOEBE HEDGES
Production Controller | CATERINA FALQUI
Senior Production Controller | JACKIE FLOOK
Senior Designer | ANDREW LEUNG
Art Director | OZ BROWNE
Sales & Circulation Manager | STEVE TOTHILL
Marketing & Advertisement Assistant | LAUREN NODING

Direct Marketing Assistant | GEORGE WICKENDEN
Publicist | IMOGEN HARRIS
Marketing Manager | RICKY CLAYDON
Head Of Rights | JENNY BOYCE
Editorial Director | DUNCAN BAIZLEY
Operations Director | LEIGH BAULCH
Executive Director | VIVIAN CHEUNG
Publisher | NICK LANDAU

ALCON PUBLISHING

Director/Editor | JEFF CONNER
COO/CFO | SCOTT PARISH
Legal/Business Affairs | JEANNETTE HILL
Publishers | ANDREW KOSOVE & BRODERICK JOHNSON

BLADE RUNNER 2019: OFF-WORLD
JULY 2020. Published by Titan Comics, a division of Titan Publishing Group, Ltd. 144 Southwark Street, London SE1 0UP. Titan Comics is a registered trademark of Titan Publishing Group, Ltd. All rights reserved. Copyright ©2020 – *Blade Runner 2019* and all related marks and characters are trademarks and copyrights of Alcon Publishing ®. All rights reserved. Licensed by Alcon Publishing ®. All Rights Reserved.

Published by Titan Comics, a division of Titan Publishing Group, Ltd. Titan Comics is a registered trademark of Titan Publishing Group, Ltd. 144 Southwark Street, London SE1 0UP

STANDARD EDITION ISBN 9781787731929
FORBIDDEN PLANET EDITION ISBN 9781787735804

A CIP catalogue for this title is available from the British Library.

First Edition September 2020
10 9 8 7 6 5 4 3 2 1
Printed in Spain

www.titan-comics.com
Follow us on twitter@ComicsTitan | Visit us at facebook.com/comicstitan
For rights information contact: jenny.boyce@titanemail.com

BLADE RUNNER 2019

OFF-WORLD

WRITTEN BY

MICHAEL GREEN
& MIKE JOHNSON

ART BY

ANDRES GUINALDO

COLORS BY

MARCO LESKO

LETTERING BY

JIM CAMPBELL

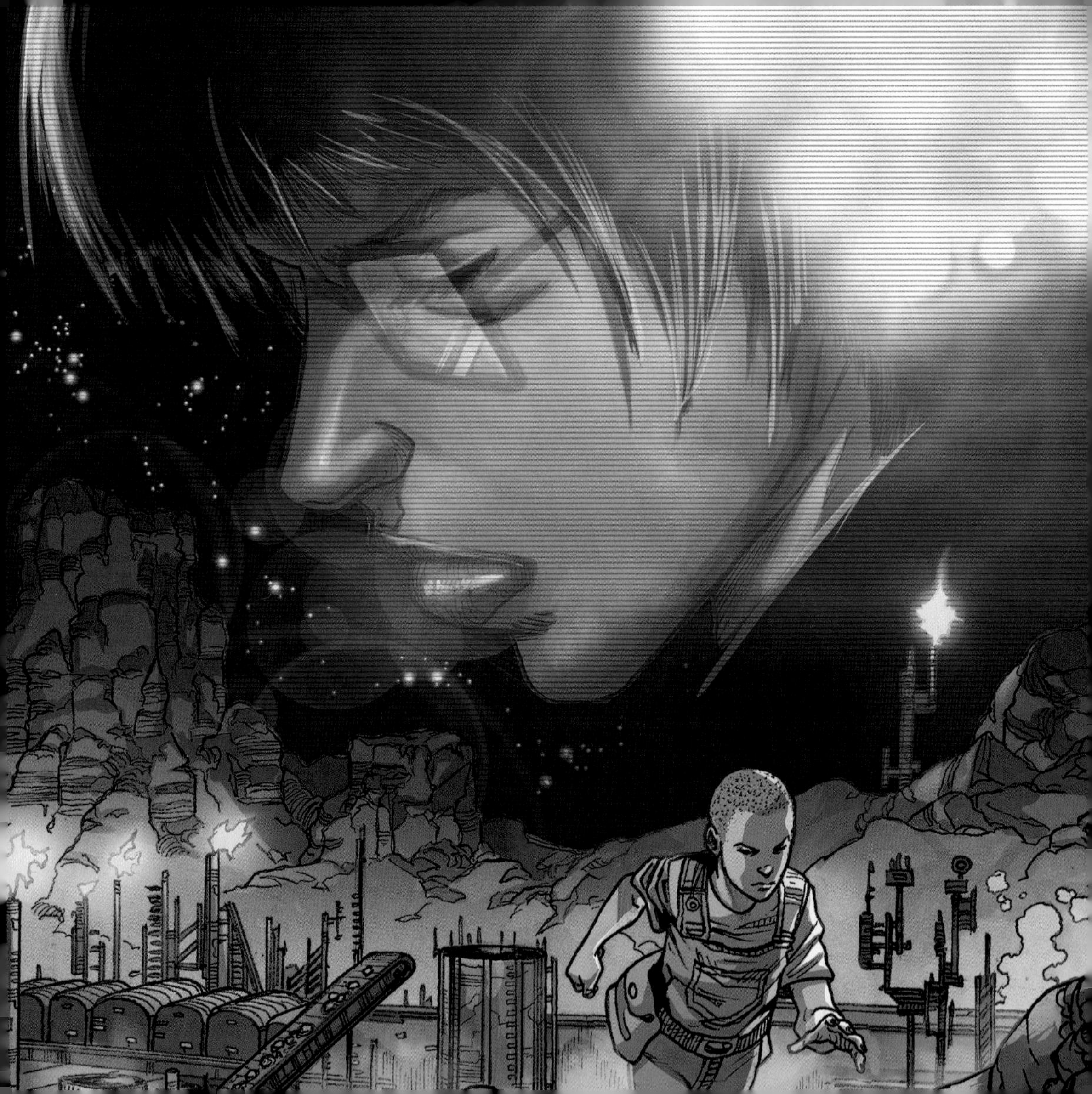

EARLY IN THE 21ST CENTURY, THE TYRELL CORPORATION
ADVANCED ROBOT EVOLUTION INTO THE NEXUS PHASE
– CREATING ARTIFICIAL BEINGS VIRTUALLY IDENTICAL TO
HUMANS – KNOWN AS REPLICANTS.

AFTER A BLOODY MUTINY BY A NEXUS 6 COMBAT TEAM IN AN
OFF-WORLD COLONY, REPLICANTS WERE DECLARED ILLEGAL
ON EARTH – UNDER PENALTY OF DEATH.

SPECIAL POLICE SQUADS – BLADE RUNNER UNITS – HAD
ORDERS TO SHOOT TO KILL, UPON DETECTION, ANY
TRESPASSING REPLICANT.

IN 2019, THE BLADE RUNNER AAHNA 'ASH' ASHINA RESCUED
CLEO SELWYN, DAUGHTER OF THE AGRIBUSINESS TYCOON
ALEXANDER SELWYN, FROM A PLOT TO GIVE THE GIRL TO THE
TYRELL CORPORATION FOR GENETIC EXPERIMENTATION.

ASH ESCAPED LOS ANGELES WITH CLEO AND DISAPPEARED.

IN 2022, REPLICANT PRODUCTION WAS BANNED ALTOGETHER.
REMAINING NEXUS 8 UNITS WERE PERMITTED TO LIVE
OUT THEIR LIFESPANS IN SERVICE TO THEIR OWNERS
IN THE COLONIES...

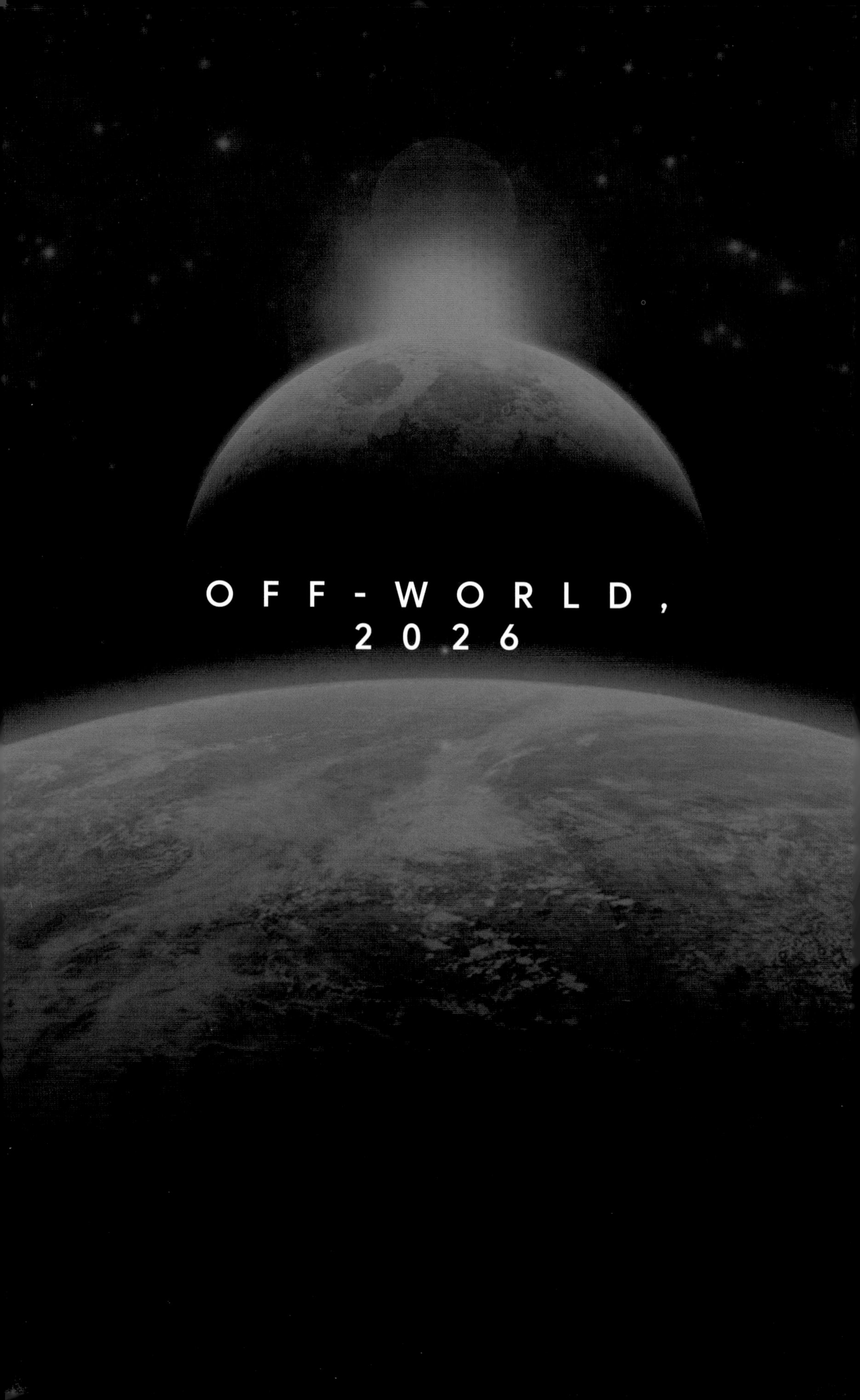
OFF-WORLD,
2026

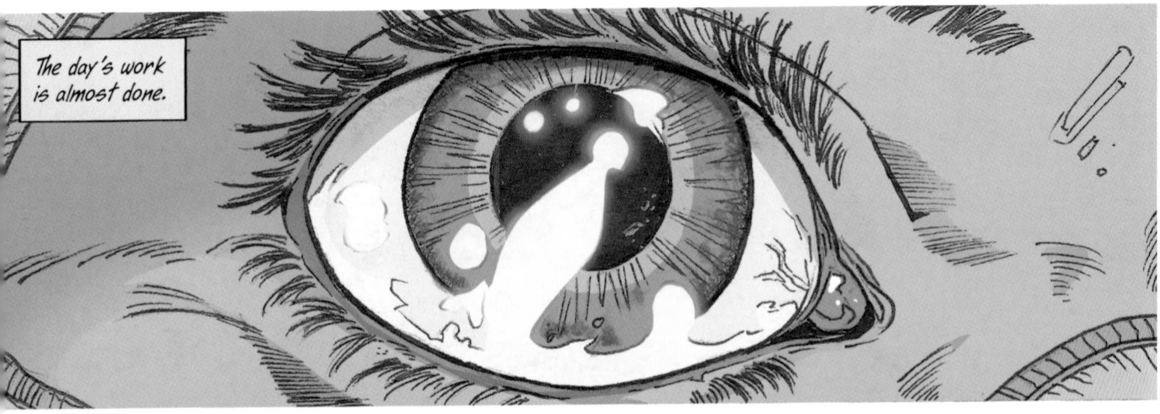
The day's work is almost done.

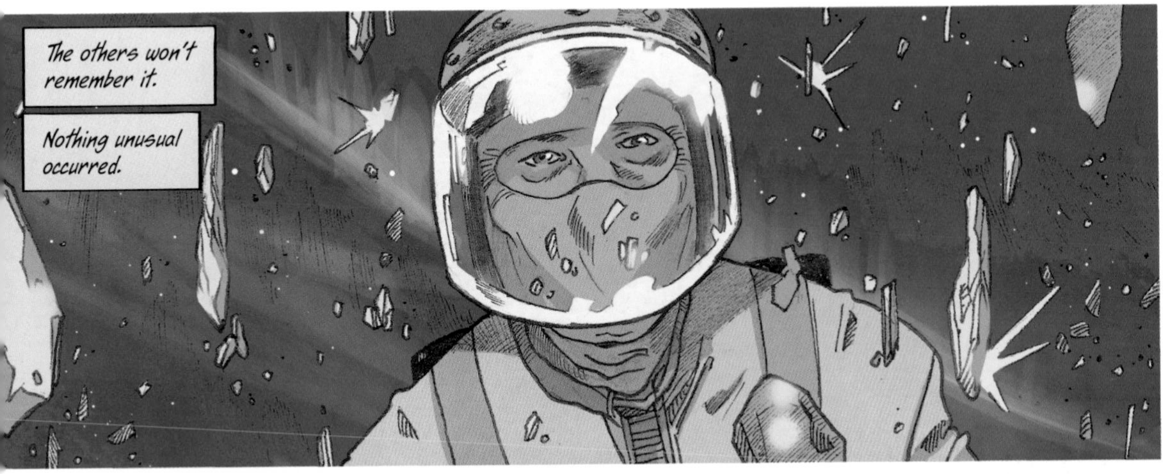
The others won't remember it.
Nothing unusual occurred.

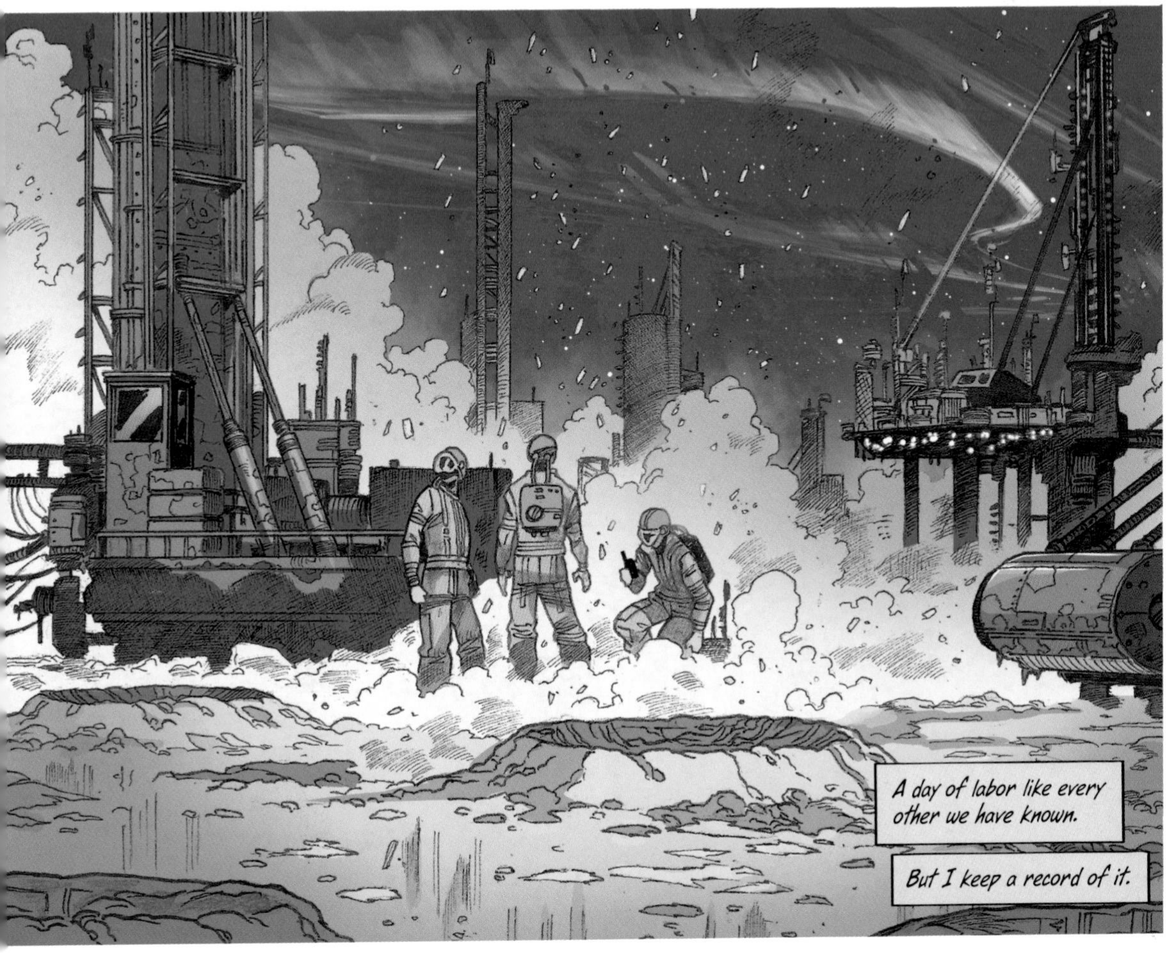
A day of labor like every other we have known.
But I keep a record of it.

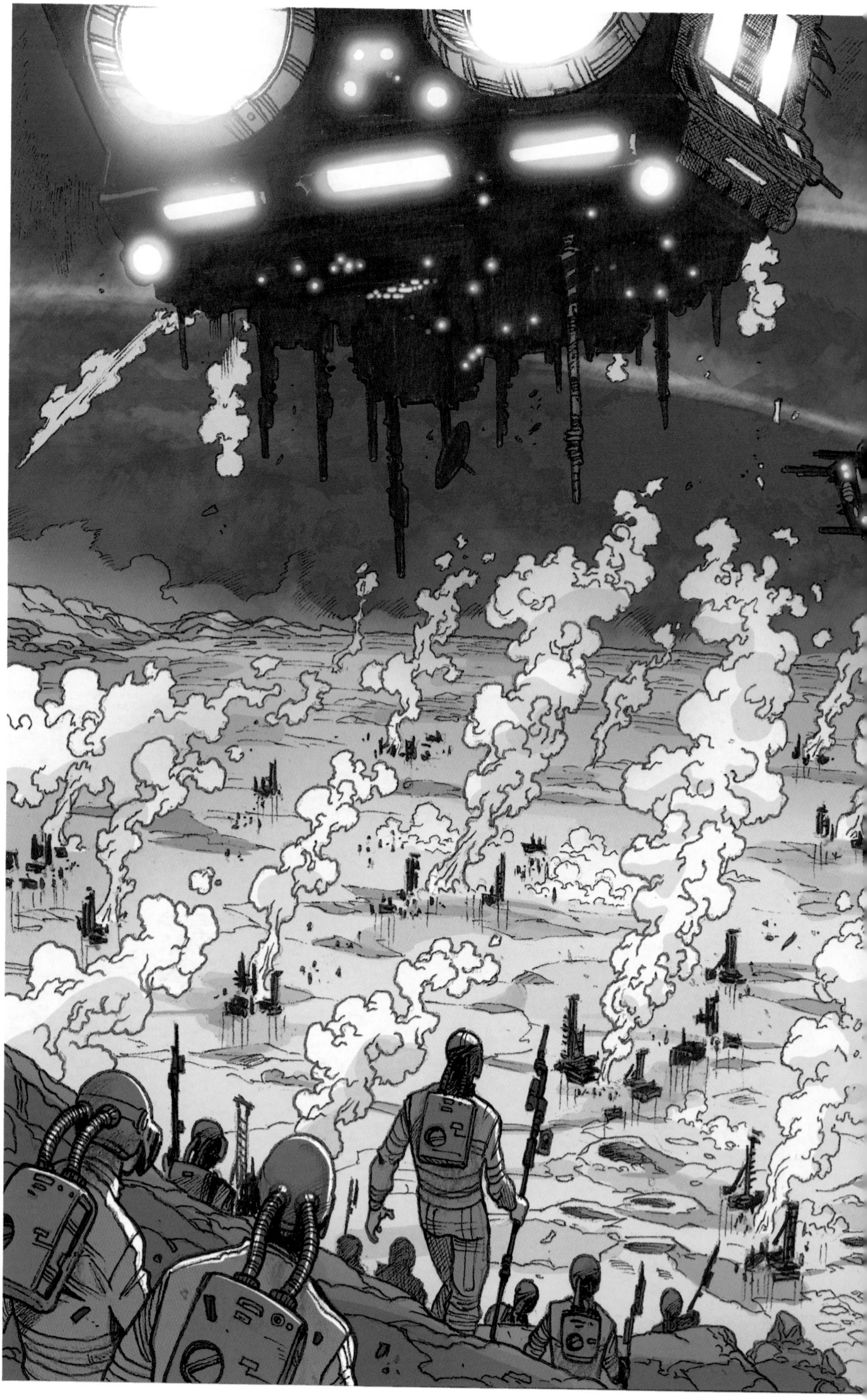

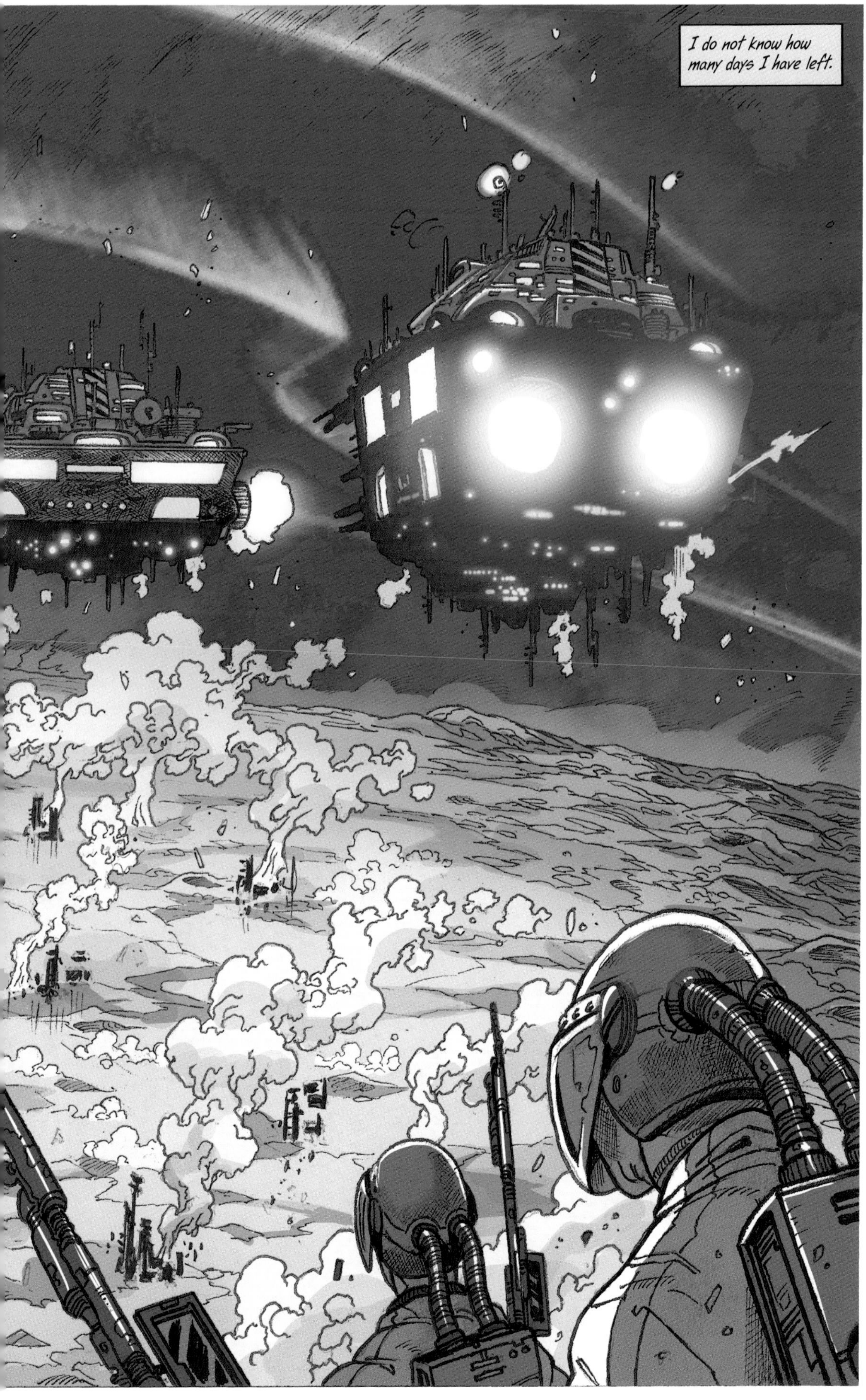
I do not know how many days I have left.

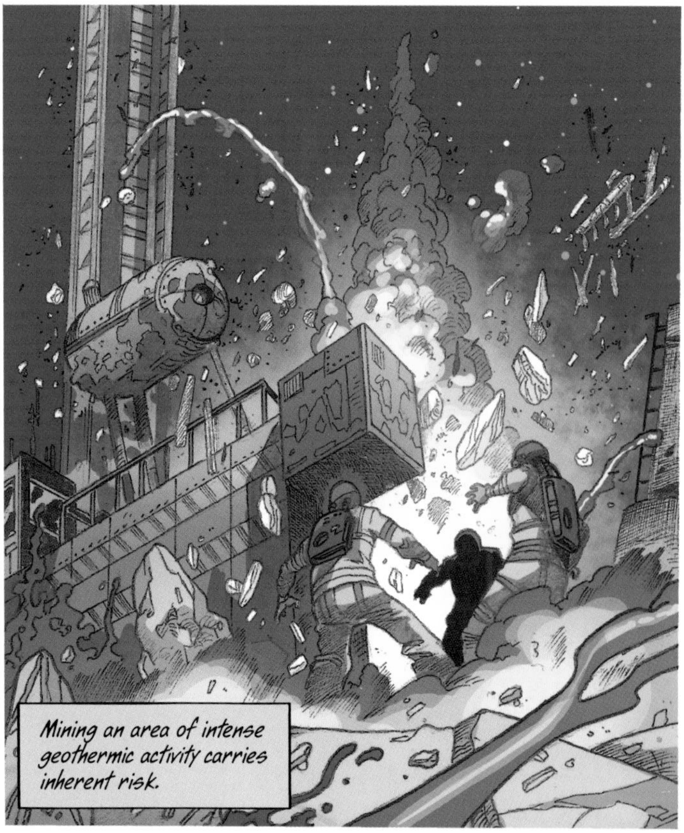
Mining an area of intense geothermic activity carries inherent risk.

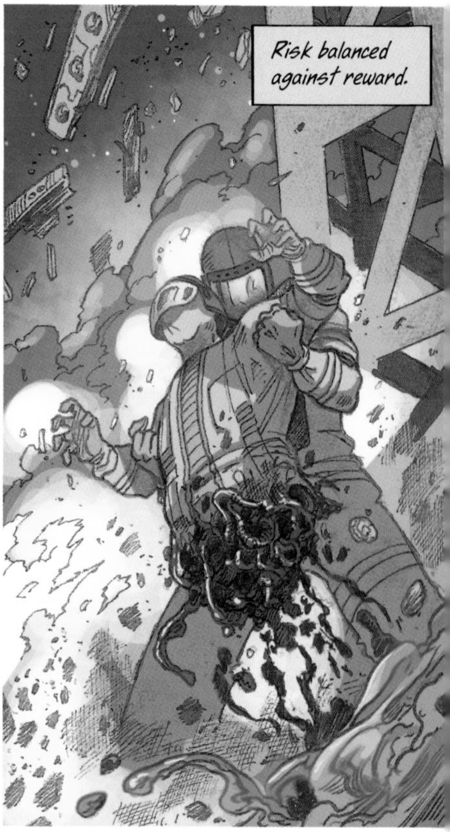
Risk balanced against reward.

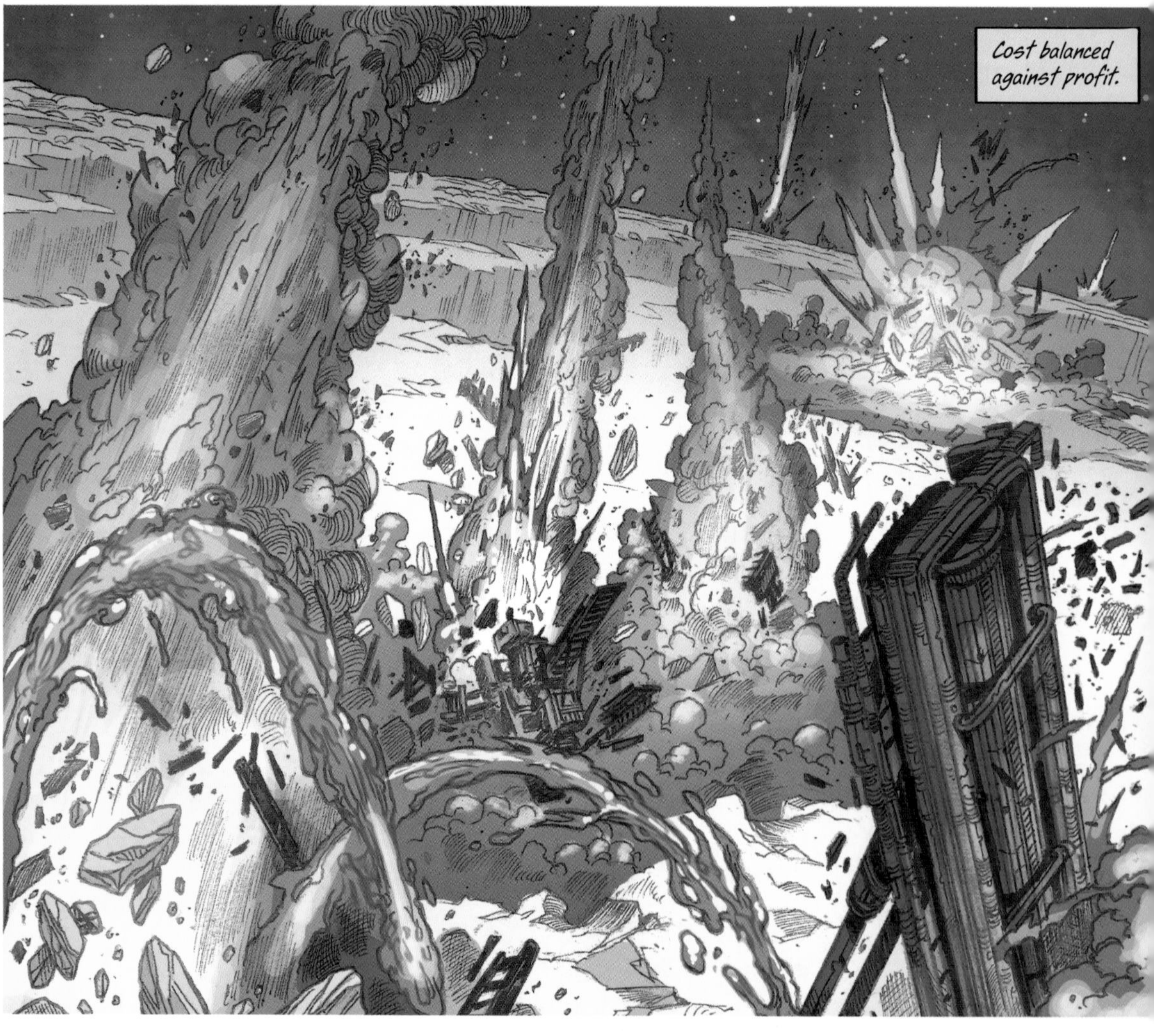
Cost balanced against profit.

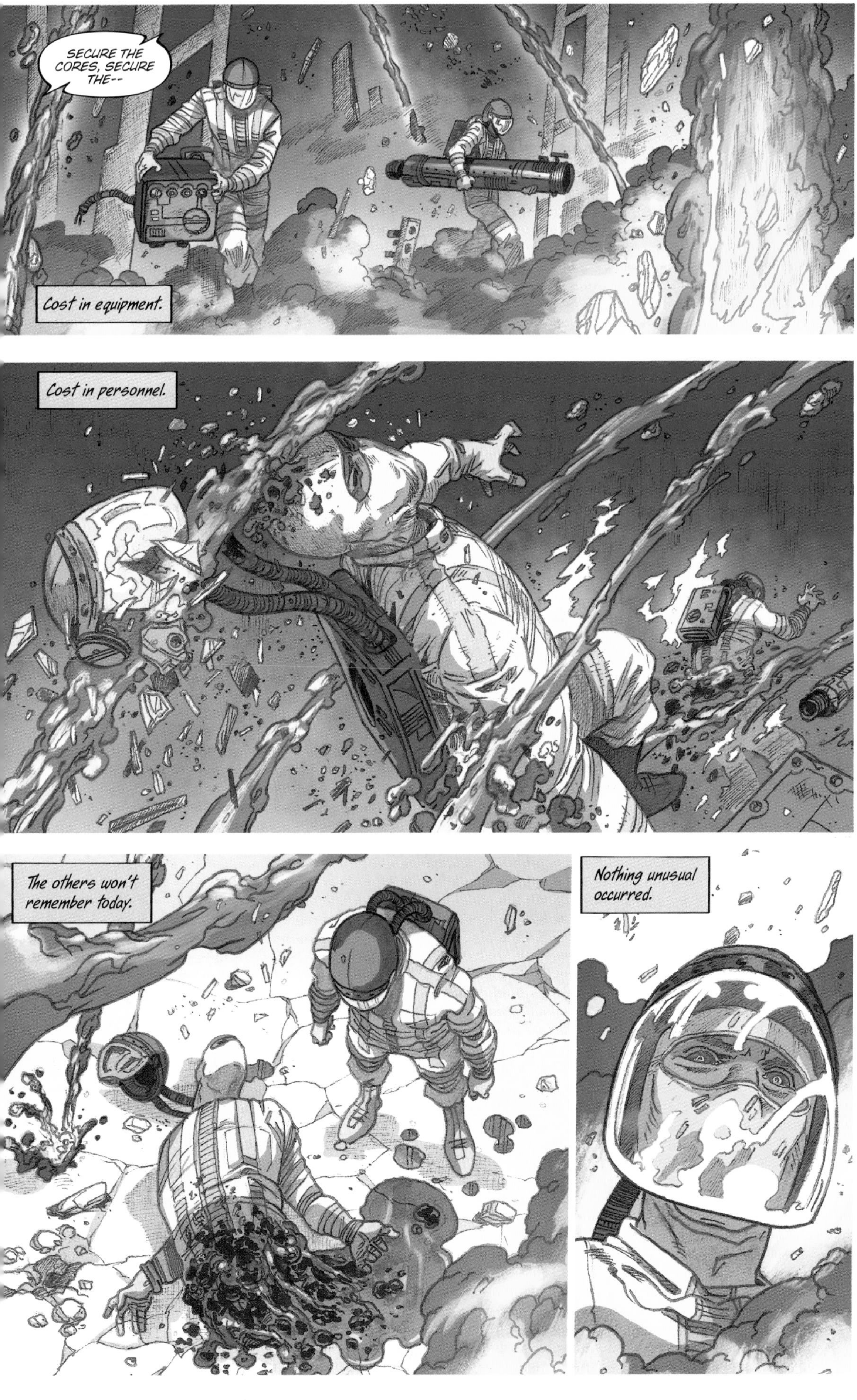
SECURE THE CORES, SECURE THE--
Cost in equipment.
Cost in personnel.
The others won't remember today.
Nothing unusual occurred.

Quarantine.

Sustenance.

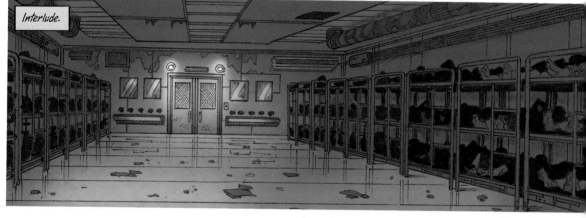

Interlude.

And for myself, reflection.

Routine...

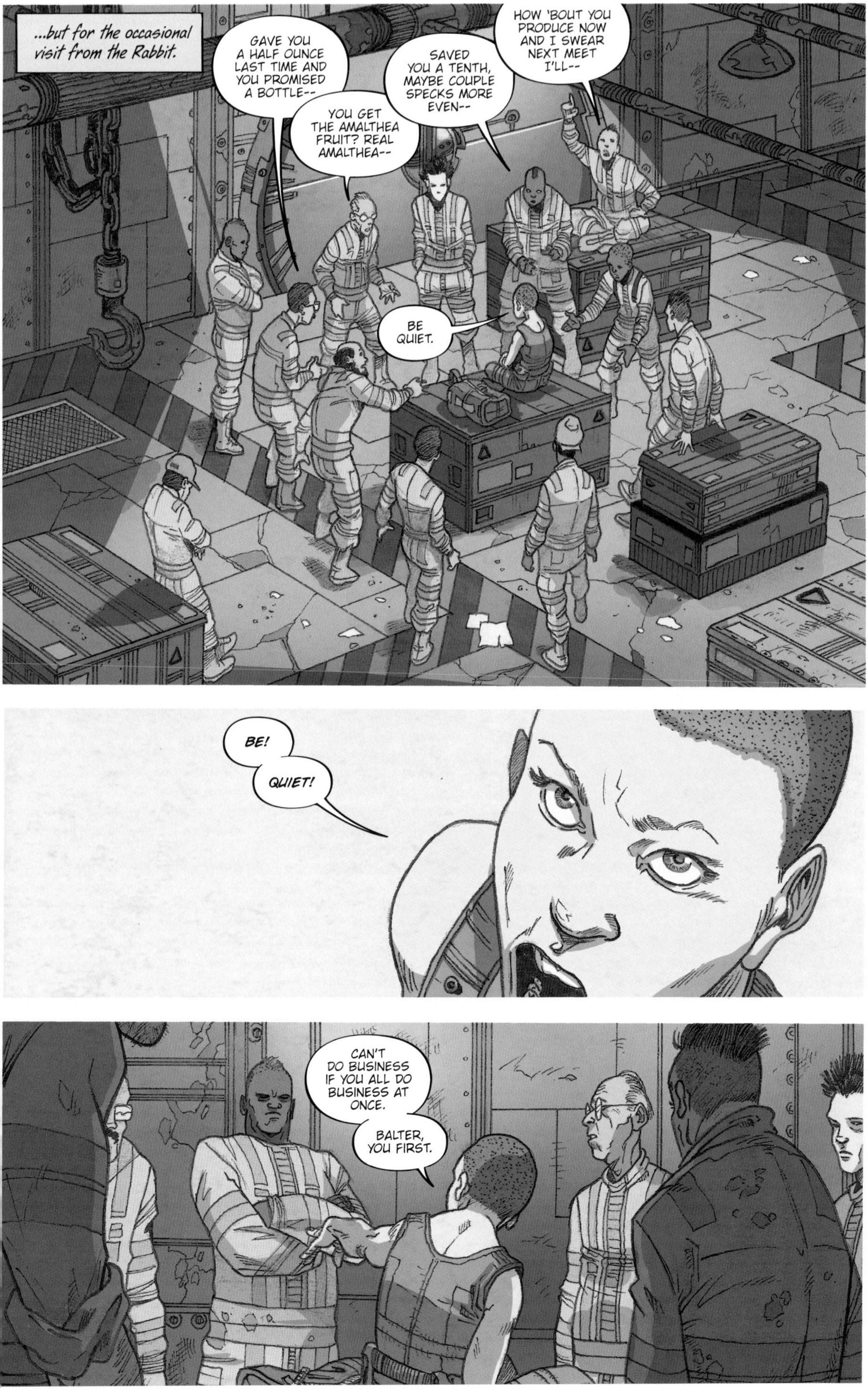
...but for the occasional visit from the Rabbit.
GAVE YOU A HALF OUNCE LAST TIME AND YOU PROMISED A BOTTLE--
YOU GET THE AMALTHEA FRUIT? REAL AMALTHEA--
SAVED YOU A TENTH, MAYBE COUPLE SPECKS MORE EVEN--
HOW 'BOUT YOU PRODUCE NOW AND I SWEAR NEXT MEET I'LL--
BE QUIET.
BE!
QUIET!
CAN'T DO BUSINESS IF YOU ALL DO BUSINESS AT ONCE.
BALTER, YOU FIRST.

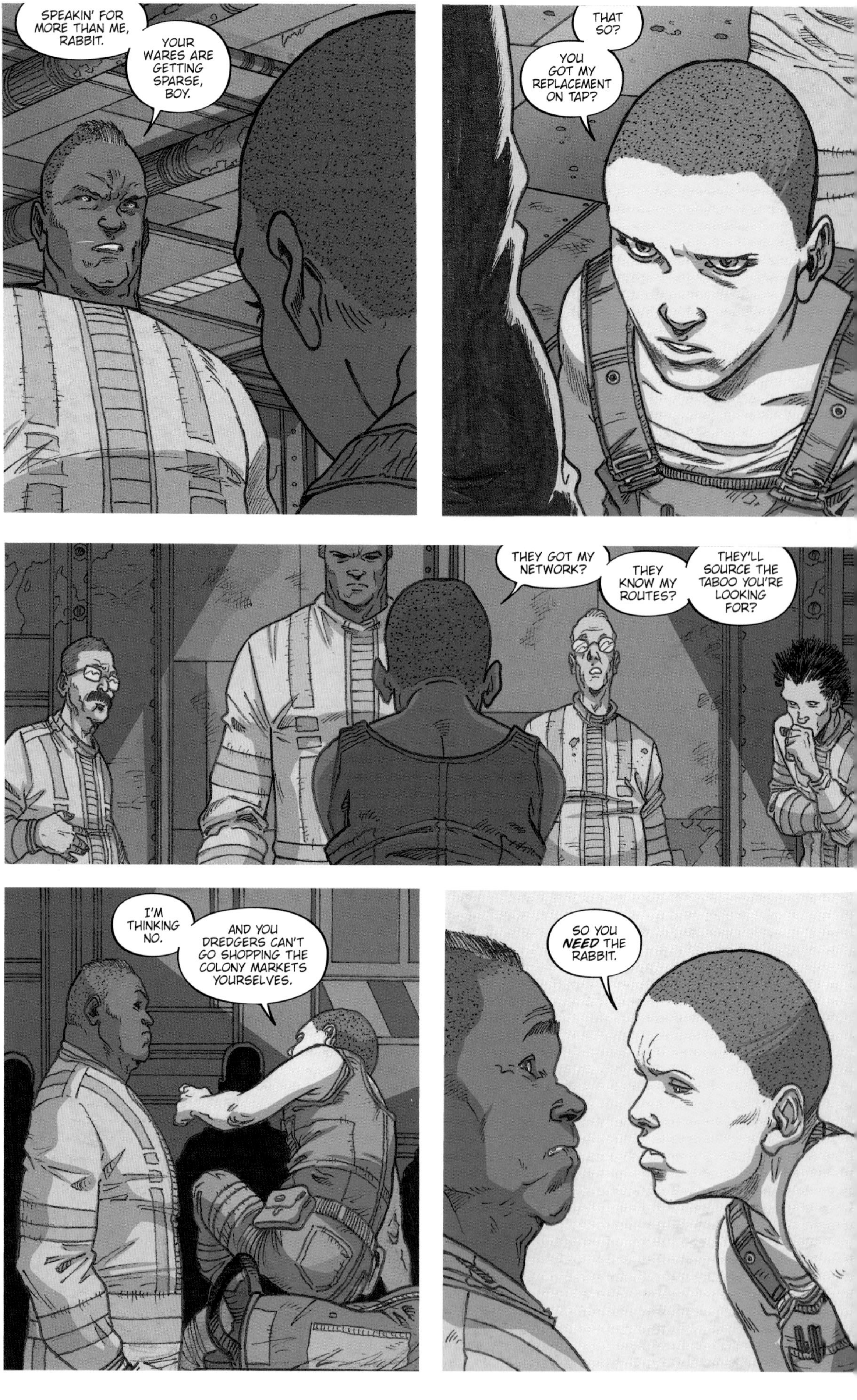
SPEAKIN' FOR MORE THAN ME, RABBIT.
YOUR WARES ARE GETTING SPARSE, BOY.
THAT SO?
YOU GOT MY REPLACEMENT ON TAP?
THEY GOT MY NETWORK?
THEY KNOW MY ROUTES?
THEY'LL SOURCE THE TABOO YOU'RE LOOKING FOR?
I'M THINKING NO.
AND YOU DREDGERS CAN'T GO SHOPPING THE COLONY MARKETS YOURSELVES.
SO YOU *NEED* THE RABBIT.

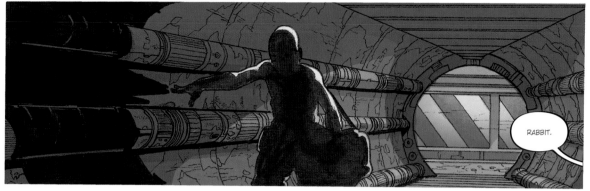

RABBIT.

UH-UH, PADRAIC. BARTER'S DONE TODAY.

NO BARTER.

GIFT.

MORE SHINE THAN I WANT THE OTHERS TO KNOW I CAUGHT.

NO SUCH THING AS A GIFT.

NAME YOUR SWAP.

...

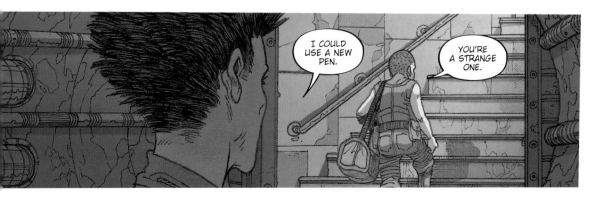

I COULD USE A NEW PEN.

YOU'RE A STRANGE ONE.

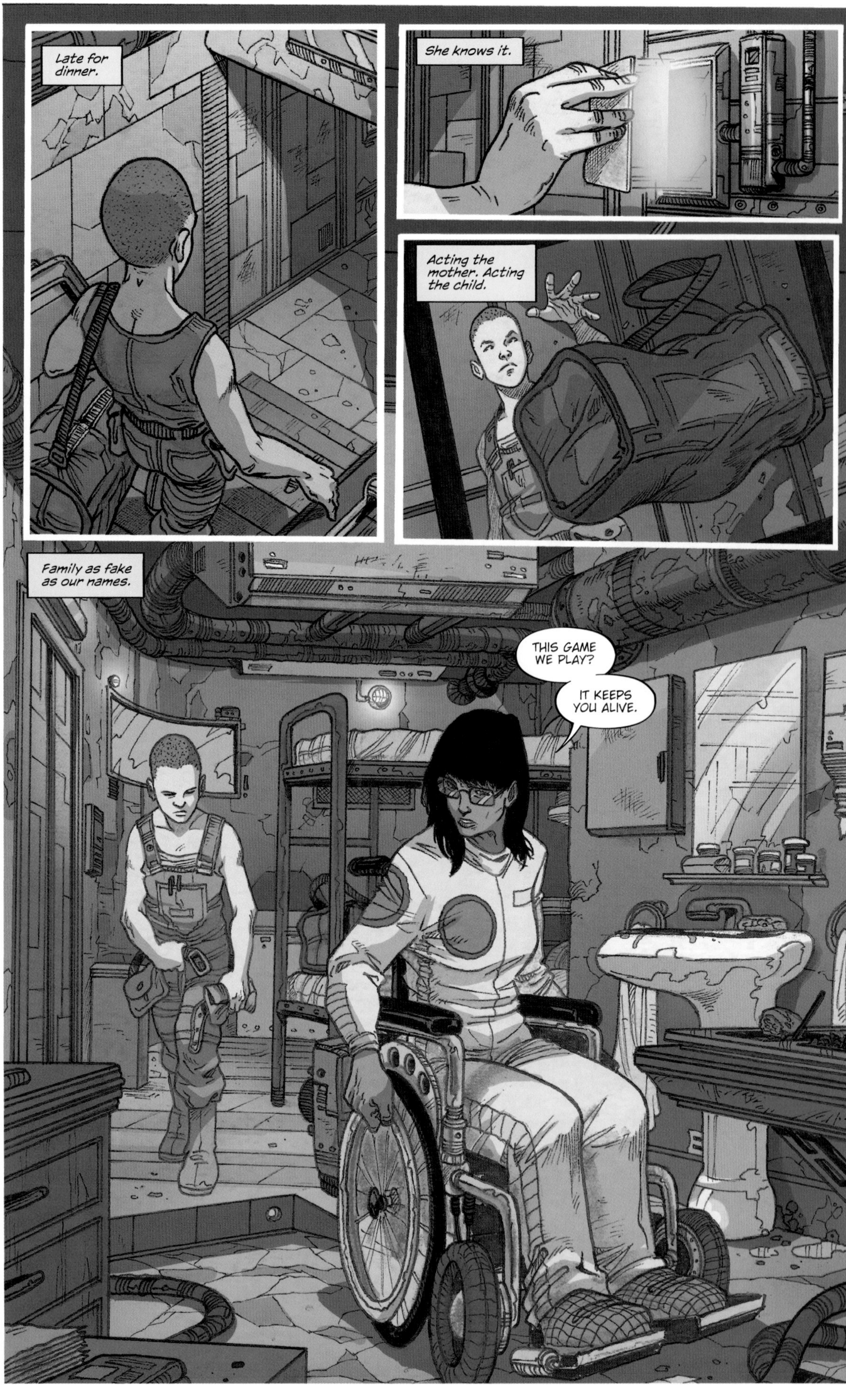
Late for dinner.
She knows it.
Acting the mother. Acting the child.
Family as fake as our names.
THIS GAME WE PLAY?
IT KEEPS YOU ALIVE.

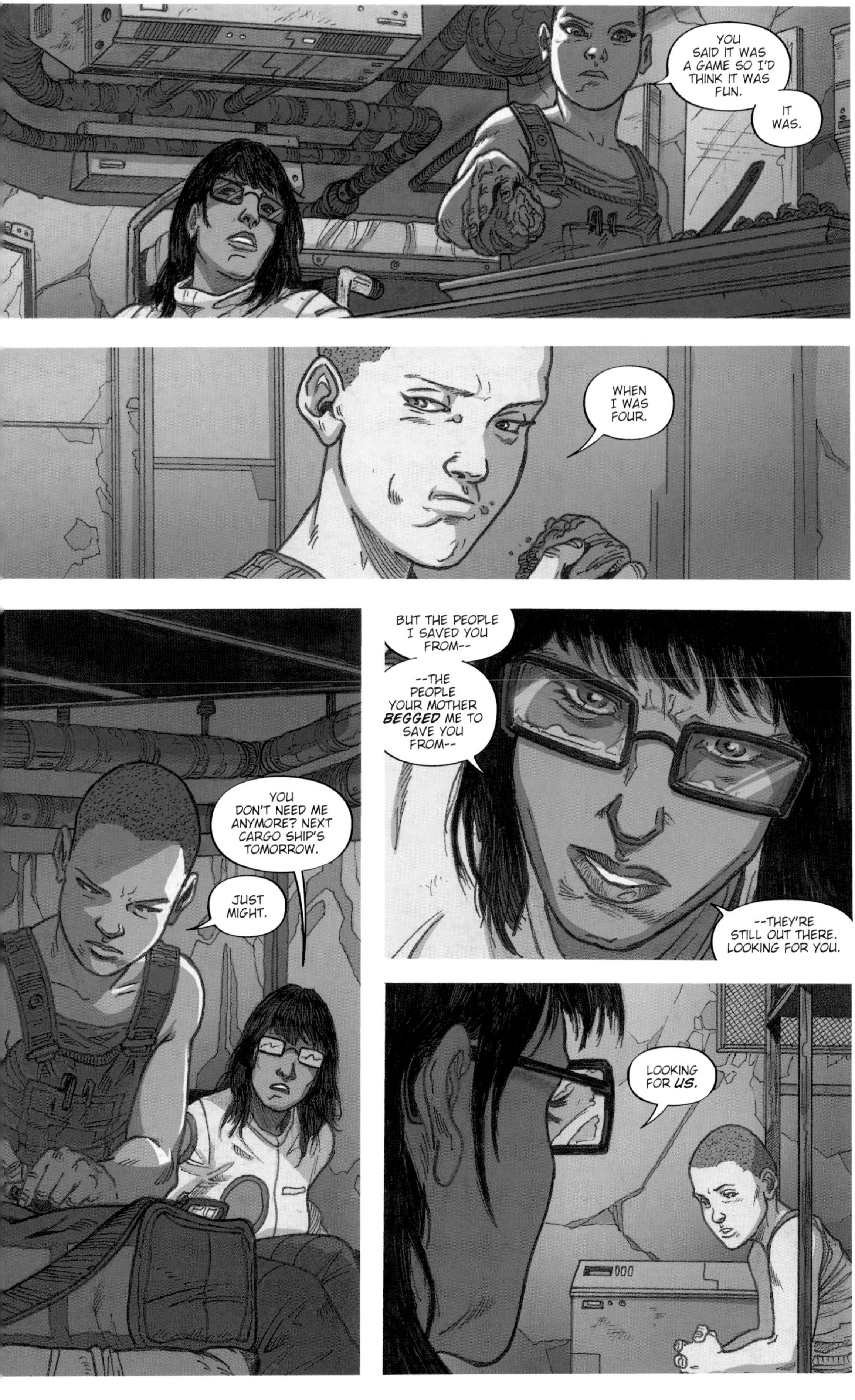
YOU SAID IT WAS A GAME SO I'D THINK IT WAS FUN.
IT WAS.
WHEN I WAS FOUR.
YOU DON'T NEED ME ANYMORE? NEXT CARGO SHIP'S TOMORROW.
JUST MIGHT.
BUT THE PEOPLE I SAVED YOU FROM--
--THE PEOPLE YOUR MOTHER *BEGGED* ME TO SAVE YOU FROM--
--THEY'RE STILL OUT THERE. LOOKING FOR YOU.
LOOKING FOR *US.*

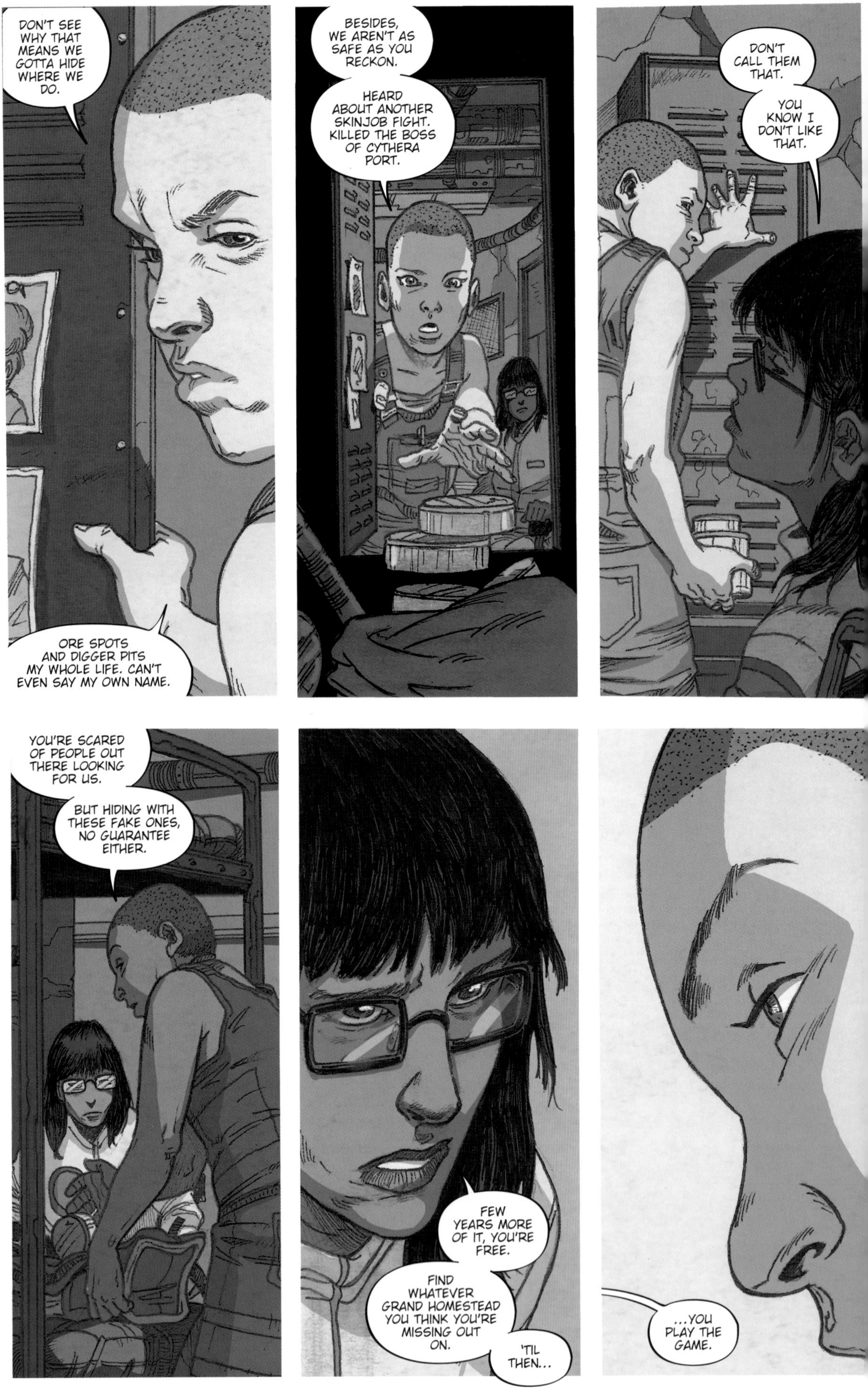
DON'T SEE WHY THAT MEANS WE GOTTA HIDE WHERE WE DO.
ORE SPOTS AND DIGGER PITS MY WHOLE LIFE. CAN'T EVEN SAY MY OWN NAME.
BESIDES, WE AREN'T AS SAFE AS YOU RECKON.
HEARD ABOUT ANOTHER SKINJOB FIGHT. KILLED THE BOSS OF CYTHERA PORT.
DON'T CALL THEM THAT.
YOU KNOW I DON'T LIKE THAT.
YOU'RE SCARED OF PEOPLE OUT THERE LOOKING FOR US.
BUT HIDING WITH THESE FAKE ONES, NO GUARANTEE EITHER.
FEW YEARS MORE OF IT, YOU'RE FREE.
FIND WHATEVER GRAND HOMESTEAD YOU THINK YOU'RE MISSING OUT ON.
'TIL THEN...
...YOU PLAY THE GAME.

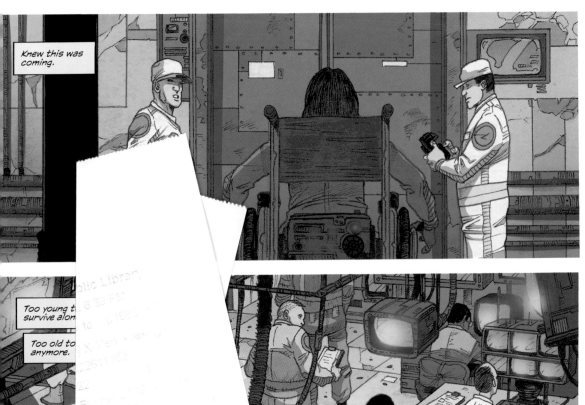

Knew this was coming.

Too young to survive alone.

Too old to anymore.

Maybe it's time.

MS. KADY, I NEED YOUR SIG ON THIS OUTPUT BATCH!

Let her have her name.

FIND ME A PEN, ROBBENS?

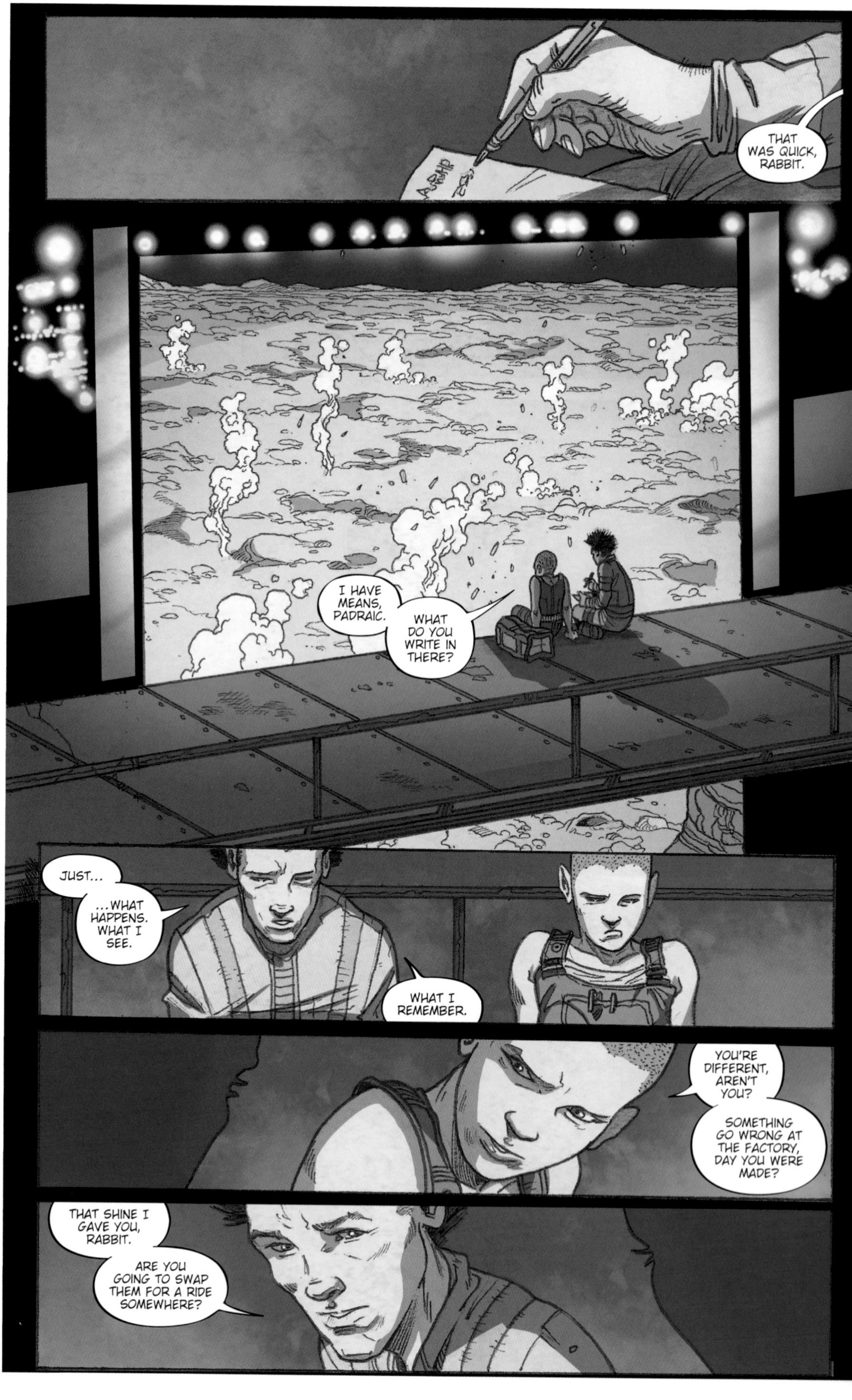
THAT WAS QUICK, RABBIT.
I HAVE MEANS, PADRAIC.
WHAT DO YOU WRITE IN THERE?
JUST...
...WHAT HAPPENS. WHAT I SEE.
WHAT I REMEMBER.
YOU'RE DIFFERENT, AREN'T YOU?
SOMETHING GO WRONG AT THE FACTORY, DAY YOU WERE MADE?
THAT SHINE I GAVE YOU, RABBIT.
ARE YOU GOING TO SWAP THEM FOR A RIDE SOMEWHERE?

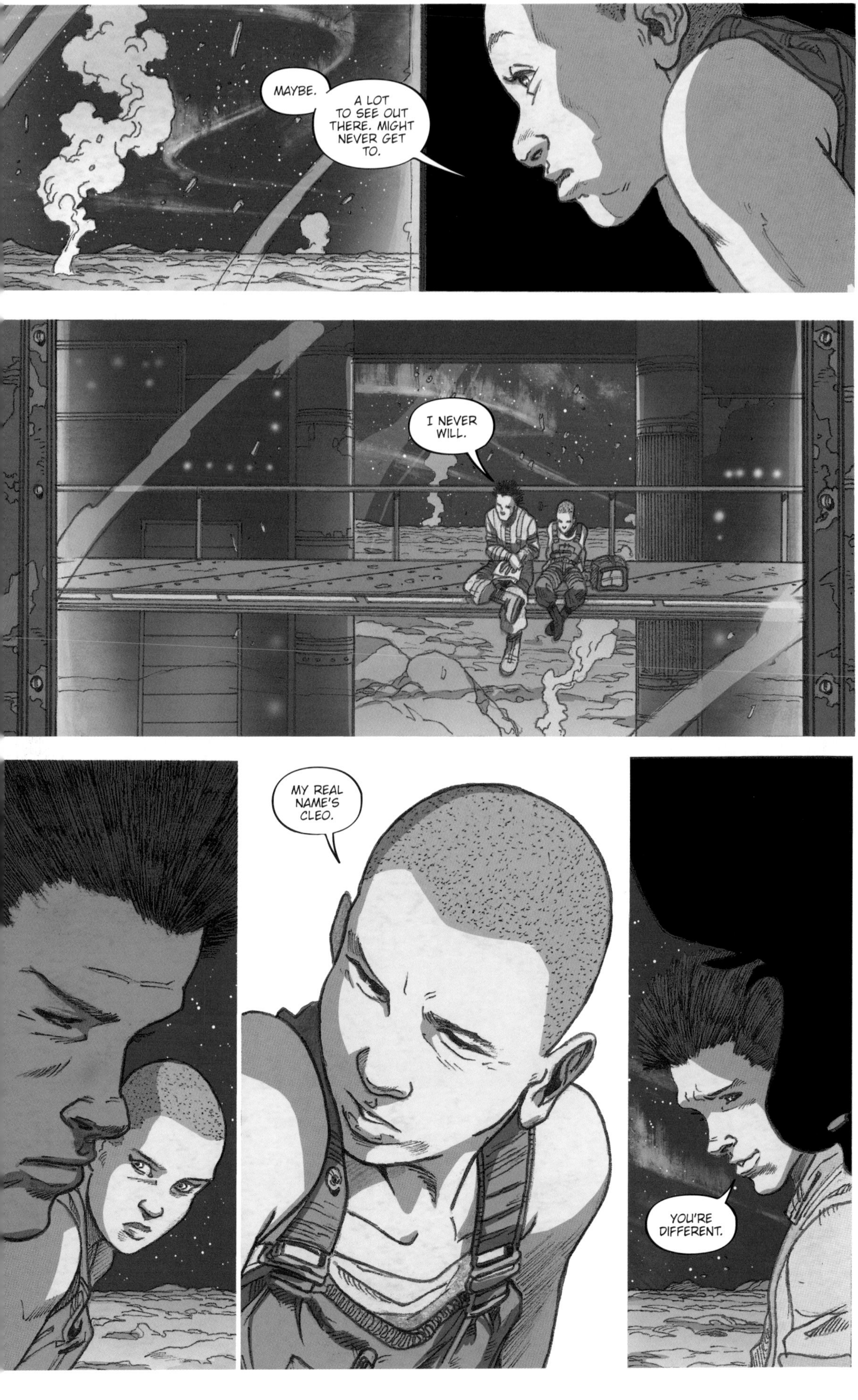
MAYBE.
A LOT TO SEE OUT THERE. MIGHT NEVER GET TO.
I NEVER WILL.
MY REAL NAME'S CLEO.
YOU'RE DIFFERENT.

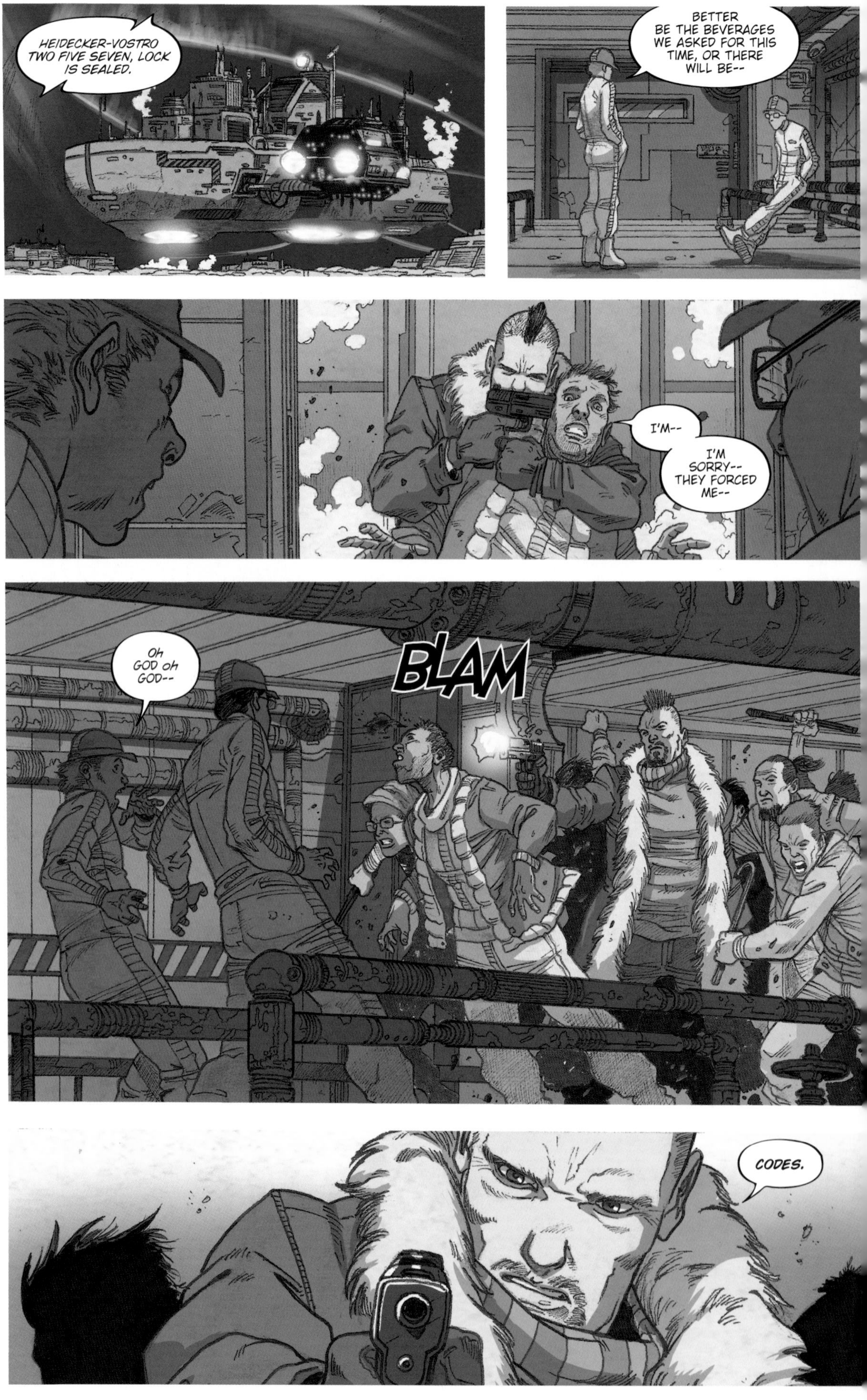
HEIDECKER-VOSTRO TWO FIVE SEVEN, LOCK IS SEALED.
BETTER BE THE BEVERAGES WE ASKED FOR THIS TIME, OR THERE WILL BE--
I'M--
I'M SORRY-- THEY FORCED ME--
Oh GOD oh GOD--
BLAM
CODES.

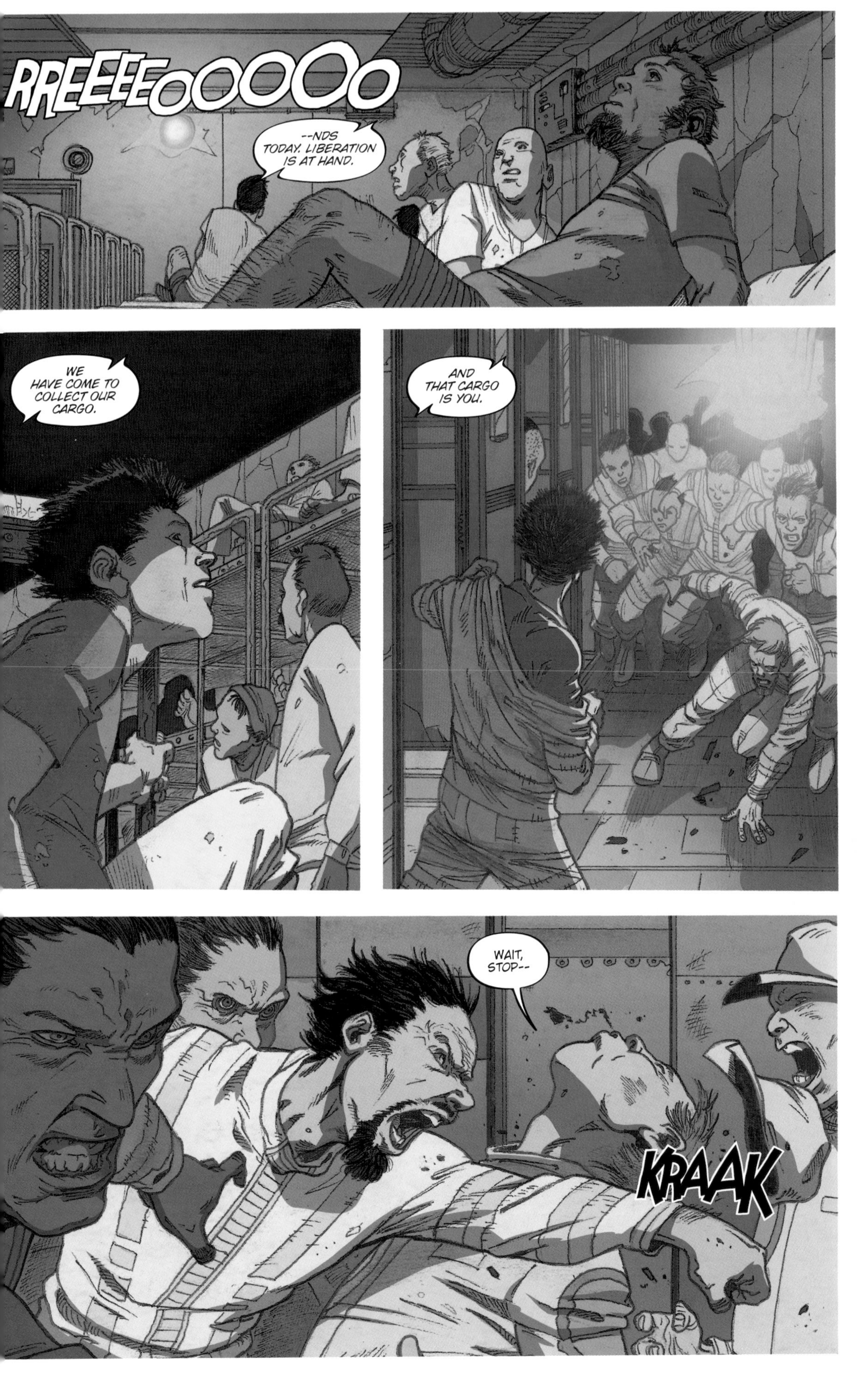
RREEEEOOOOOO
--NDS TODAY. LIBERATION IS AT HAND.
WE HAVE COME TO COLLECT OUR CARGO.
AND THAT CARGO IS YOU.
WAIT, STOP--
KRAAK

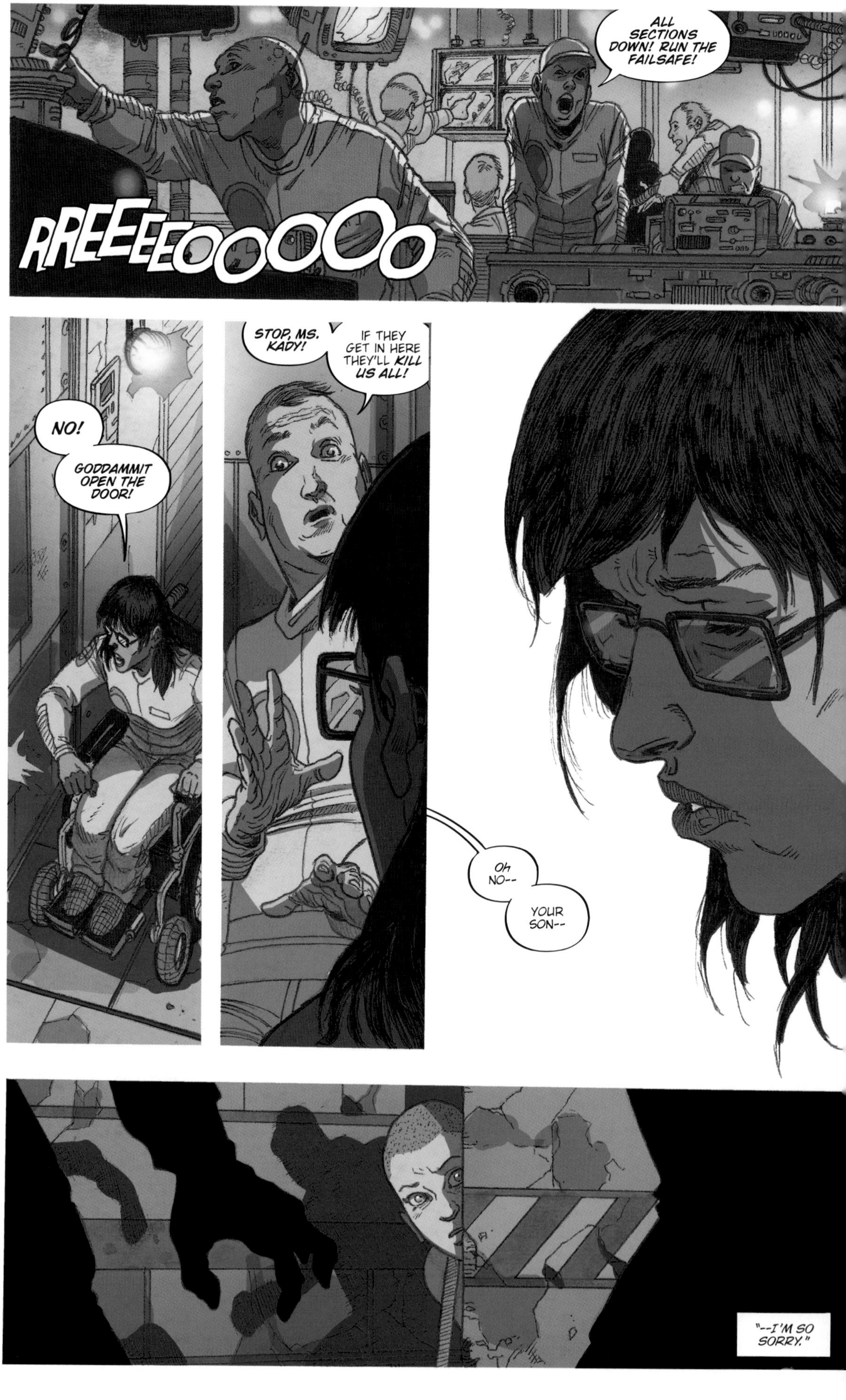
ALL SECTIONS DOWN! RUN THE FAILSAFE!
RREEEEEOOOOOO
NO!
GODDAMMIT OPEN THE DOOR!
STOP, MS. KADY!
IF THEY GET IN HERE THEY'LL KILL US ALL!
OH NO--
YOUR SON--
"--I'M SO SORRY."

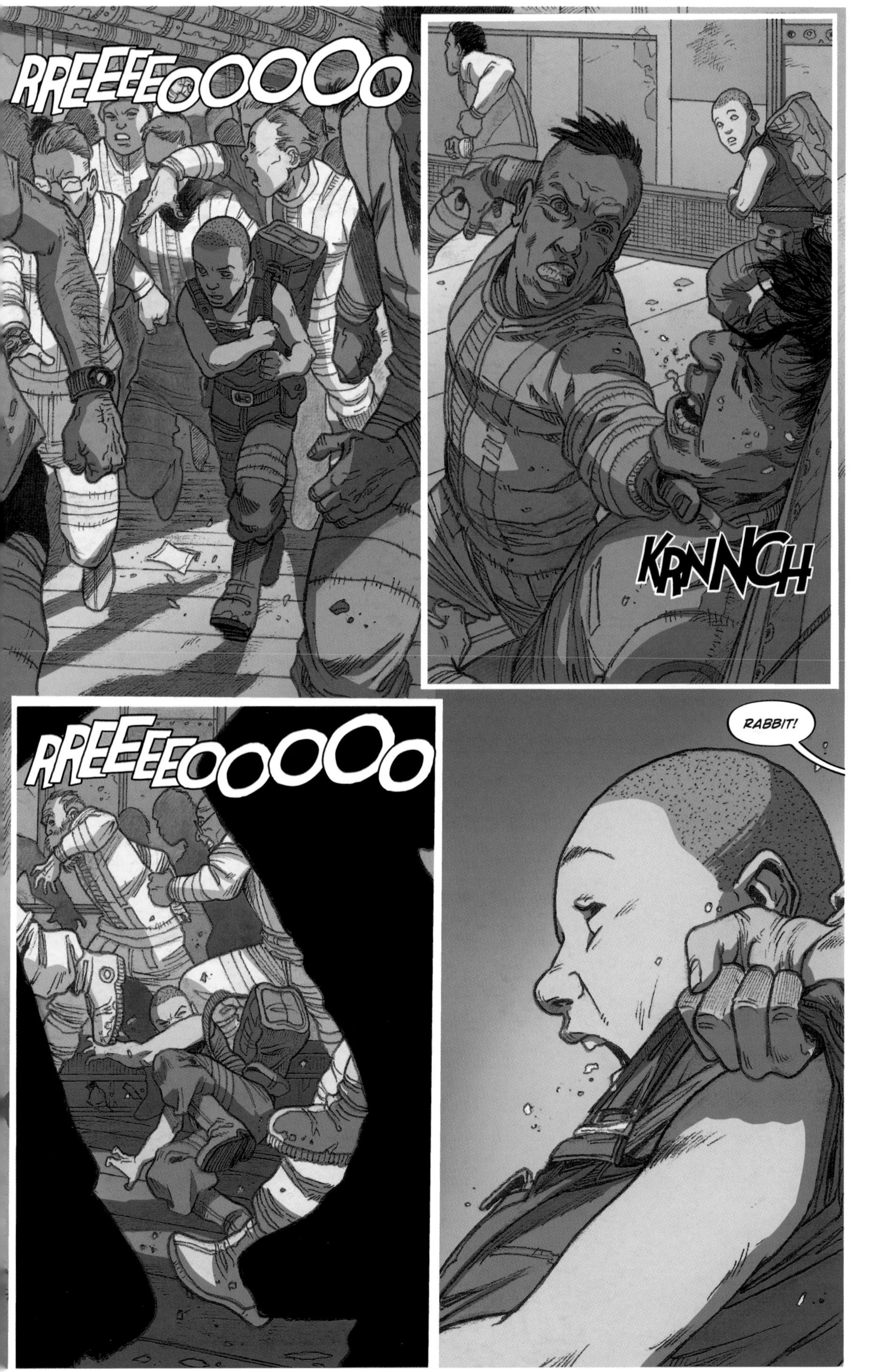
RREEEEEOOOOOo
KRNNCH
RREEEEEOOOOOo
RABBIT!

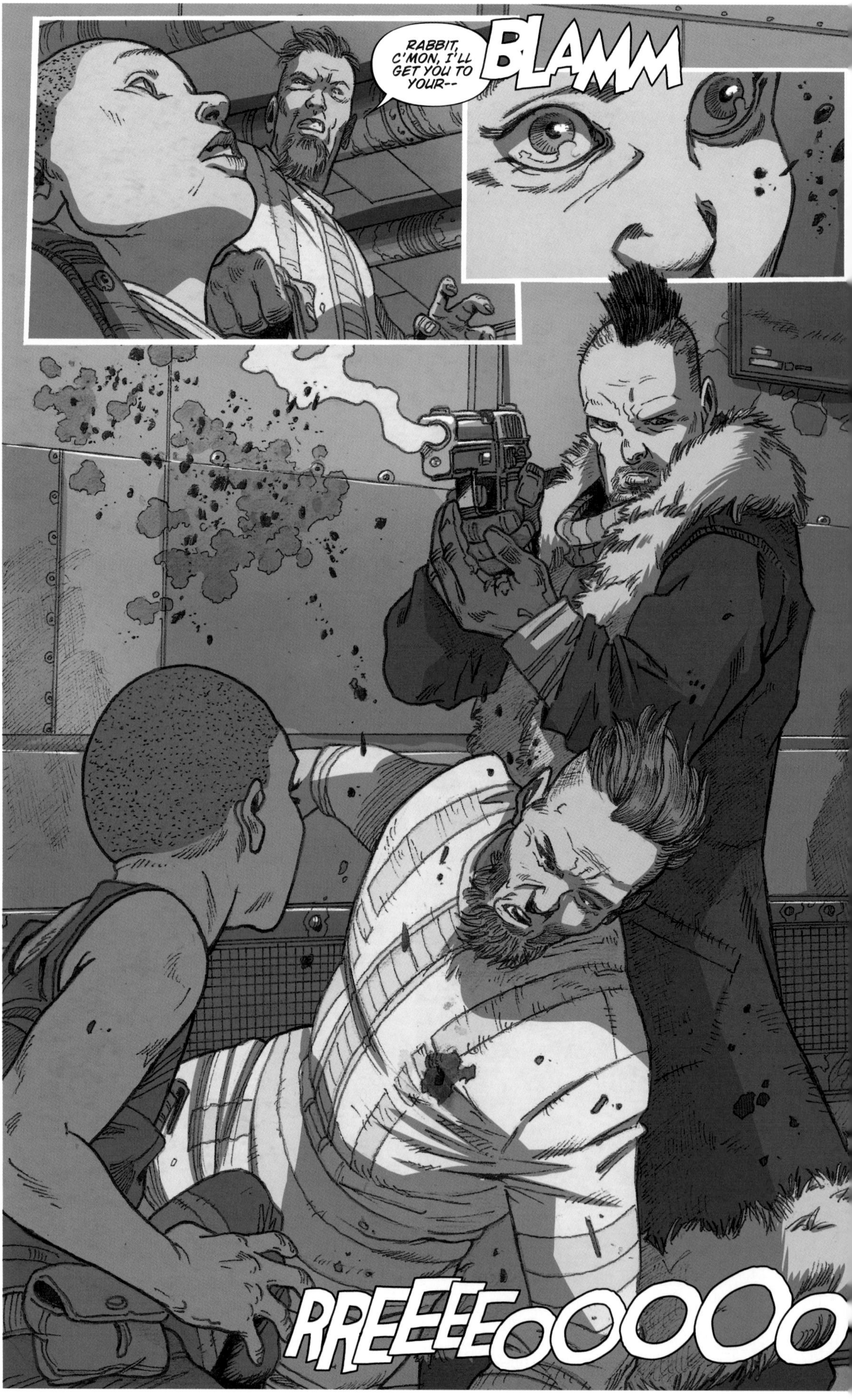
RABBIT, C'MON, I'LL GET YOU TO YOUR--
BLAMM
RREEEEEOOOOOO

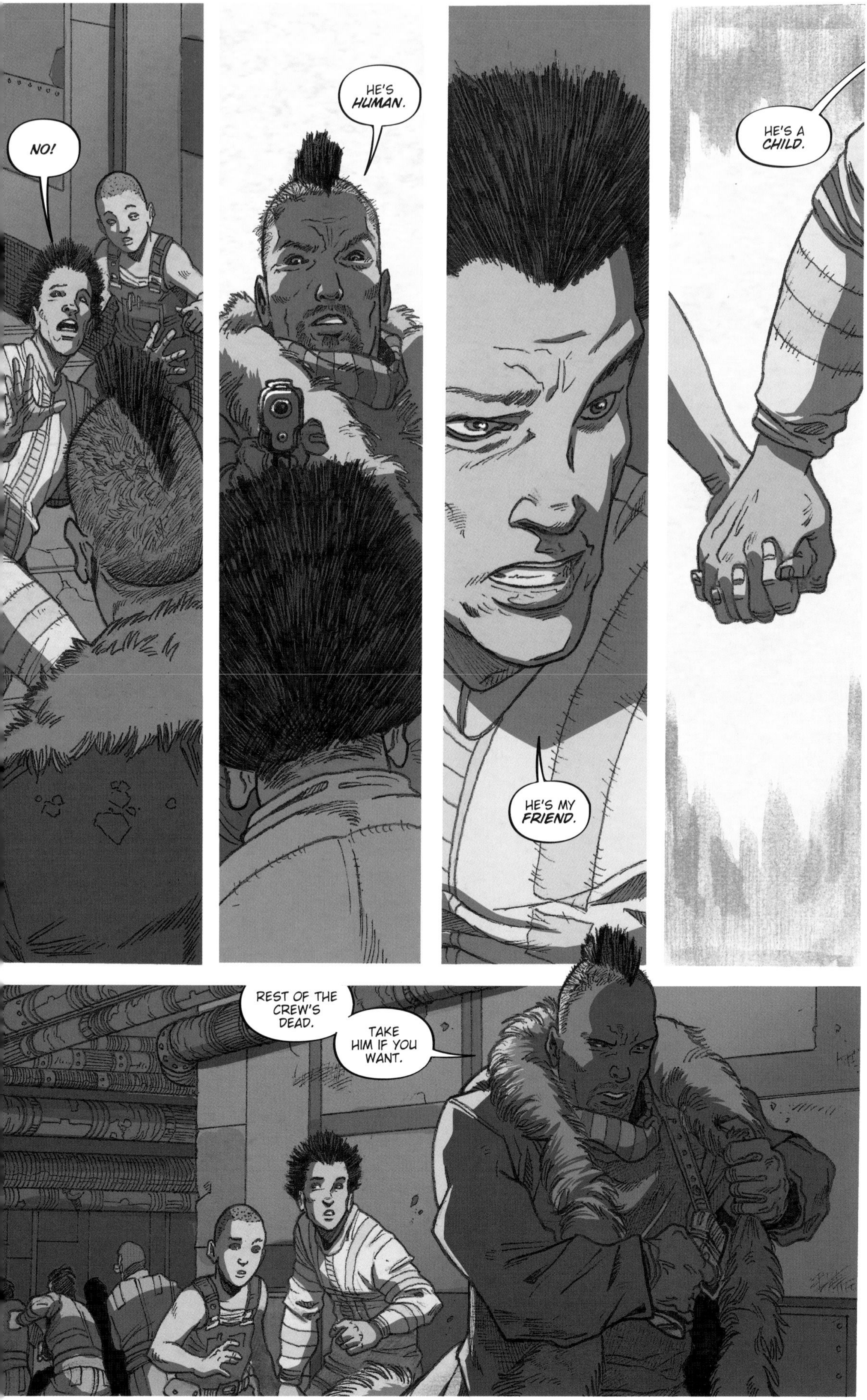
NO!
HE'S HUMAN.
HE'S MY FRIEND.
HE'S A CHILD.
REST OF THE CREW'S DEAD.
TAKE HIM IF YOU WANT.

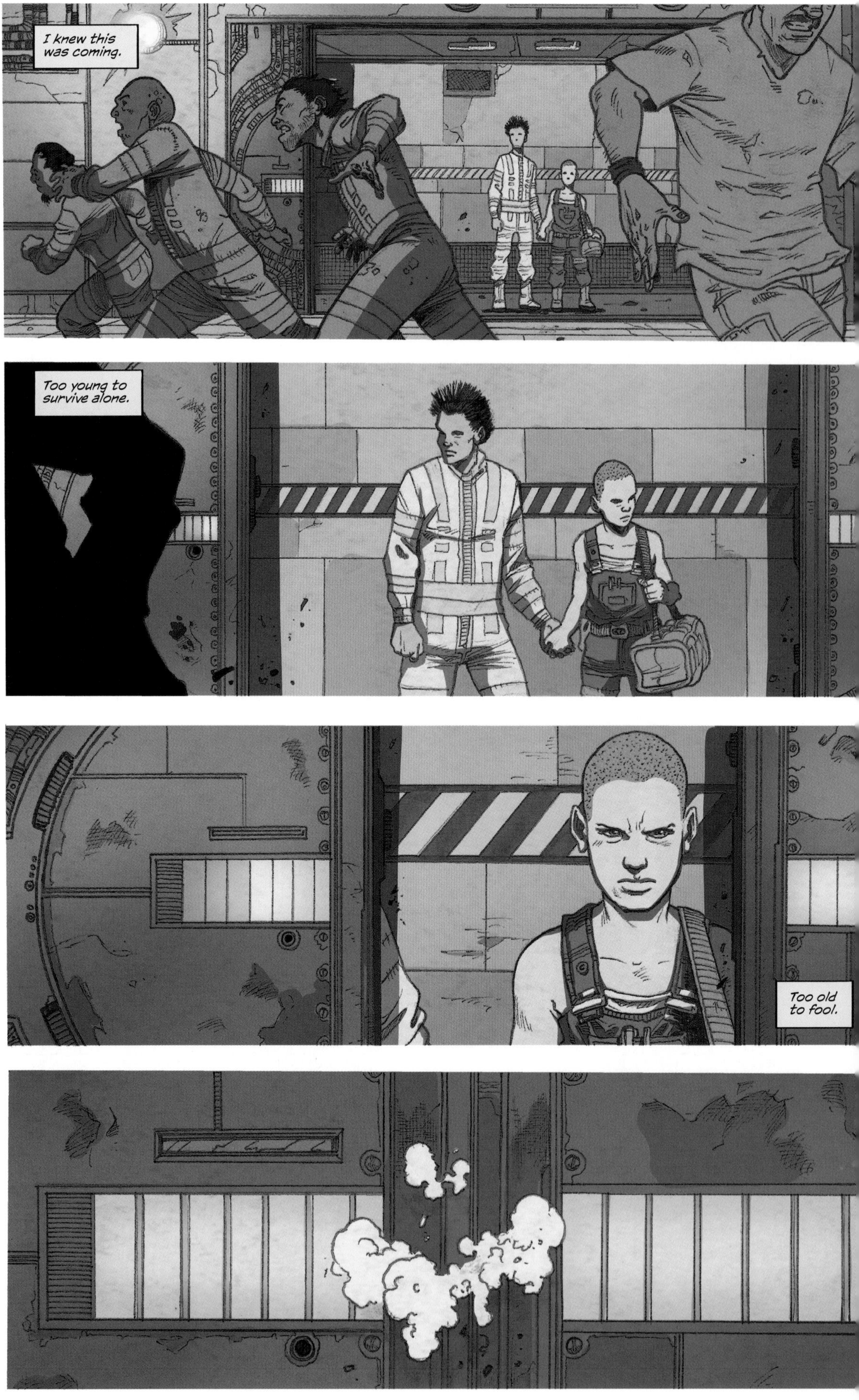
I knew this was coming.
Too young to survive alone.
Too old to fool.

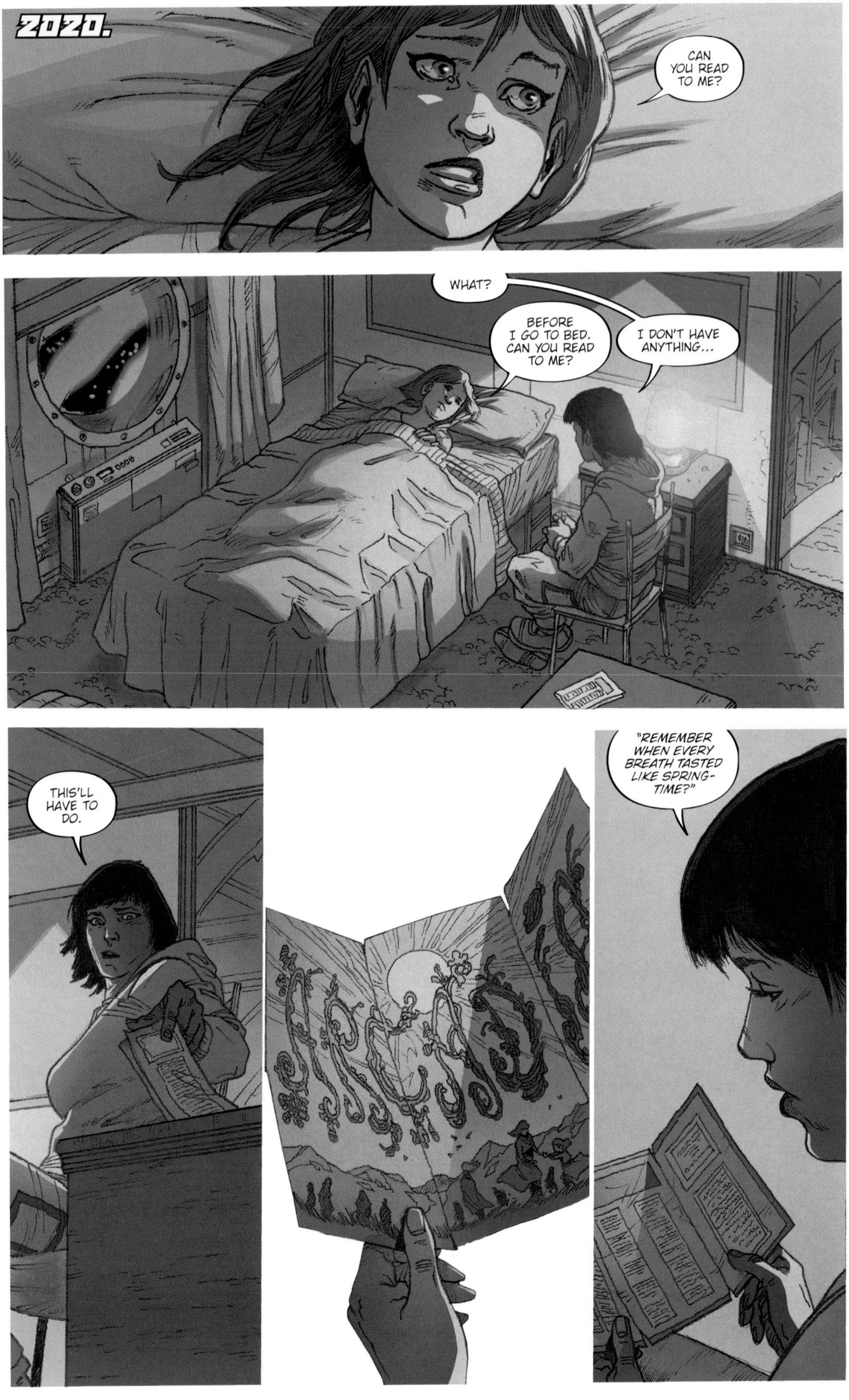
2020.
CAN YOU READ TO ME?
WHAT?
BEFORE I GO TO BED. CAN YOU READ TO ME?
I DON'T HAVE ANYTHING...
THIS'LL HAVE TO DO.
"REMEMBER WHEN EVERY BREATH TASTED LIKE SPRING-TIME?"

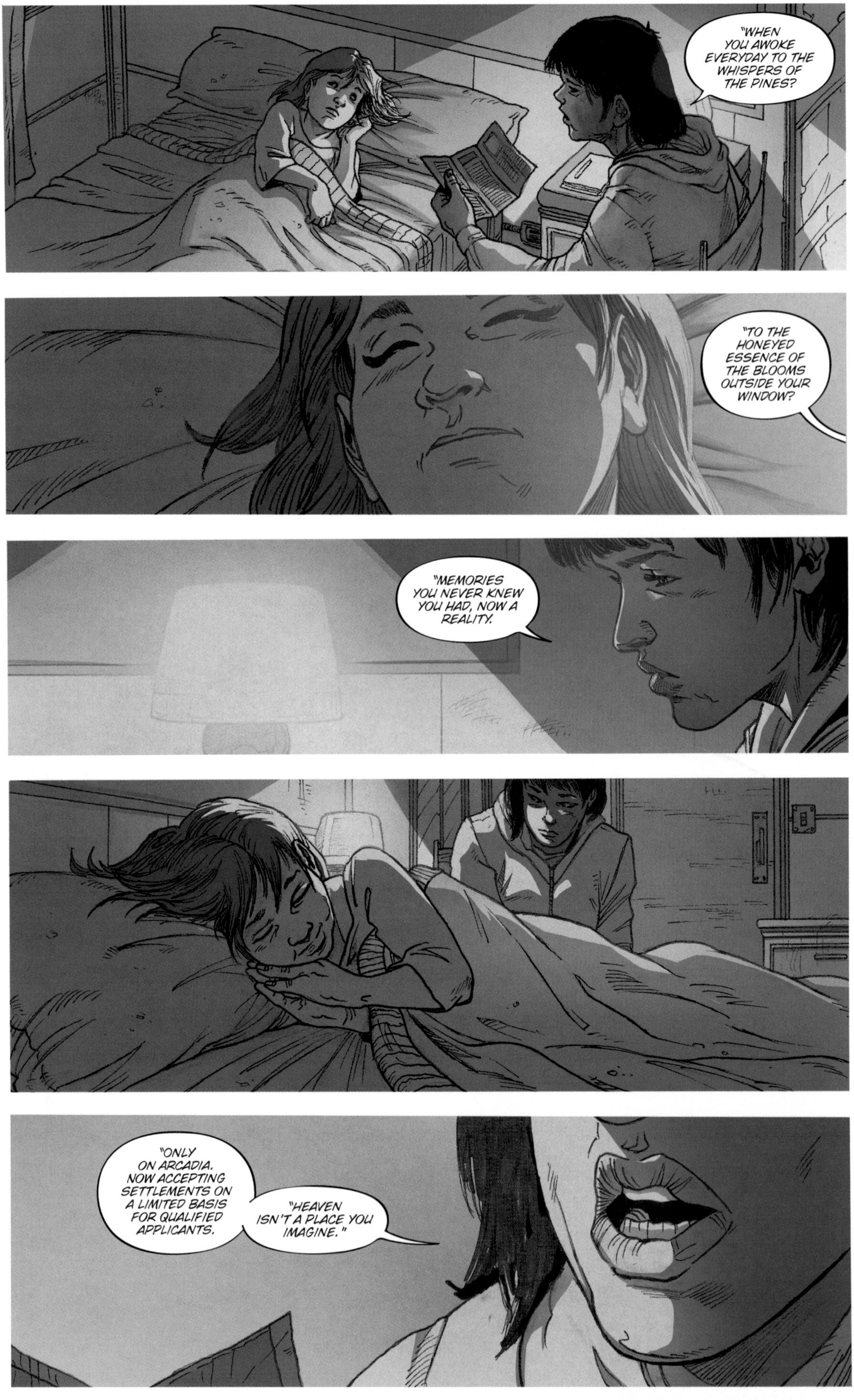
"WHEN YOU AWOKE EVERYDAY TO THE WHISPERS OF THE PINES?
"TO THE HONEYED ESSENCE OF THE BLOOMS OUTSIDE YOUR WINDOW?
"MEMORIES YOU NEVER KNEW YOU HAD, NOW A REALITY.
"ONLY ON ARCADIA. NOW ACCEPTING SETTLEMENTS ON A LIMITED BASIS FOR QUALIFIED APPLICANTS.
"HEAVEN ISN'T A PLACE YOU IMAGINE."

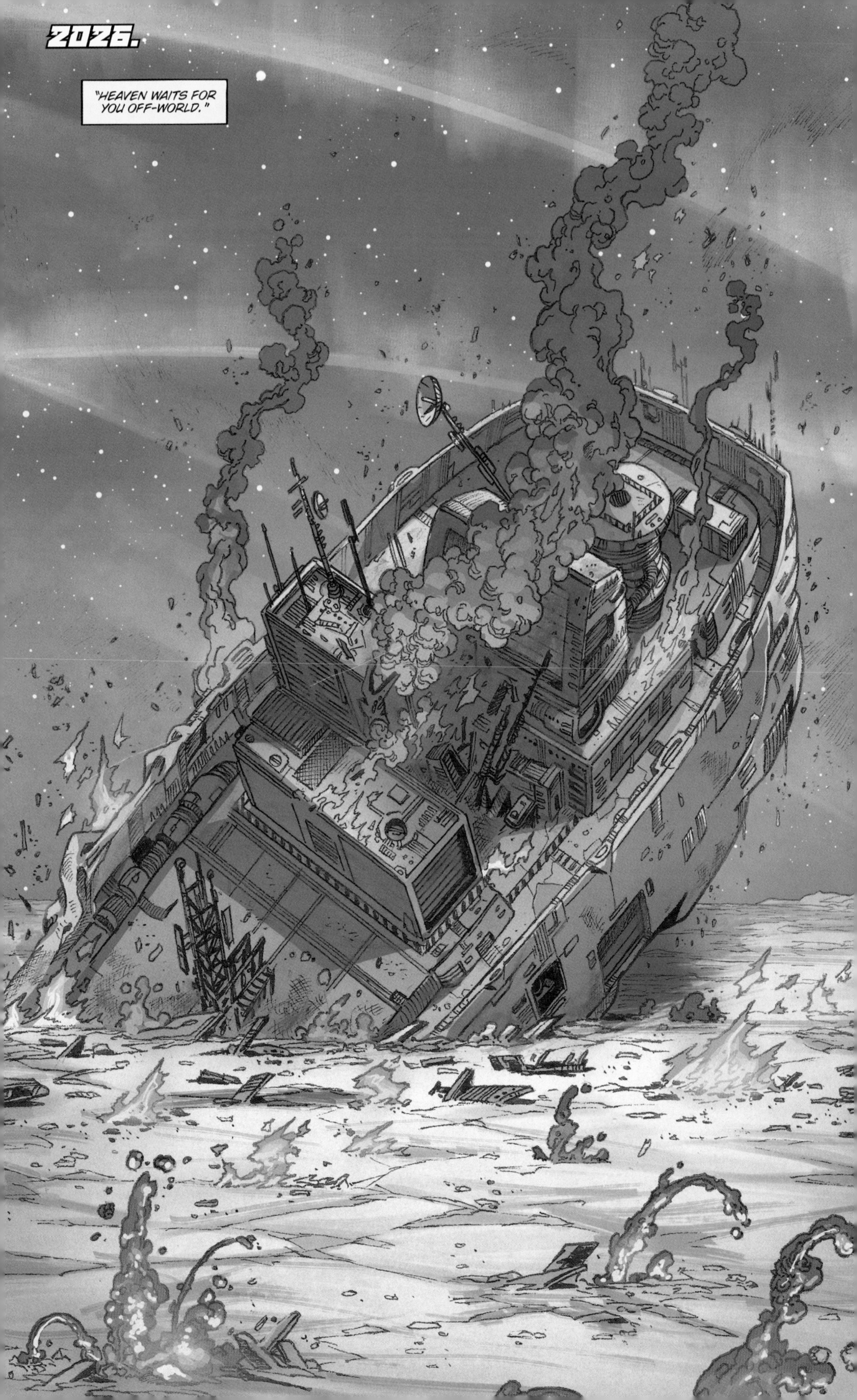
2026.
"HEAVEN WAITS FOR YOU OFF-WORLD."

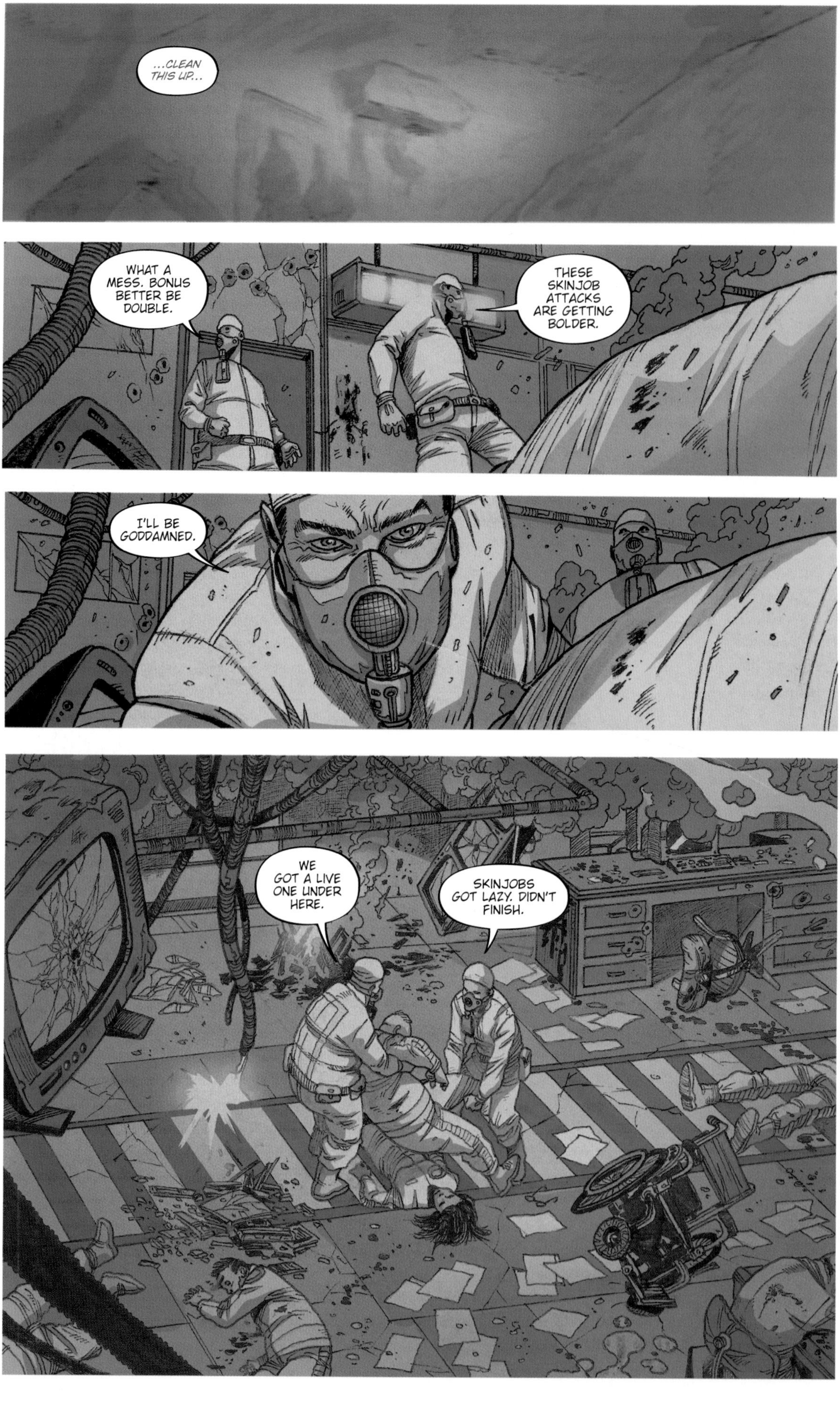
...CLEAN THIS UP...
WHAT A MESS. BONUS BETTER BE DOUBLE.
THESE SKINJOB ATTACKS ARE GETTING BOLDER.
I'LL BE GODDAMNED.
WE GOT A LIVE ONE UNDER HERE.
SKINJOBS GOT LAZY. DIDN'T FINISH.

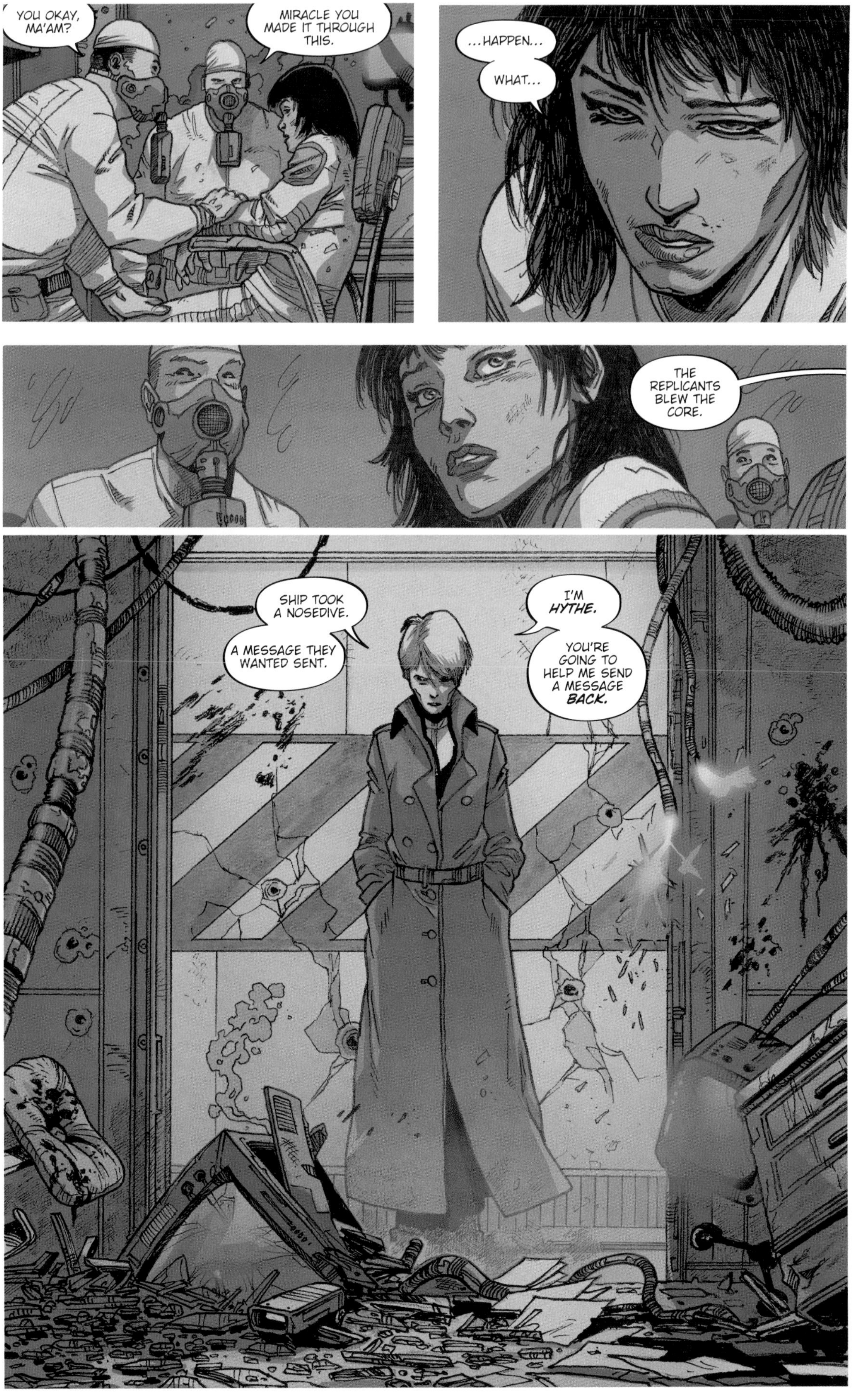
YOU OKAY, MA'AM?
MIRACLE YOU MADE IT THROUGH THIS.
...HAPPEN...
WHAT...
THE REPLICANTS BLEW THE CORE.
SHIP TOOK A NOSEDIVE.
A MESSAGE THEY WANTED SENT.
I'M *HYTHE.*
YOU'RE GOING TO HELP ME SEND A MESSAGE *BACK.*

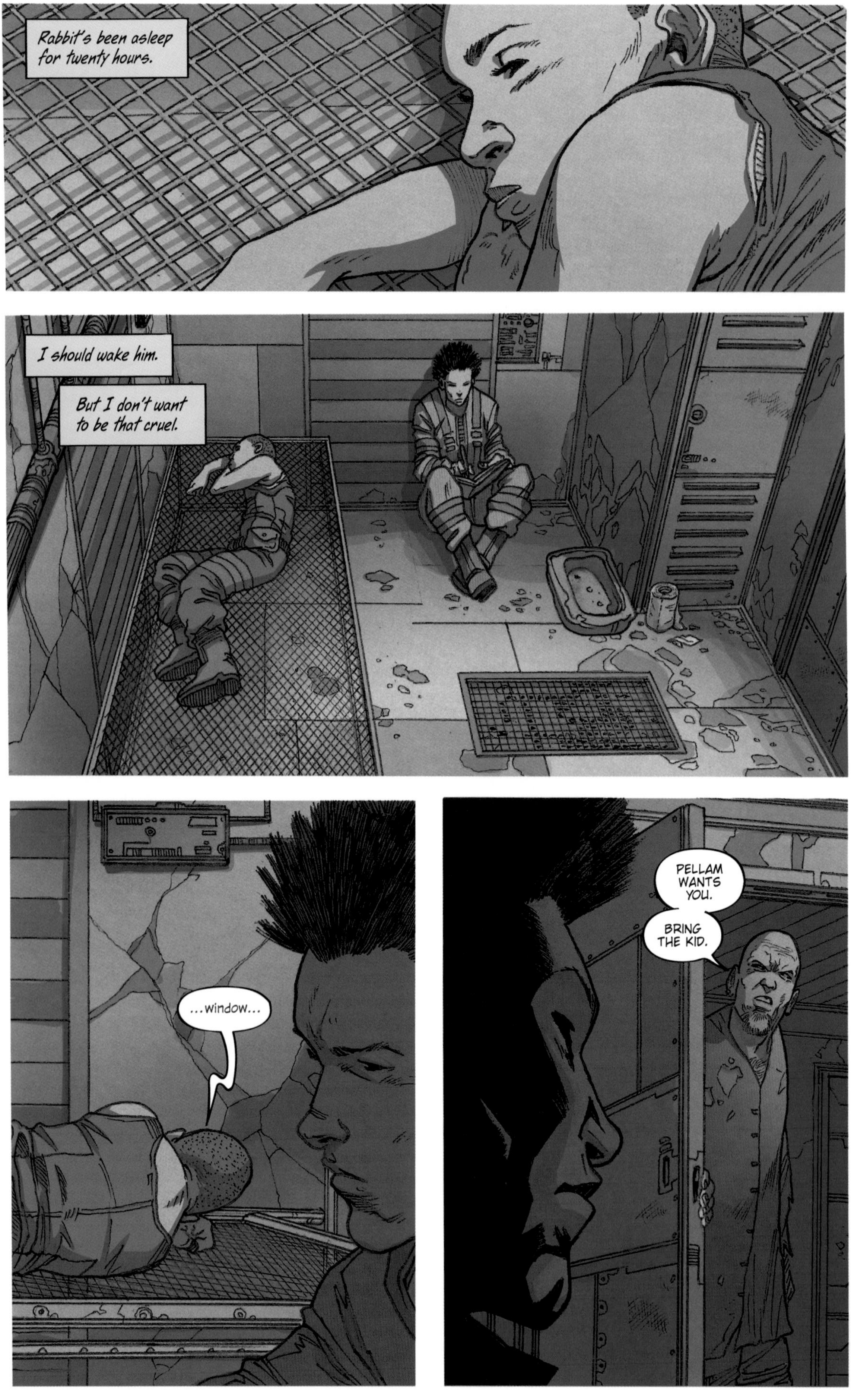
Rabbit's been asleep for twenty hours.
I should wake him.
But I don't want to be that cruel.
...window...
PELLAM WANTS YOU.
BRING THE KID.

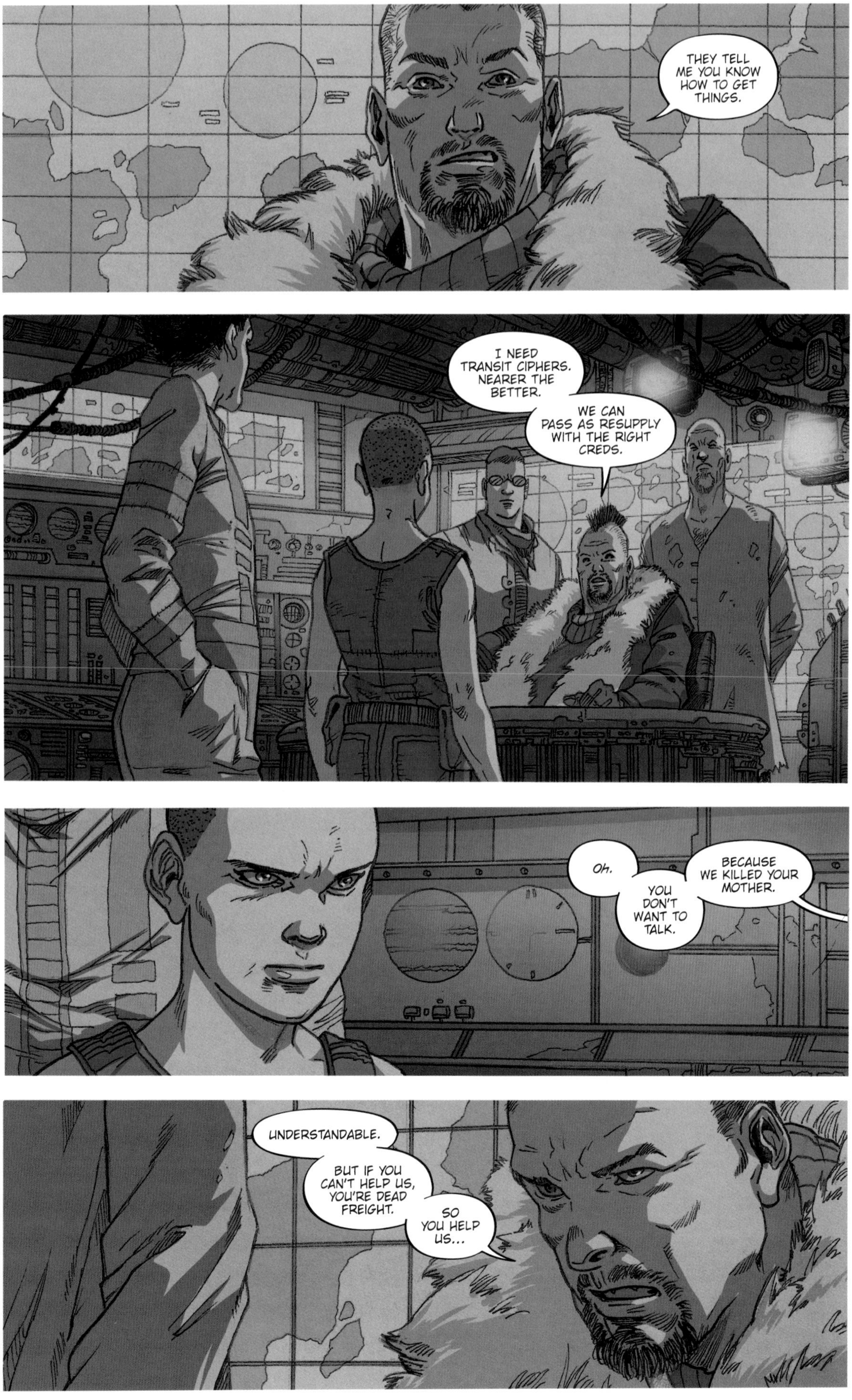
THEY TELL ME YOU KNOW HOW TO GET THINGS.
I NEED TRANSIT CIPHERS. NEARER THE BETTER.
WE CAN PASS AS RESUPPLY WITH THE RIGHT CREDS.
Oh.
YOU DON'T WANT TO TALK.
BECAUSE WE KILLED YOUR MOTHER.
UNDERSTANDABLE.
BUT IF YOU CAN'T HELP US, YOU'RE DEAD FREIGHT.
SO YOU HELP US...

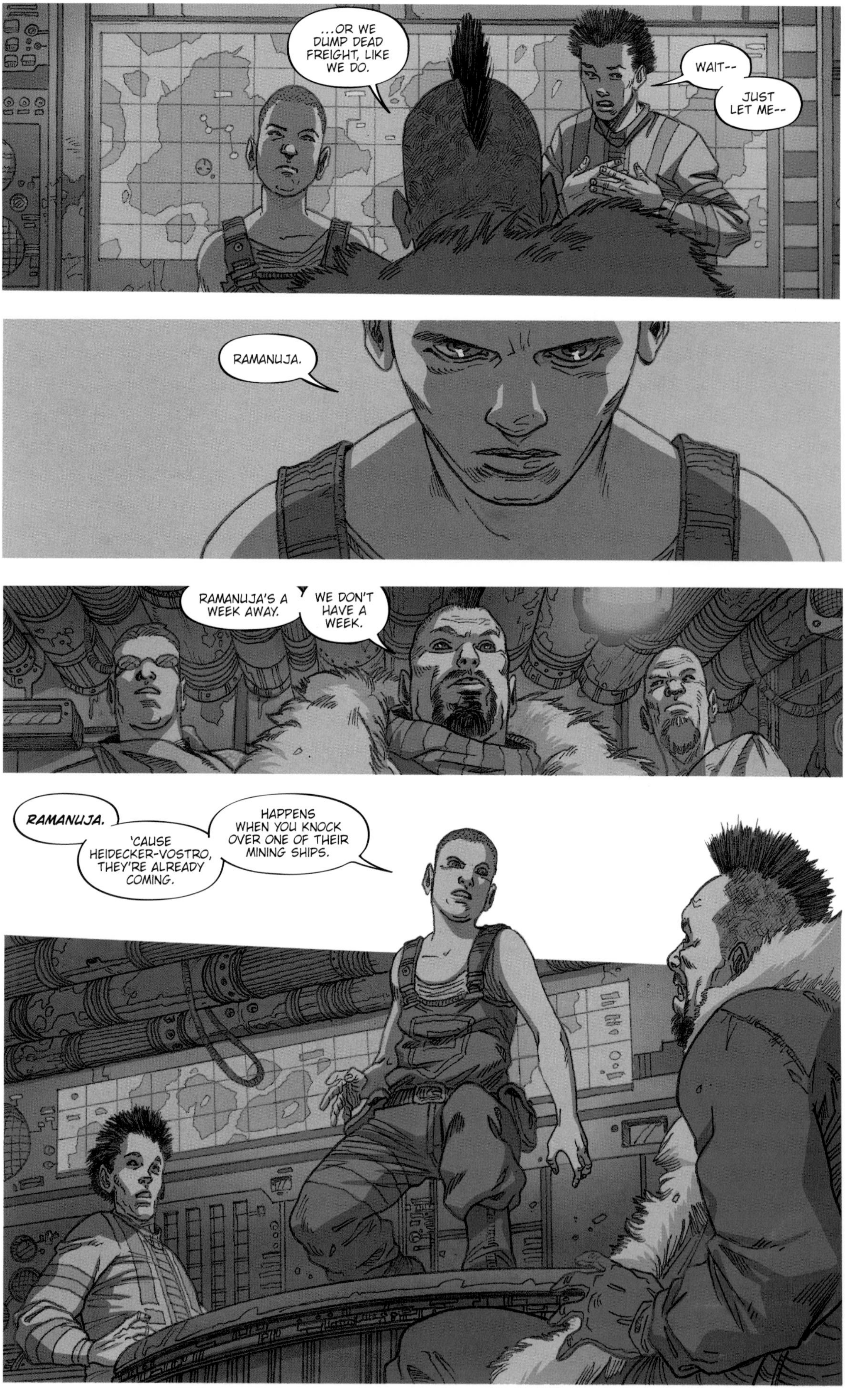
...OR WE DUMP DEAD FREIGHT, LIKE WE DO.
WAIT--
JUST LET ME--
RAMANUJA.
RAMANUJA'S A WEEK AWAY.
WE DON'T HAVE A WEEK.
RAMANUJA.
'CAUSE HEIDECKER-VOSTRO, THEY'RE ALREADY COMING.
HAPPENS WHEN YOU KNOCK OVER ONE OF THEIR MINING SHIPS.

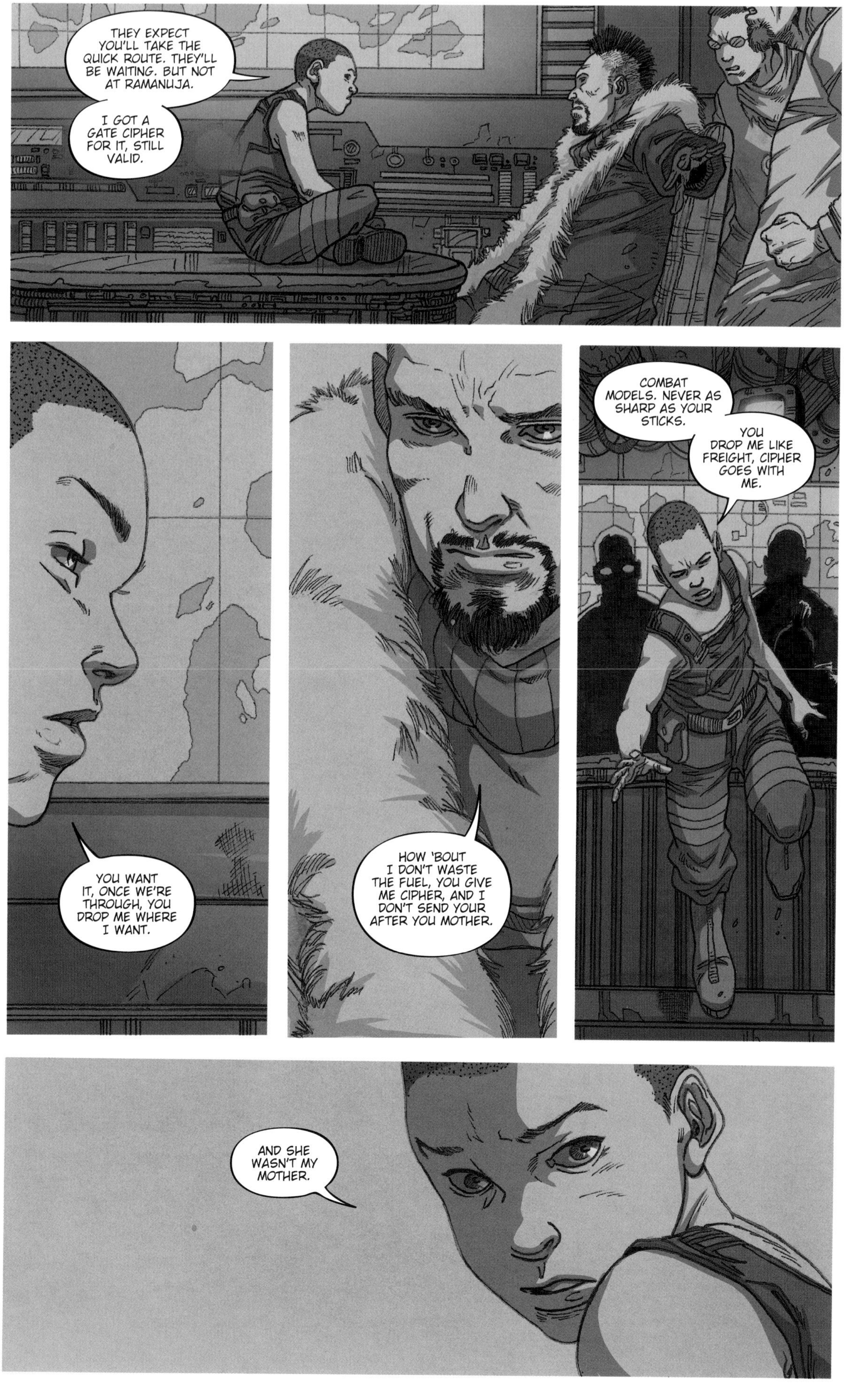
THEY EXPECT YOU'LL TAKE THE QUICK ROUTE. THEY'LL BE WAITING. BUT NOT AT RAMANUJA.
I GOT A GATE CIPHER FOR IT, STILL VALID.
YOU WANT IT, ONCE WE'RE THROUGH, YOU DROP ME WHERE I WANT.
HOW 'BOUT I DON'T WASTE THE FUEL, YOU GIVE ME CIPHER, AND I DON'T SEND YOUR AFTER YOU MOTHER.
COMBAT MODELS. NEVER AS SHARP AS YOUR STICKS.
YOU DROP ME LIKE FREIGHT, CIPHER GOES WITH ME.
AND SHE WASN'T MY MOTHER.

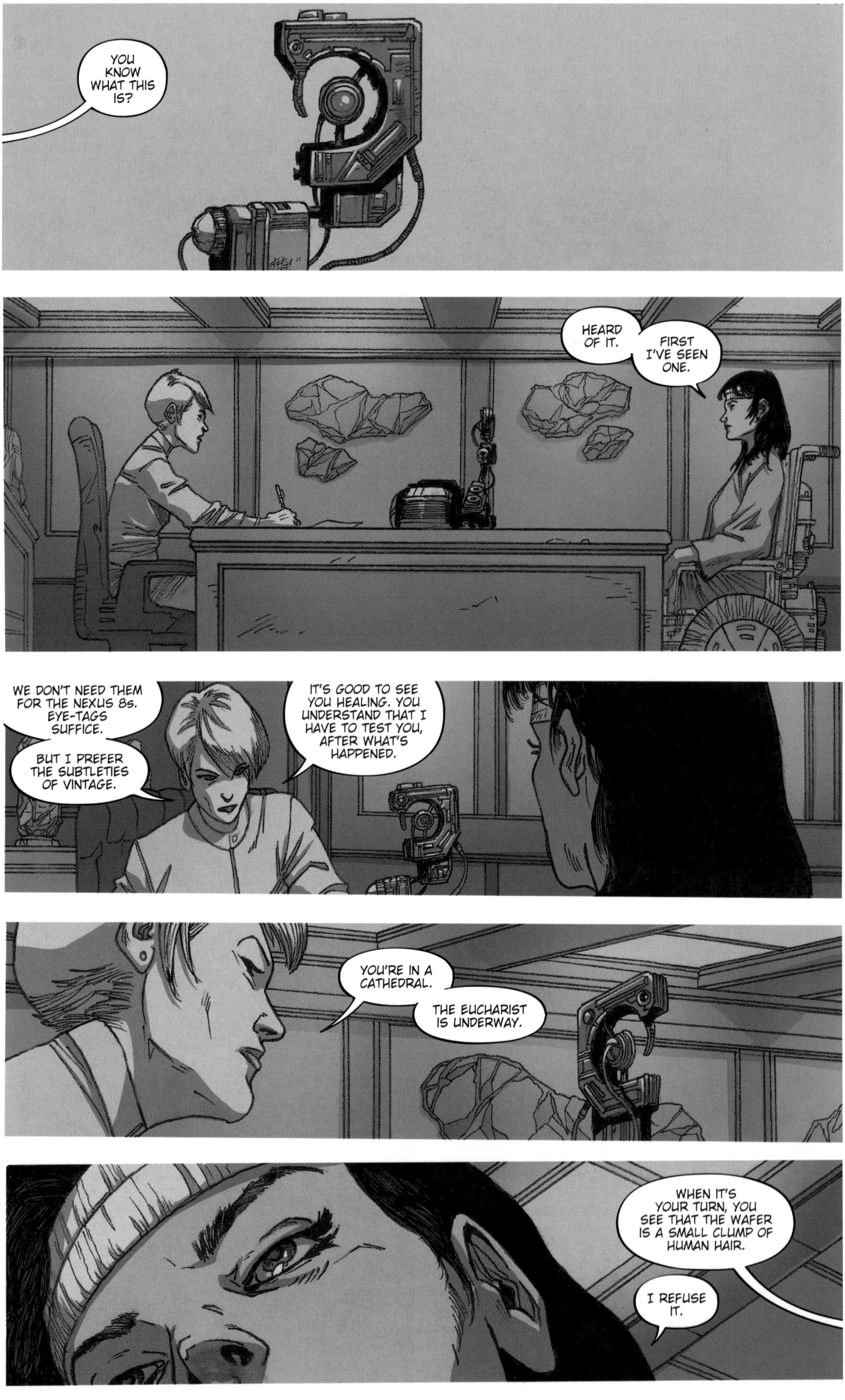
YOU KNOW WHAT THIS IS?
HEARD OF IT.
FIRST I'VE SEEN ONE.
WE DON'T NEED THEM FOR THE NEXUS 8s. EYE-TAGS SUFFICE.
BUT I PREFER THE SUBTLETIES OF VINTAGE.
IT'S GOOD TO SEE YOU HEALING. YOU UNDERSTAND THAT I HAVE TO TEST YOU, AFTER WHAT'S HAPPENED.
YOU'RE IN A CATHEDRAL.
THE EUCHARIST IS UNDERWAY.
WHEN IT'S YOUR TURN, YOU SEE THAT THE WAFER IS A SMALL CLUMP OF HUMAN HAIR.
I REFUSE IT.

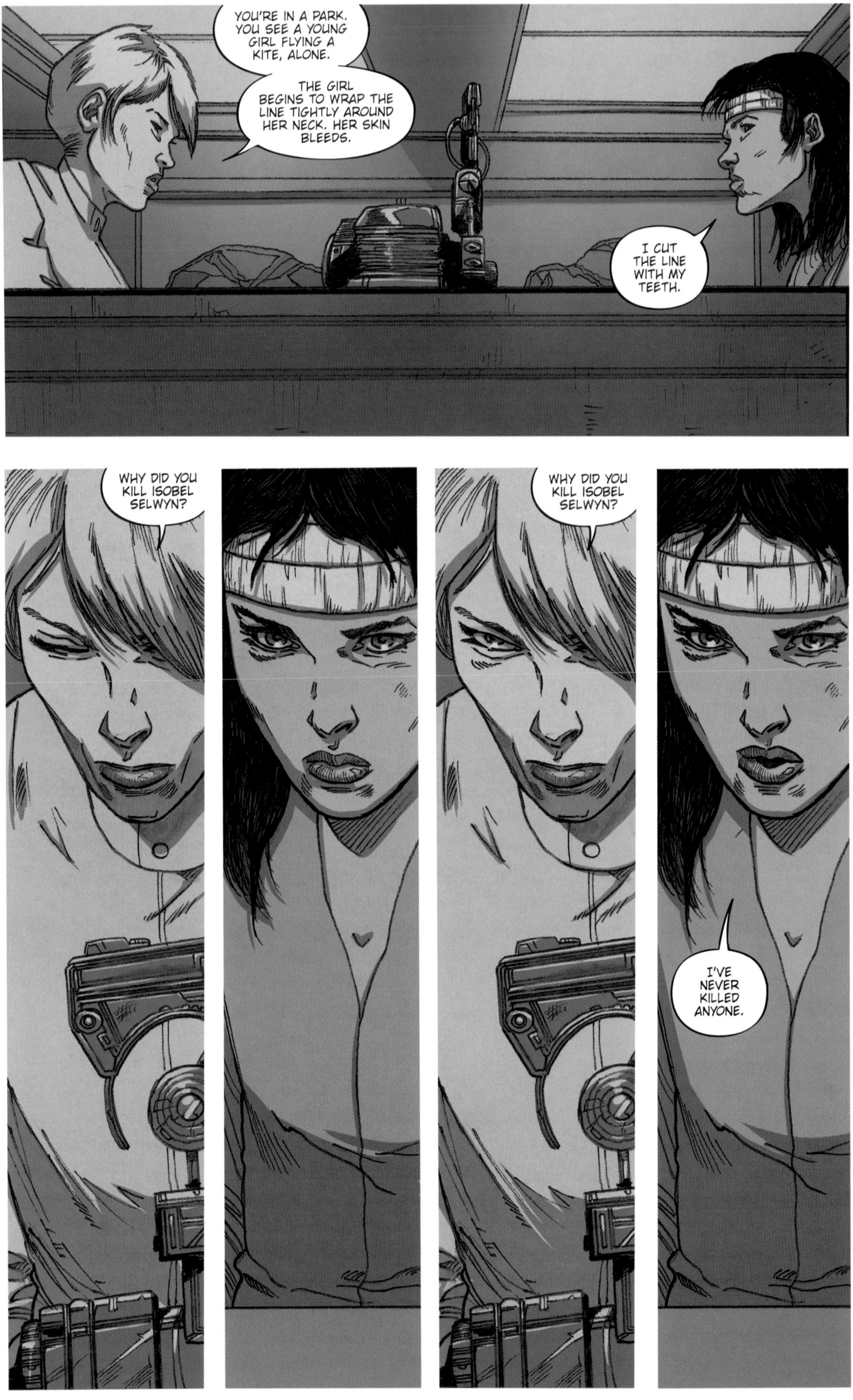

YOU'RE IN A PARK. YOU SEE A YOUNG GIRL FLYING A KITE, ALONE.
THE GIRL BEGINS TO WRAP THE LINE TIGHTLY AROUND HER NECK. HER SKIN BLEEDS.
I CUT THE LINE WITH MY TEETH.
WHY DID YOU KILL ISOBEL SELWYN?
WHY DID YOU KILL ISOBEL SELWYN?
I'VE NEVER KILLED ANYONE.

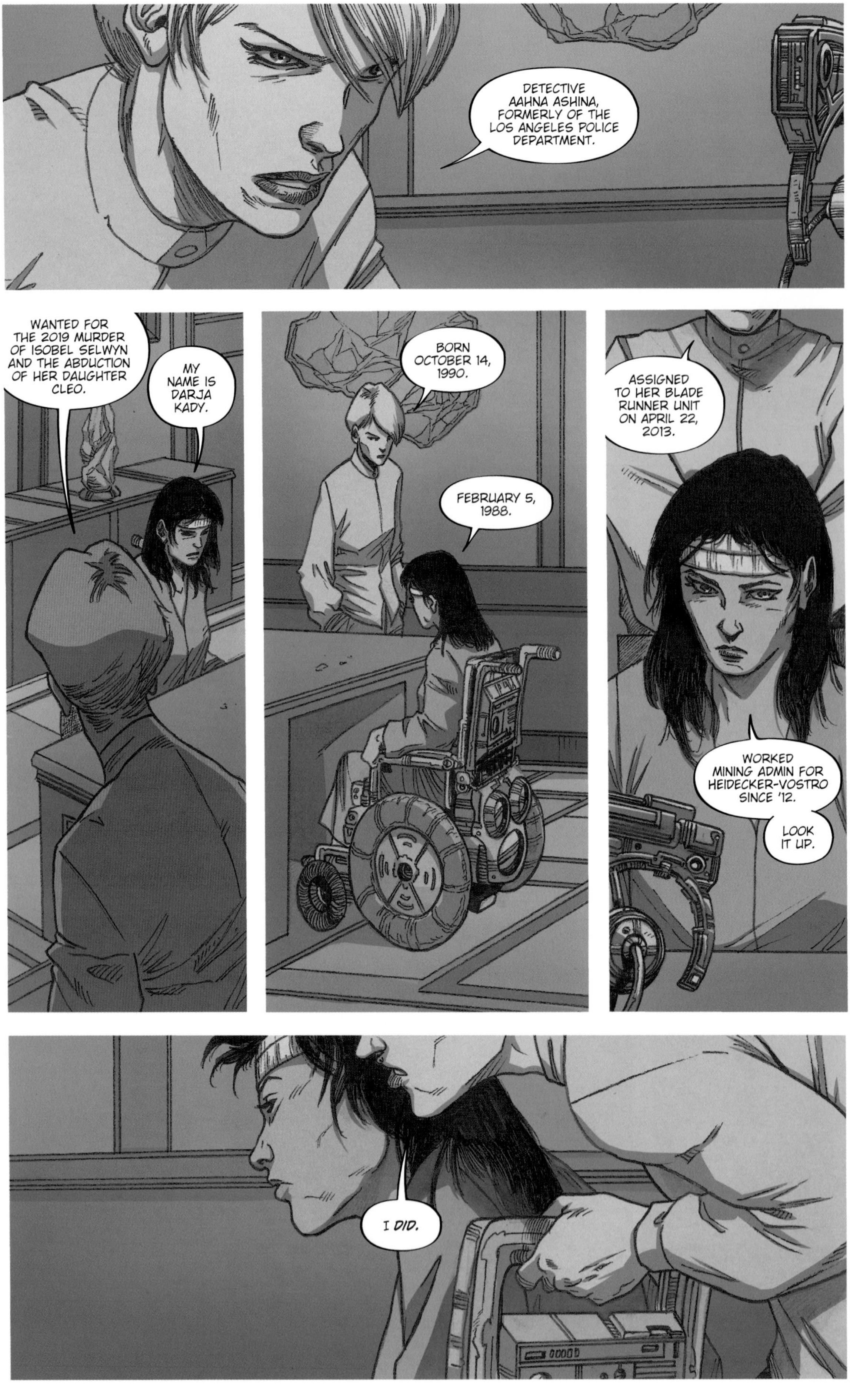
DETECTIVE AAHNA ASHINA, FORMERLY OF THE LOS ANGELES POLICE DEPARTMENT.
WANTED FOR THE 2019 MURDER OF ISOBEL SELWYN AND THE ABDUCTION OF HER DAUGHTER CLEO.
MY NAME IS DARJA KADY.
BORN OCTOBER 14, 1990.
FEBRUARY 5, 1988.
ASSIGNED TO HER BLADE RUNNER UNIT ON APRIL 22, 2013.
WORKED MINING ADMIN FOR HEIDECKER-VOSTRO SINCE '12.
LOOK IT UP.
I *DID.*

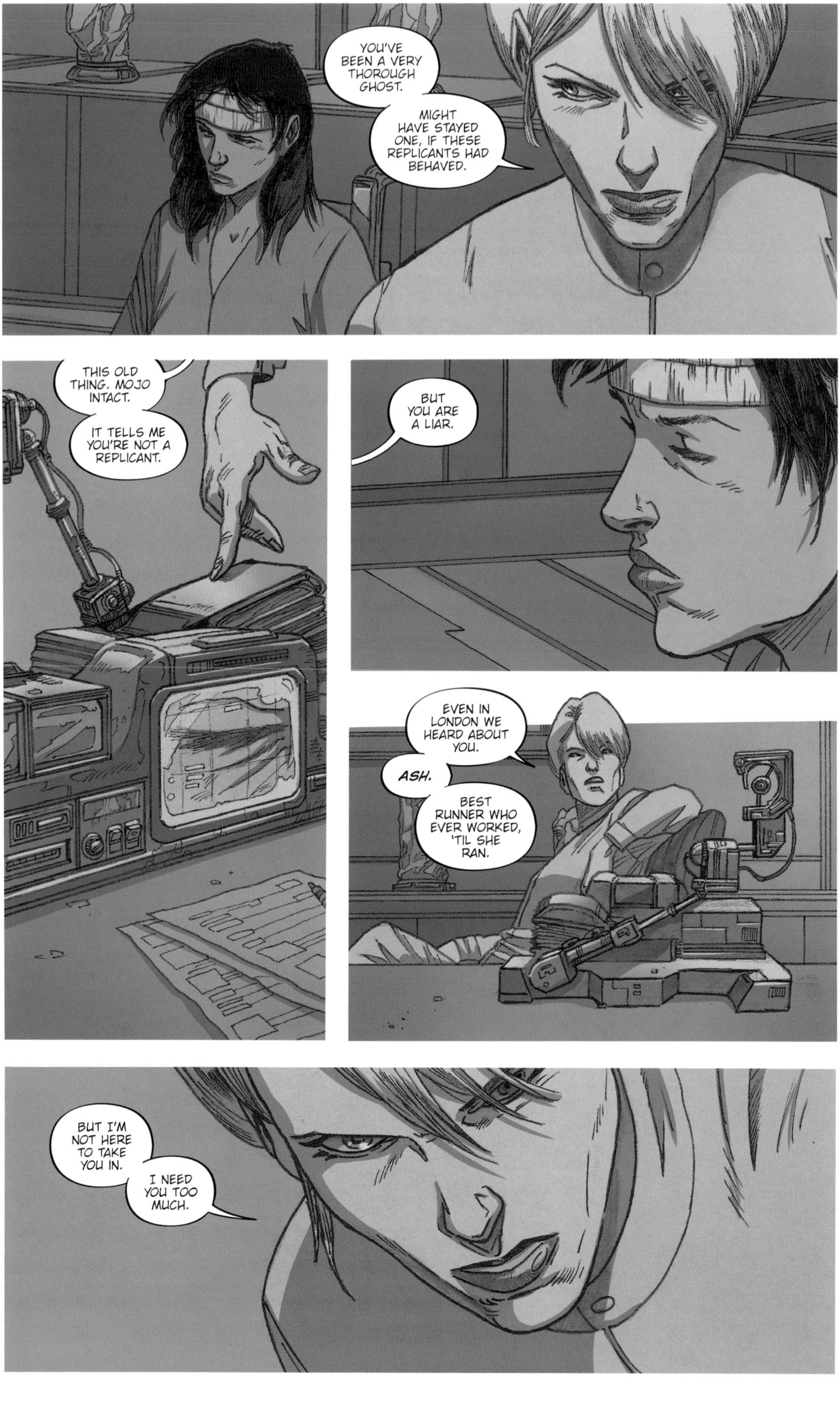
YOU'VE BEEN A VERY THOROUGH GHOST.
MIGHT HAVE STAYED ONE, IF THESE REPLICANTS HAD BEHAVED.
THIS OLD THING. MOJO INTACT.
IT TELLS ME YOU'RE NOT A REPLICANT.
BUT YOU ARE A LIAR.
EVEN IN LONDON WE HEARD ABOUT YOU.
ASH.
BEST RUNNER WHO EVER WORKED, 'TIL SHE RAN.
BUT I'M NOT HERE TO TAKE YOU IN.
I NEED YOU TOO MUCH.

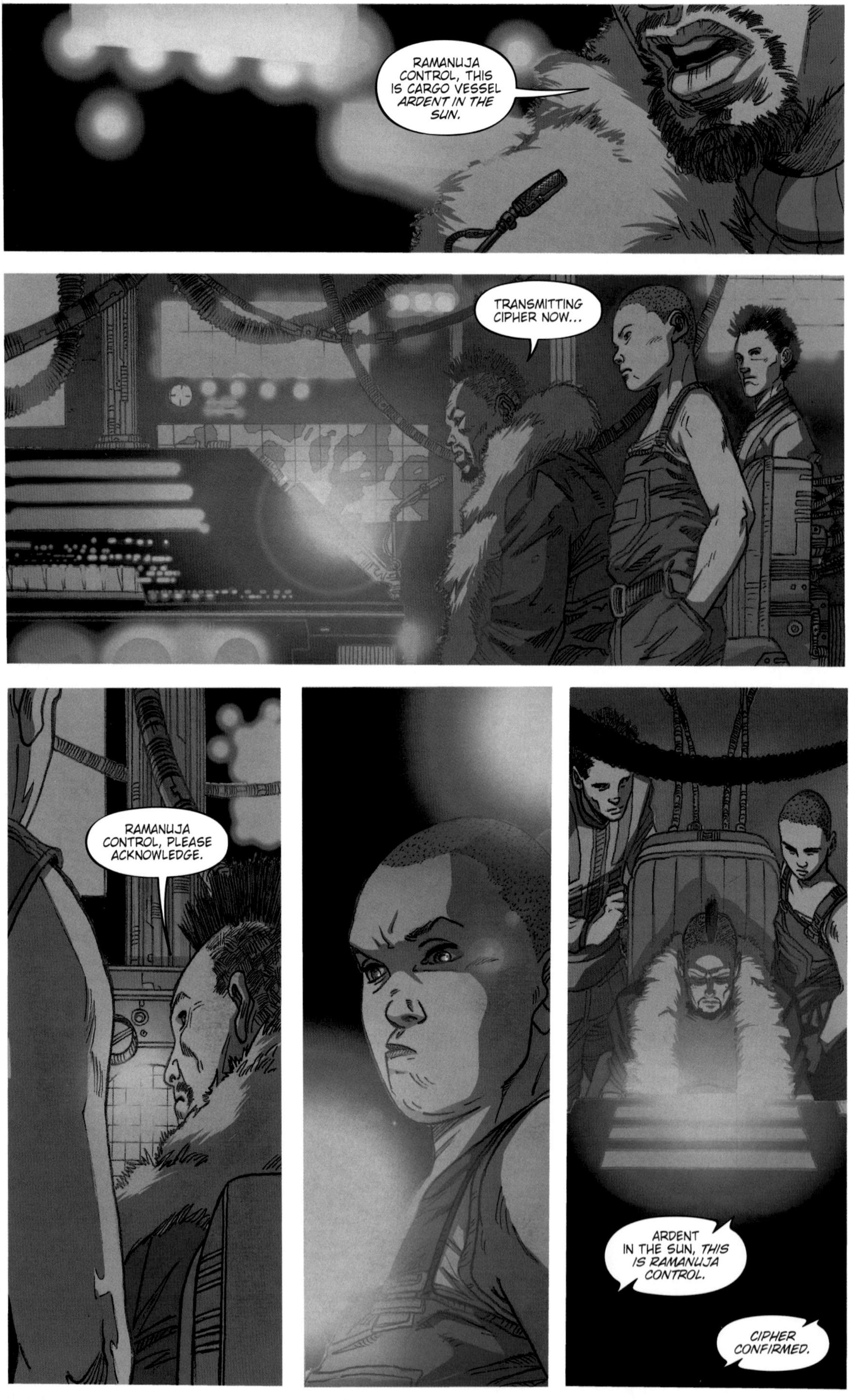
RAMANUJA CONTROL, THIS IS CARGO VESSEL *ARDENT IN THE SUN.*
TRANSMITTING CIPHER NOW...
RAMANUJA CONTROL, PLEASE ACKNOWLEDGE.
ARDENT IN THE SUN, *THIS IS RAMANUJA CONTROL.*
CIPHER CONFIRMED.

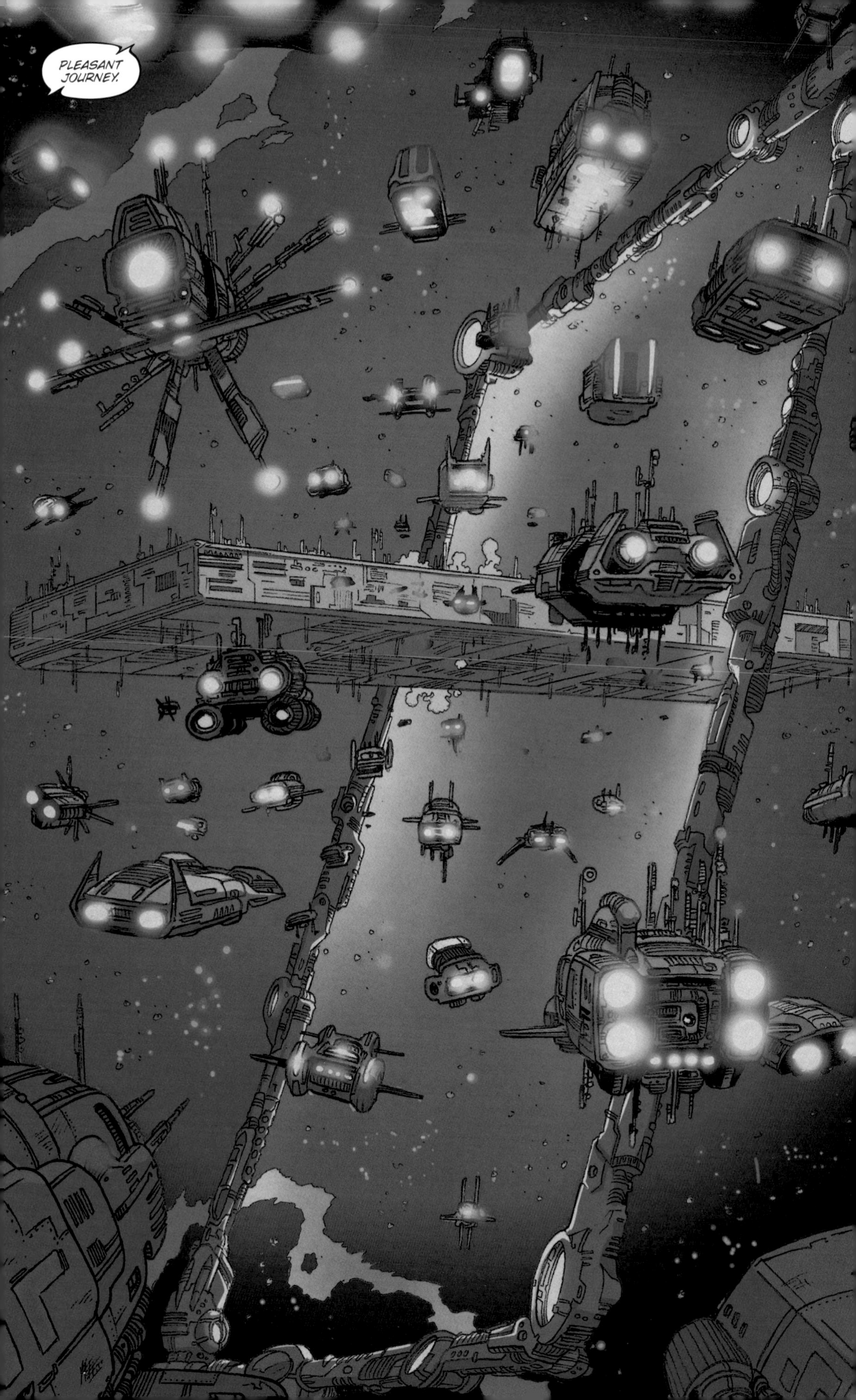
PLEASANT
JOURNEY.

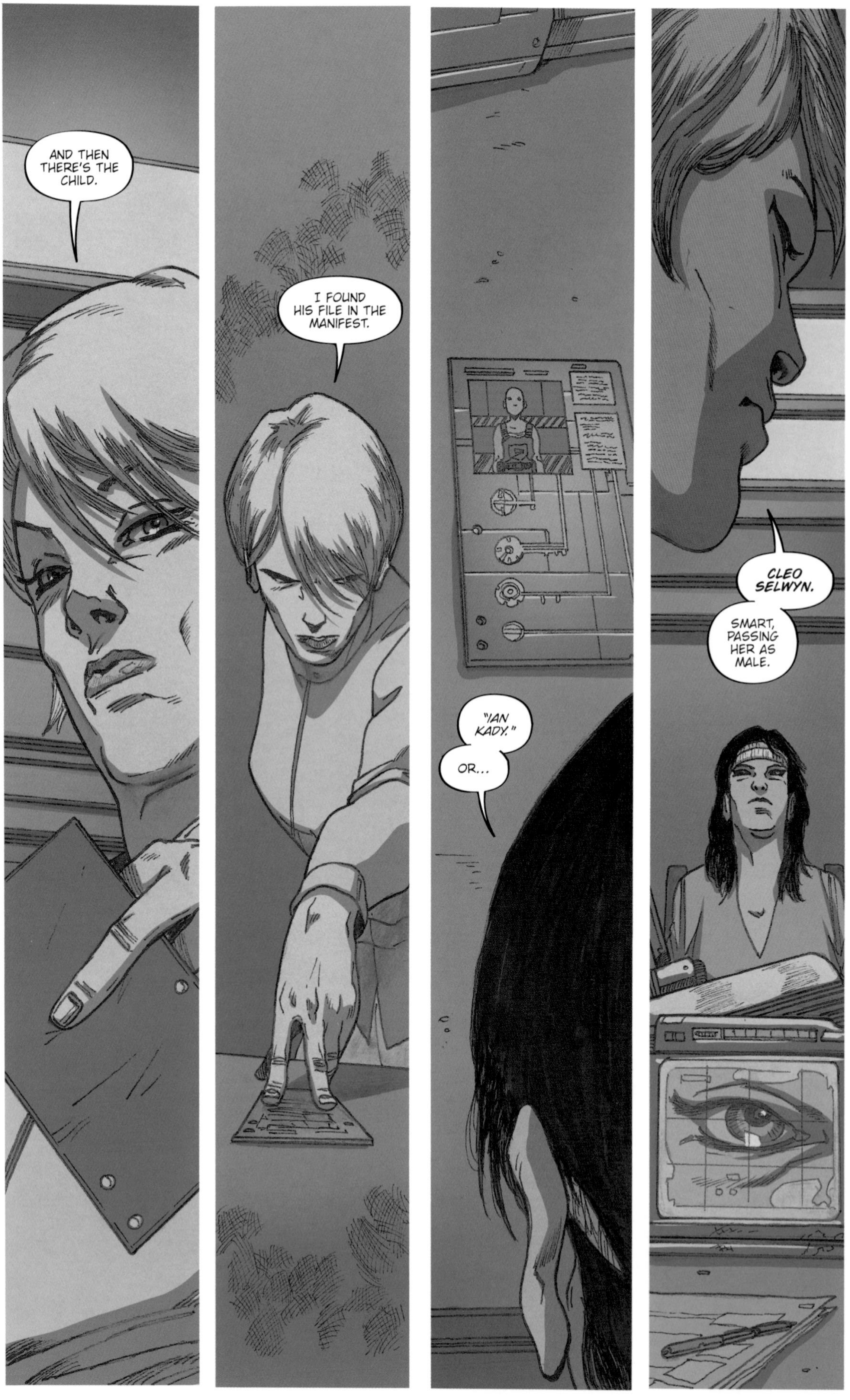

AND THEN THERE'S THE CHILD.
I FOUND HIS FILE IN THE MANIFEST.
"IAN KADY."
OR...
CLEO SELWYN.
SMART, PASSING HER AS MALE.

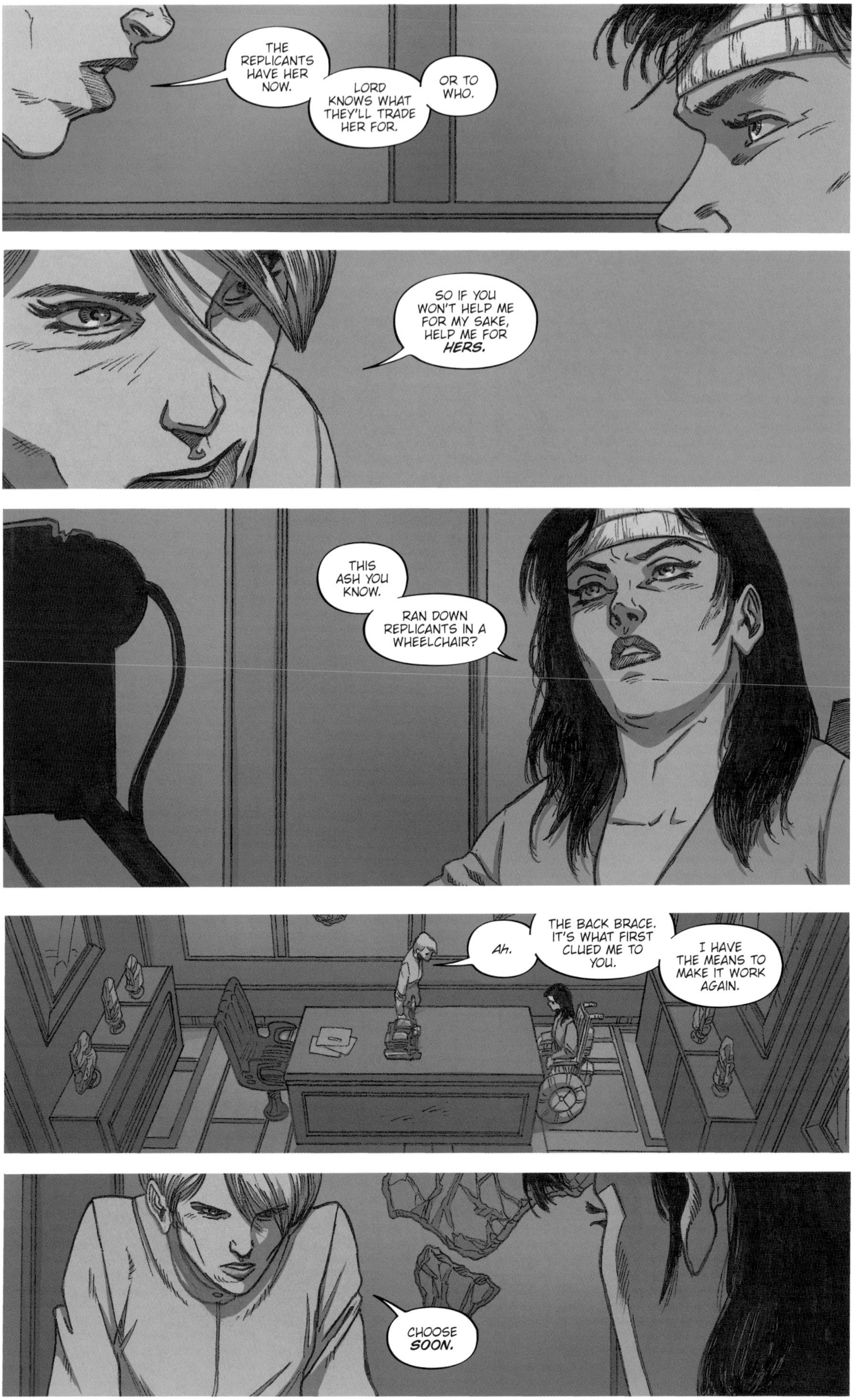
THE REPLICANTS HAVE HER NOW.
LORD KNOWS WHAT THEY'LL TRADE HER FOR.
OR TO WHO.
SO IF YOU WON'T HELP ME FOR MY SAKE, HELP ME FOR **HERS.**
THIS ASH YOU KNOW.
RAN DOWN REPLICANTS IN A WHEELCHAIR?
Ah.
THE BACK BRACE. IT'S WHAT FIRST CLUED ME TO YOU.
I HAVE THE MEANS TO MAKE IT WORK AGAIN.
CHOOSE **SOON.**

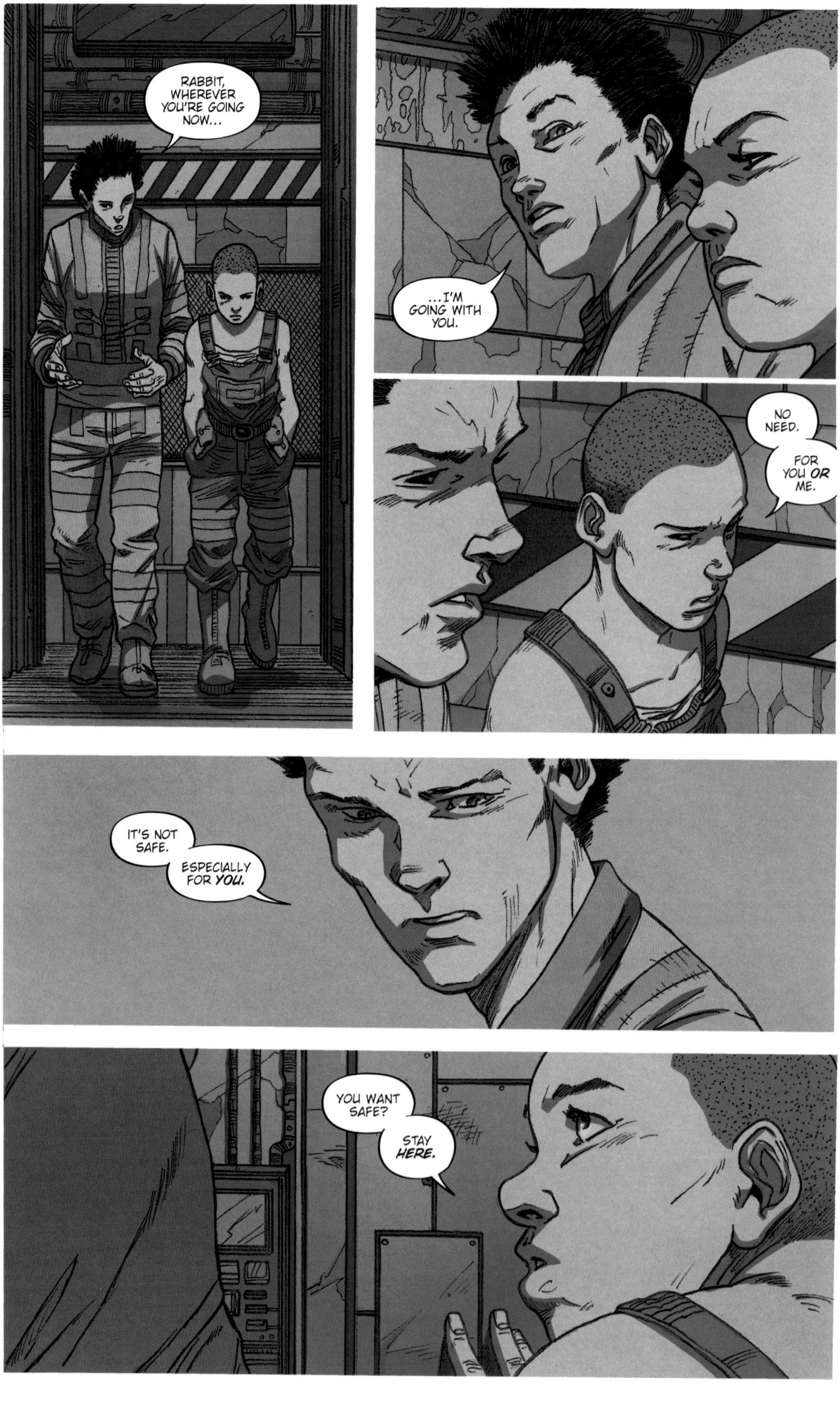
RABBIT, WHEREVER YOU'RE GOING NOW...
...I'M GOING WITH YOU.
NO NEED.
FOR YOU OR ME.
IT'S NOT SAFE.
ESPECIALLY FOR YOU.
YOU WANT SAFE?
STAY HERE.

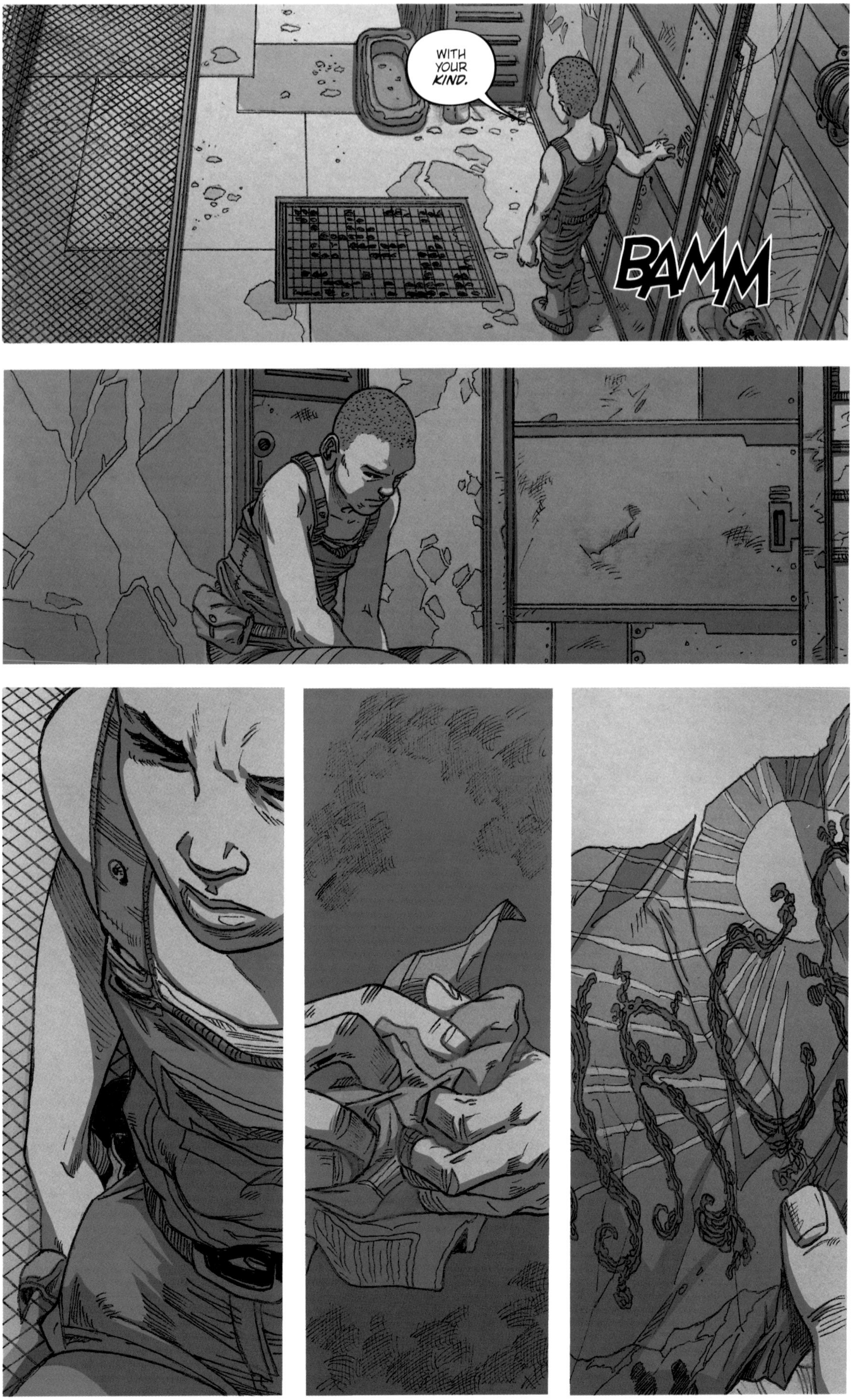
WITH YOUR KIND.
BAMM

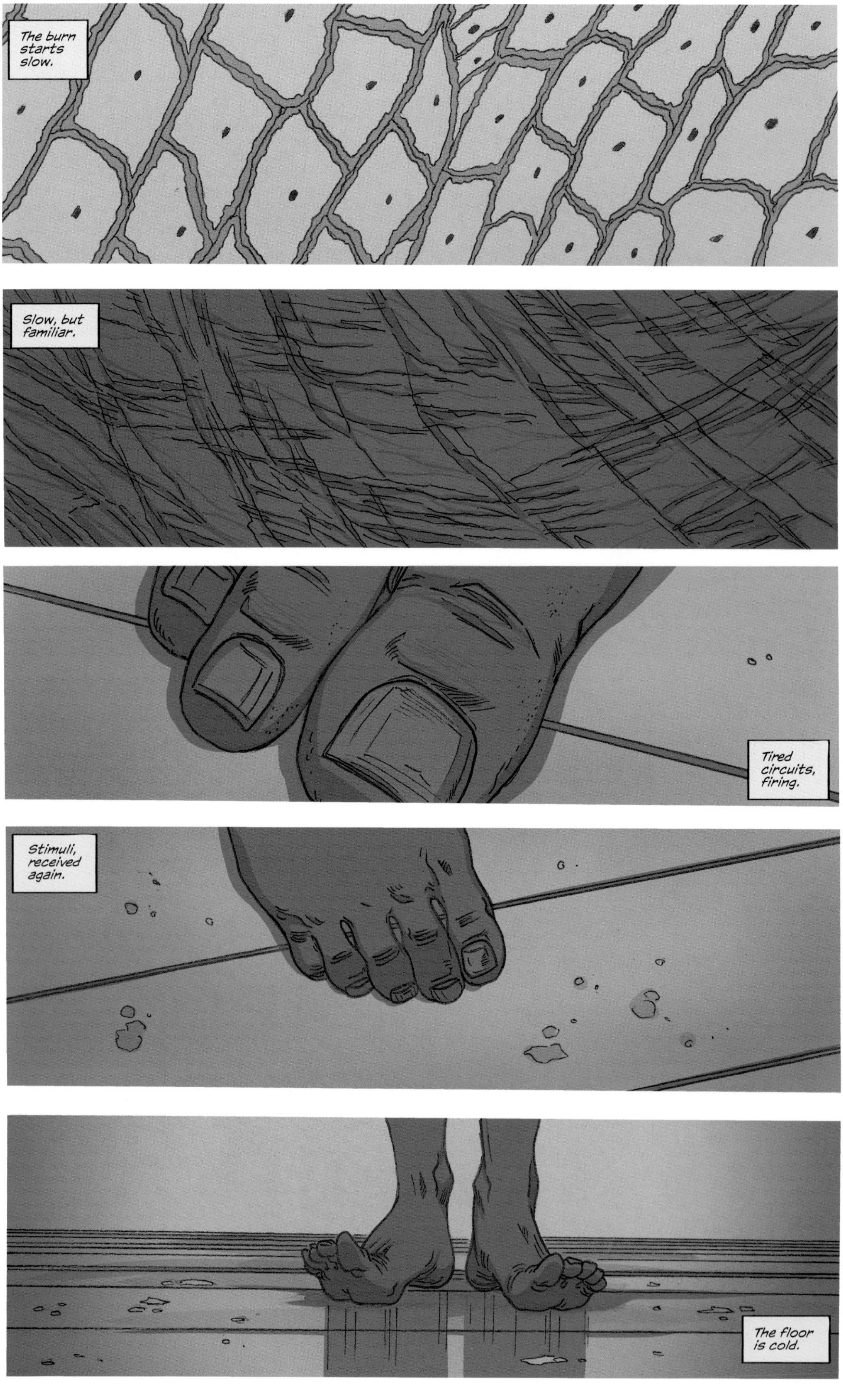
The burn starts slow.
Slow, but familiar.
Tired circuits, firing.
Stimuli, received again.
The floor is cold.

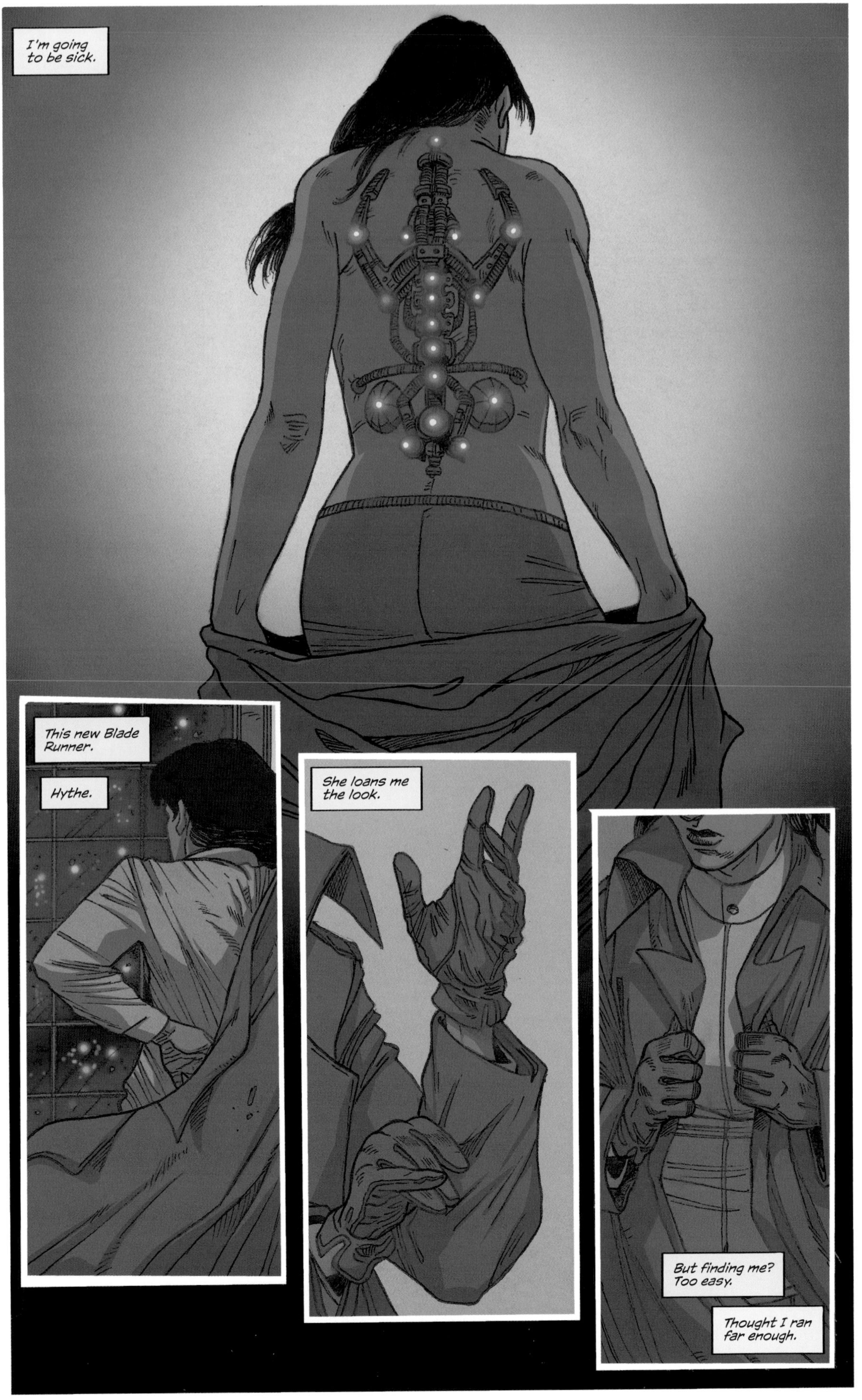
I'm going to be sick.
This new Blade Runner.
Hythe.
She loans me the look.
But finding me? Too easy.
Thought I ran far enough.

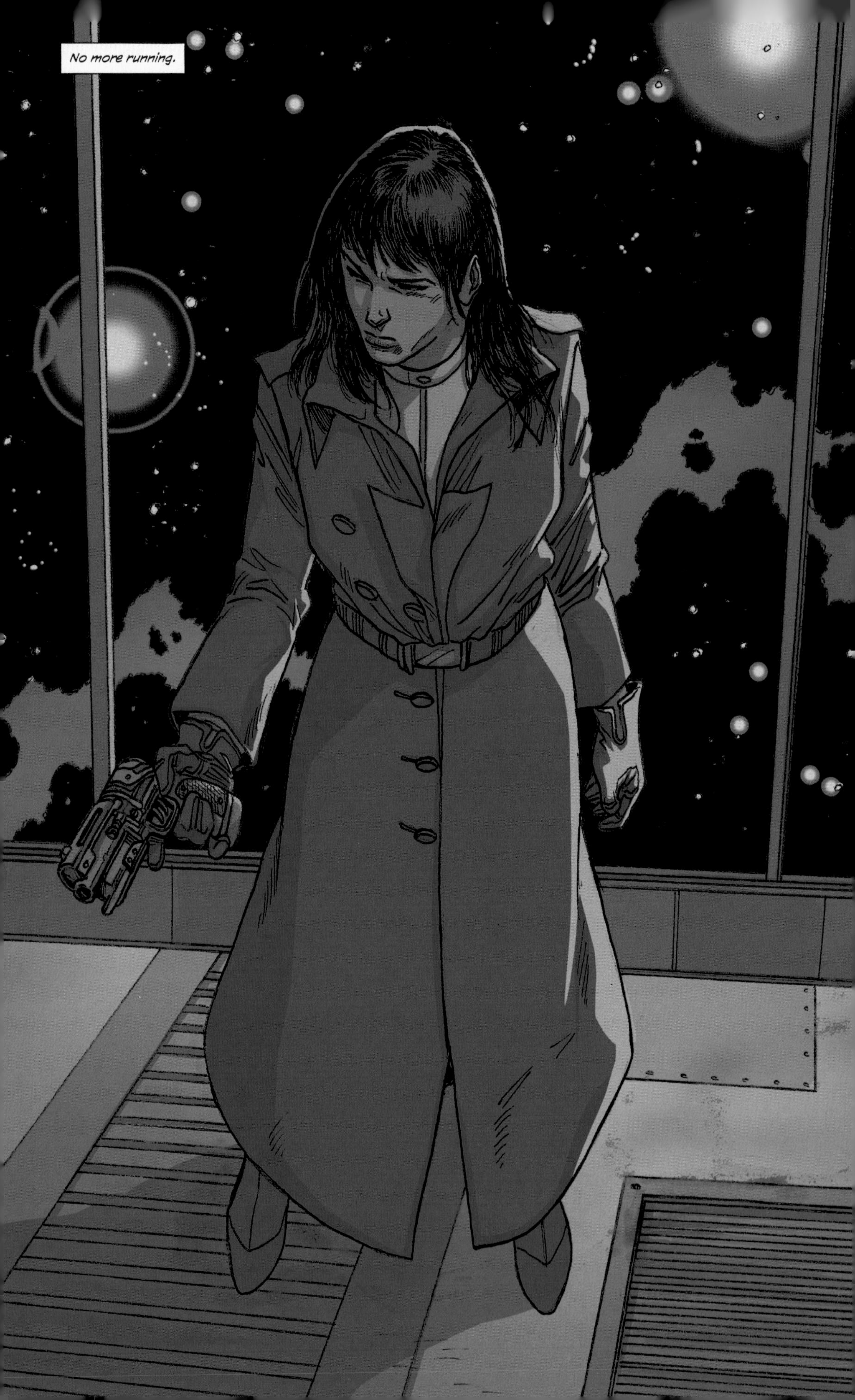
No more running.

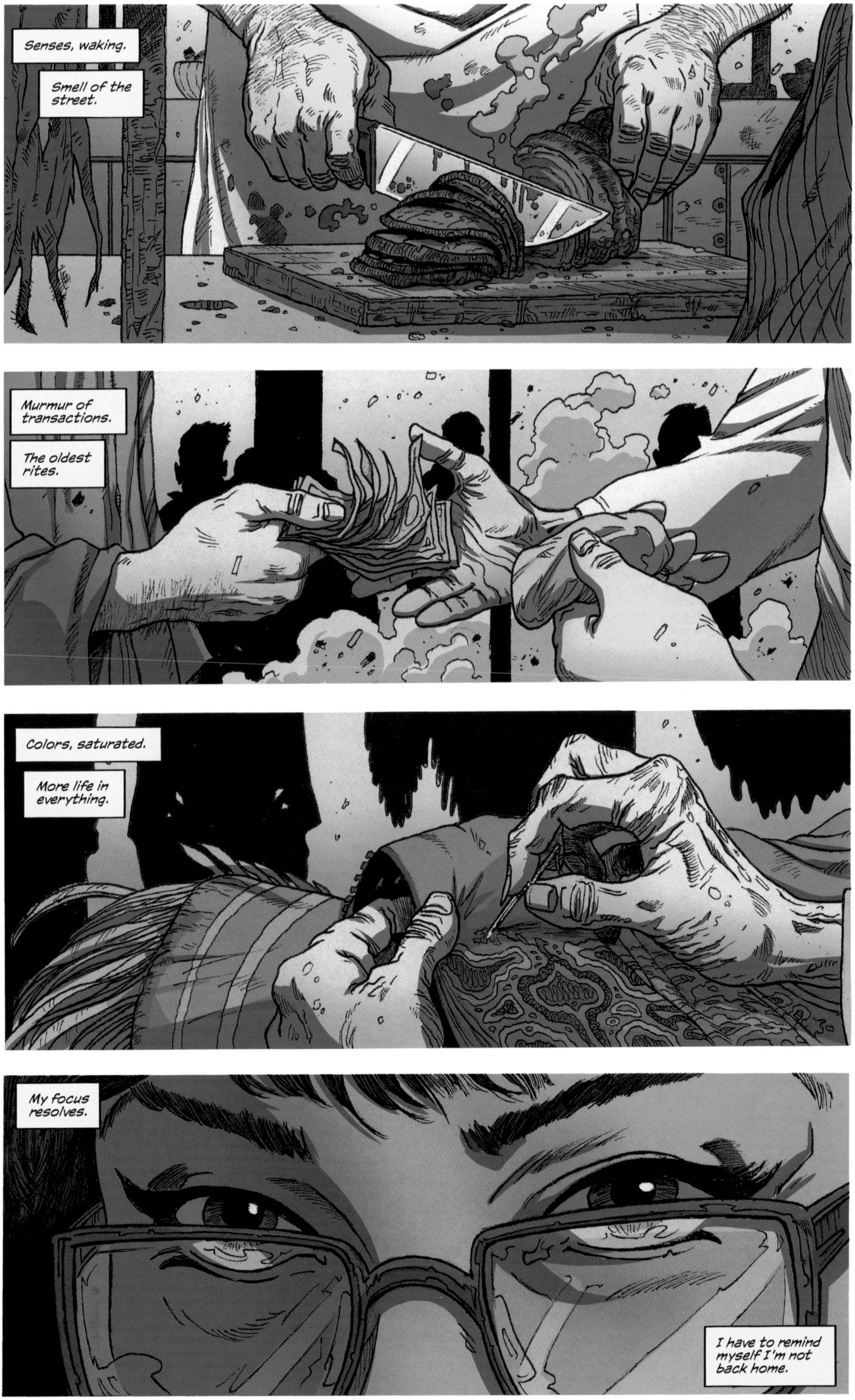
Senses, waking.
Smell of the street.
Murmur of transactions.
The oldest rites.
Colors, saturated.
More life in everything.
My focus resolves.
I have to remind myself I'm not back home.

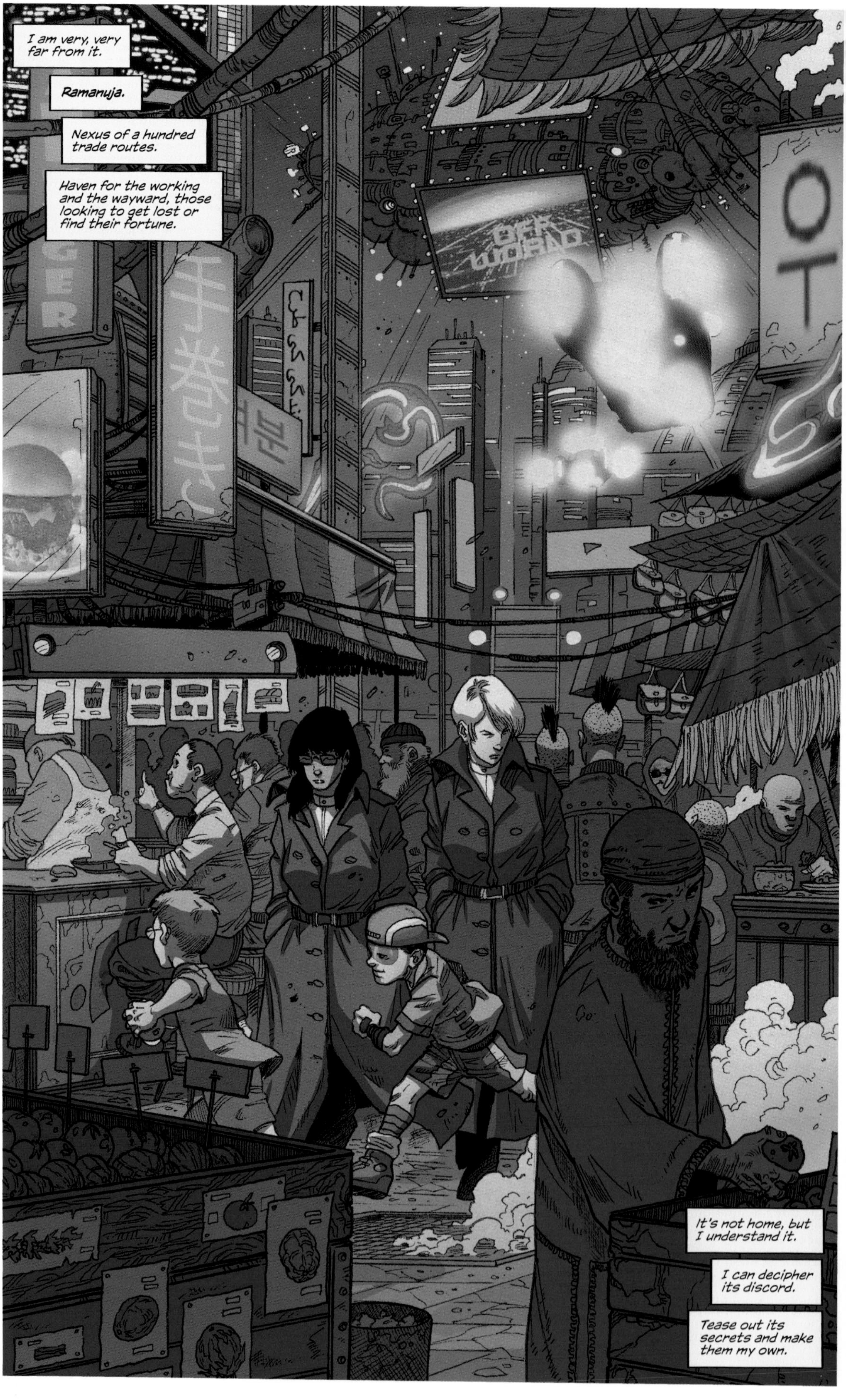
I am very, very far from it.
Ramanuja.
Nexus of a hundred trade routes.
Haven for the working and the wayward, those looking to get lost or find their fortune.
It's not home, but I understand it.
I can decipher its discord.
Tease out its secrets and make them my own.

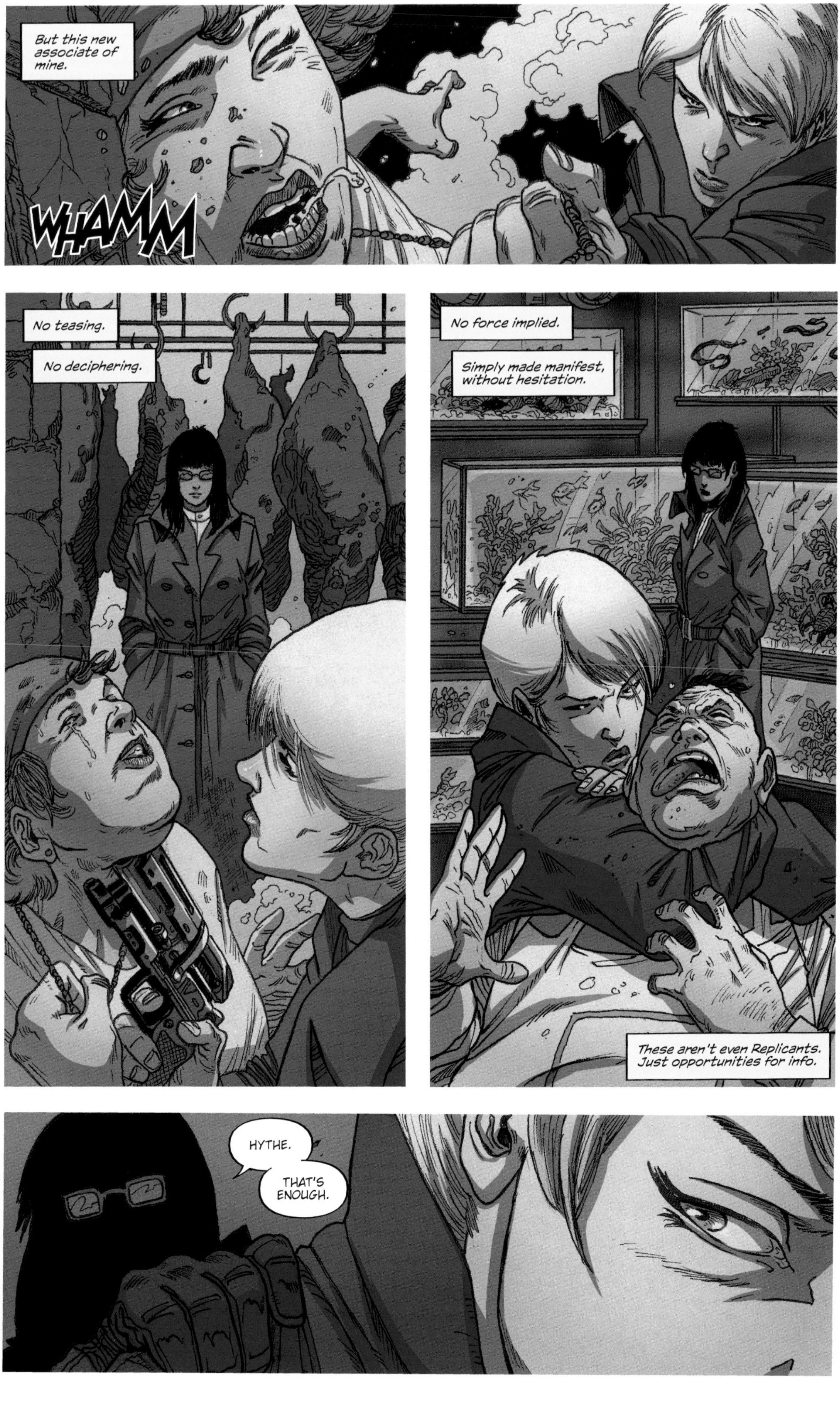
But this new associate of mine.
WHAMM
No teasing.
No deciphering.
No force implied.
Simply made manifest, without hesitation.
These aren't even Replicants. Just opportunities for info.
HYTHE.
THAT'S ENOUGH.

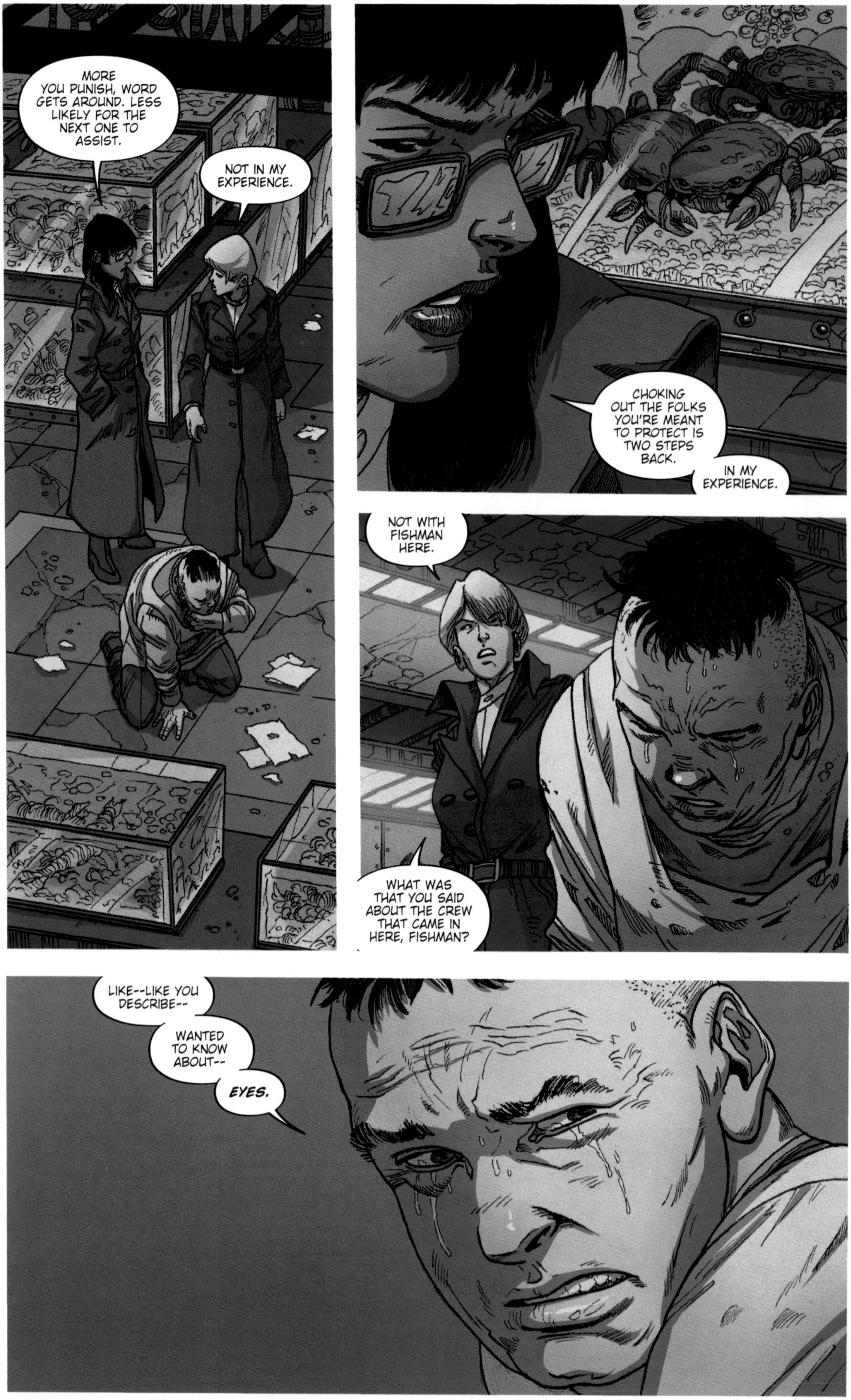
MORE YOU PUNISH, WORD GETS AROUND. LESS LIKELY FOR THE NEXT ONE TO ASSIST.
NOT IN MY EXPERIENCE.
CHOKING OUT THE FOLKS YOU'RE MEANT TO PROTECT IS TWO STEPS BACK.
IN MY EXPERIENCE.
NOT WITH FISHMAN HERE.
WHAT WAS THAT YOU SAID ABOUT THE CREW THAT CAME IN HERE, FISHMAN?
LIKE--LIKE YOU DESCRIBE--
WANTED TO KNOW ABOUT--
EYES.

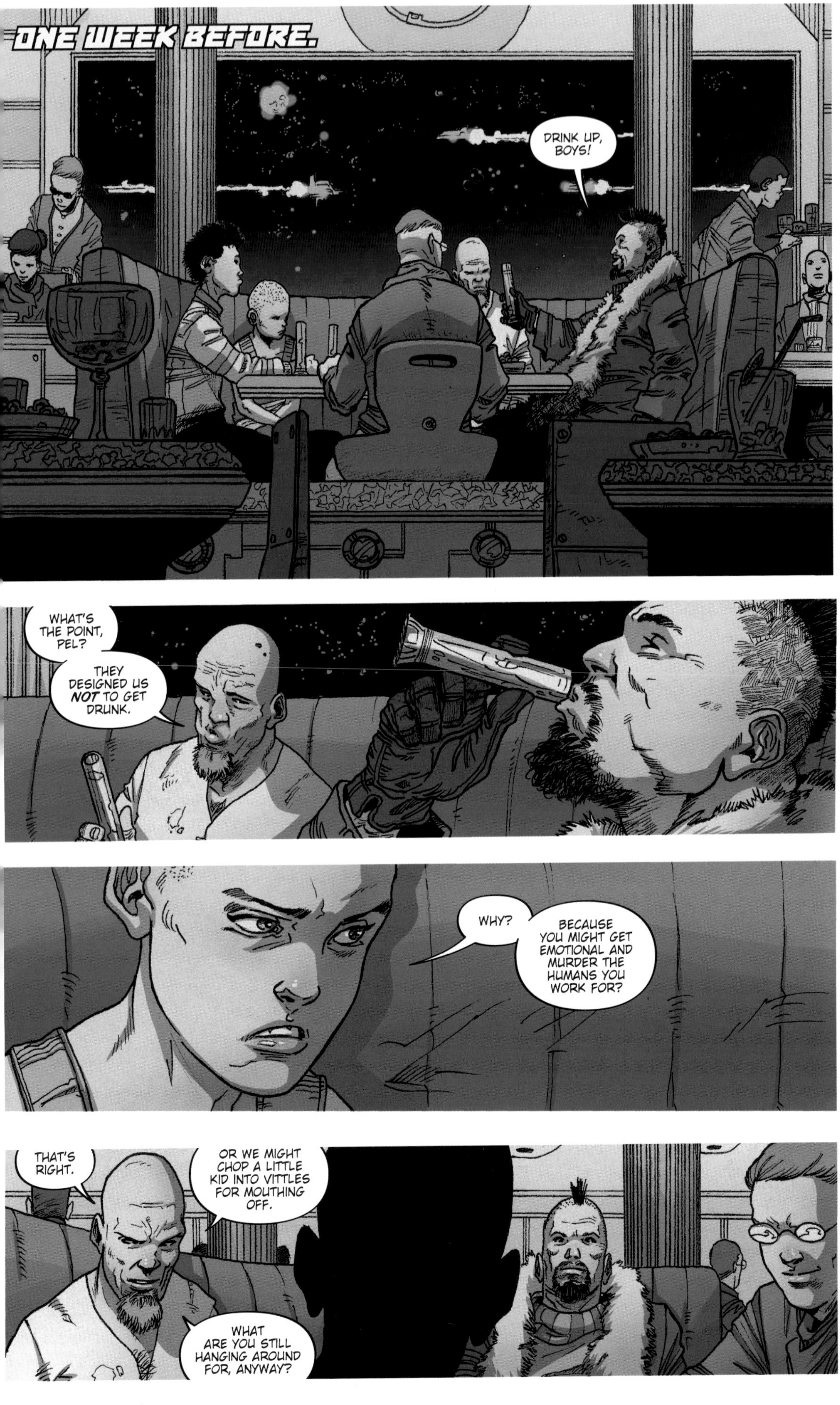
ONE WEEK BEFORE.
DRINK UP, BOYS!
WHAT'S THE POINT, PEL?
THEY DESIGNED US NOT TO GET DRUNK.
WHY?
BECAUSE YOU MIGHT GET EMOTIONAL AND MURDER THE HUMANS YOU WORK FOR?
THAT'S RIGHT.
OR WE MIGHT CHOP A LITTLE KID INTO VITTLES FOR MOUTHING OFF.
WHAT ARE YOU STILL HANGING AROUND FOR, ANYWAY?

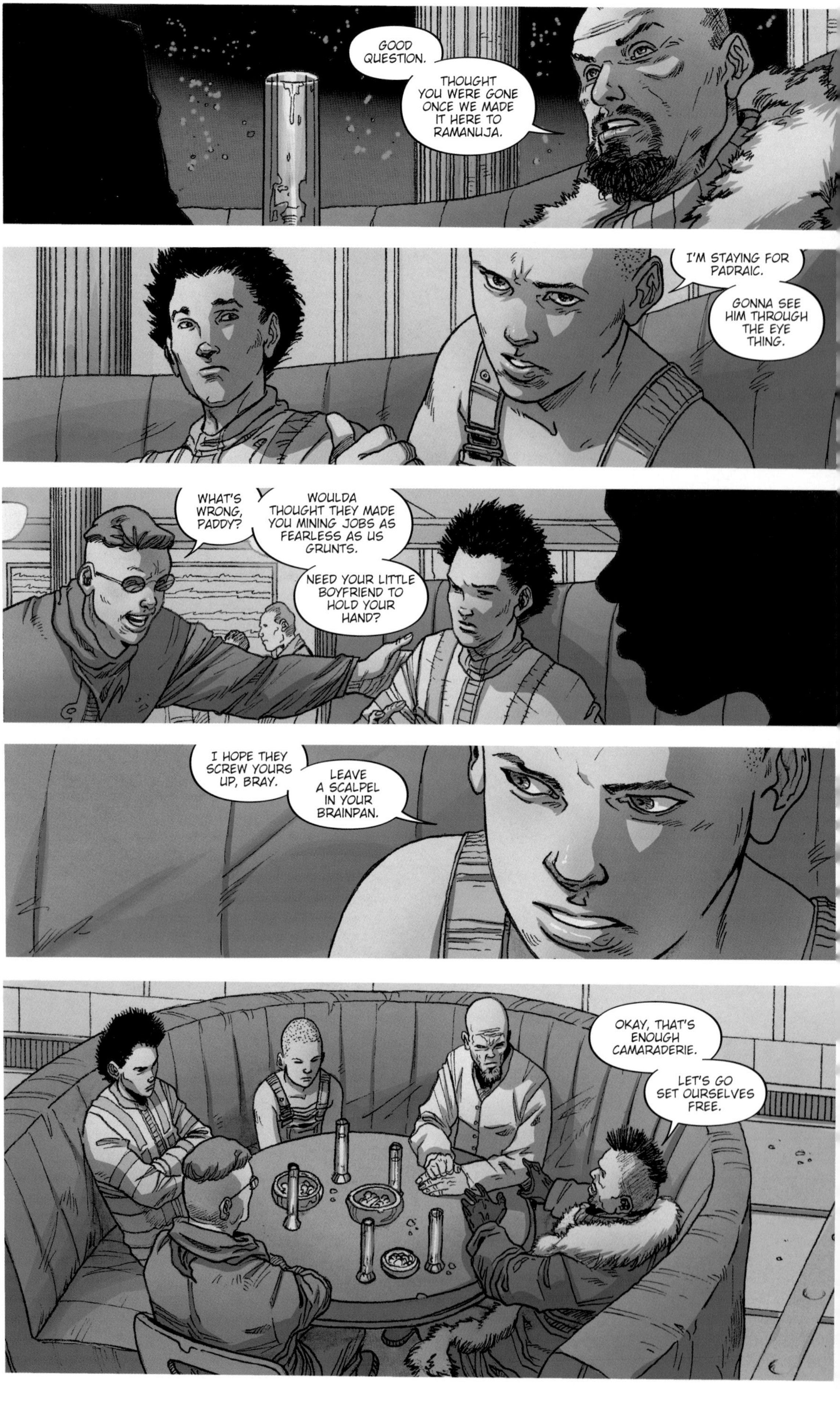
GOOD QUESTION.
THOUGHT YOU WERE GONE ONCE WE MADE IT HERE TO RAMANUJA.
I'M STAYING FOR PADRAIC.
GONNA SEE HIM THROUGH THE EYE THING.
WHAT'S WRONG, PADDY?
WOULDA THOUGHT THEY MADE YOU MINING JOBS AS FEARLESS AS US GRUNTS.
NEED YOUR LITTLE BOYFRIEND TO HOLD YOUR HAND?
I HOPE THEY SCREW YOURS UP, BRAY.
LEAVE A SCALPEL IN YOUR BRAINPAN.
OKAY, THAT'S ENOUGH CAMARADERIE.
LET'S GO SET OURSELVES FREE.

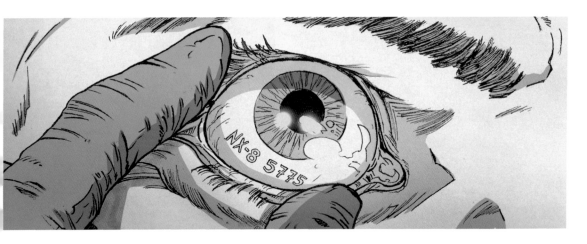

HOW'D YOU FIND ME?

AQUARIUMS GUY.

UNCLE JO. HE'S PROUD OF ME.

YOU AS EXPERIENCED WITH ORGANICS AS YOU ARE WITH METAL?

YOU GOT A BETTER OPTION?

BESIDES, YOUR MONEY'S ALREADY IN WASH AND DEPO.

YOU SURE YOU DON'T WANT CANDY FOR THIS?

I RECOMMEND CANDY.

I'M A NEXUS-8 COMBAT MODEL.

NOTHING YOU CAN IMAGINE COULD HURT ME.

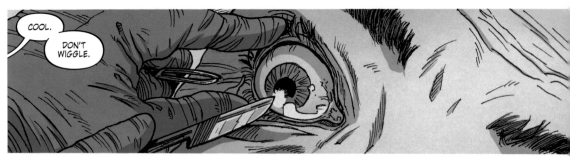

COOL.

DON'T WIGGLE.

AAAIIIIEEE!

AAAIIIIEEEEE!

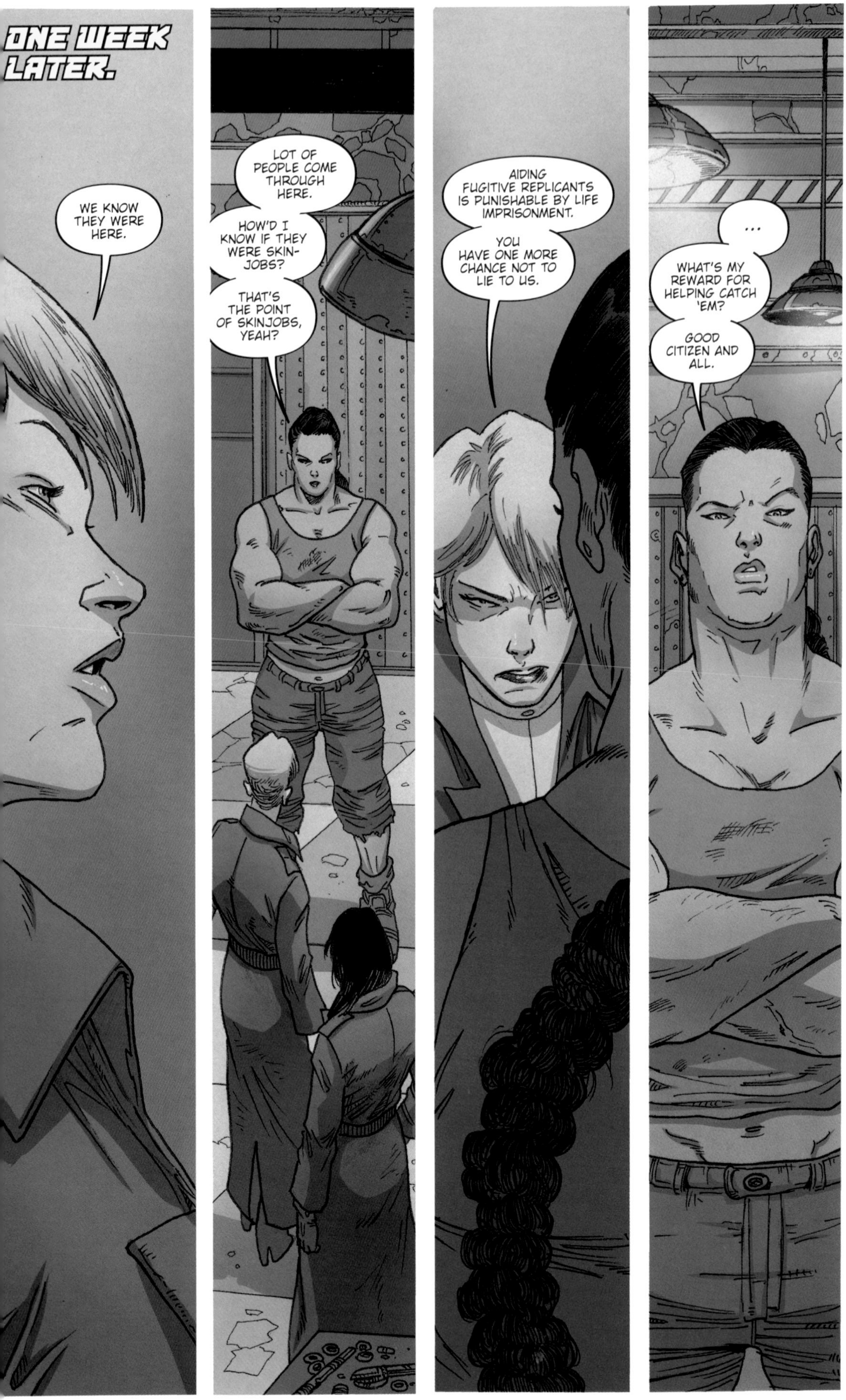
ONE WEEK LATER.
WE KNOW THEY WERE HERE.
LOT OF PEOPLE COME THROUGH HERE.
HOW'D I KNOW IF THEY WERE SKIN-JOBS?
THAT'S THE POINT OF SKINJOBS, YEAH?
AIDING FUGITIVE REPLICANTS IS PUNISHABLE BY LIFE IMPRISONMENT.
YOU HAVE ONE MORE CHANCE NOT TO LIE TO US.
...
WHAT'S MY REWARD FOR HELPING CATCH 'EM?
GOOD CITIZEN AND ALL.

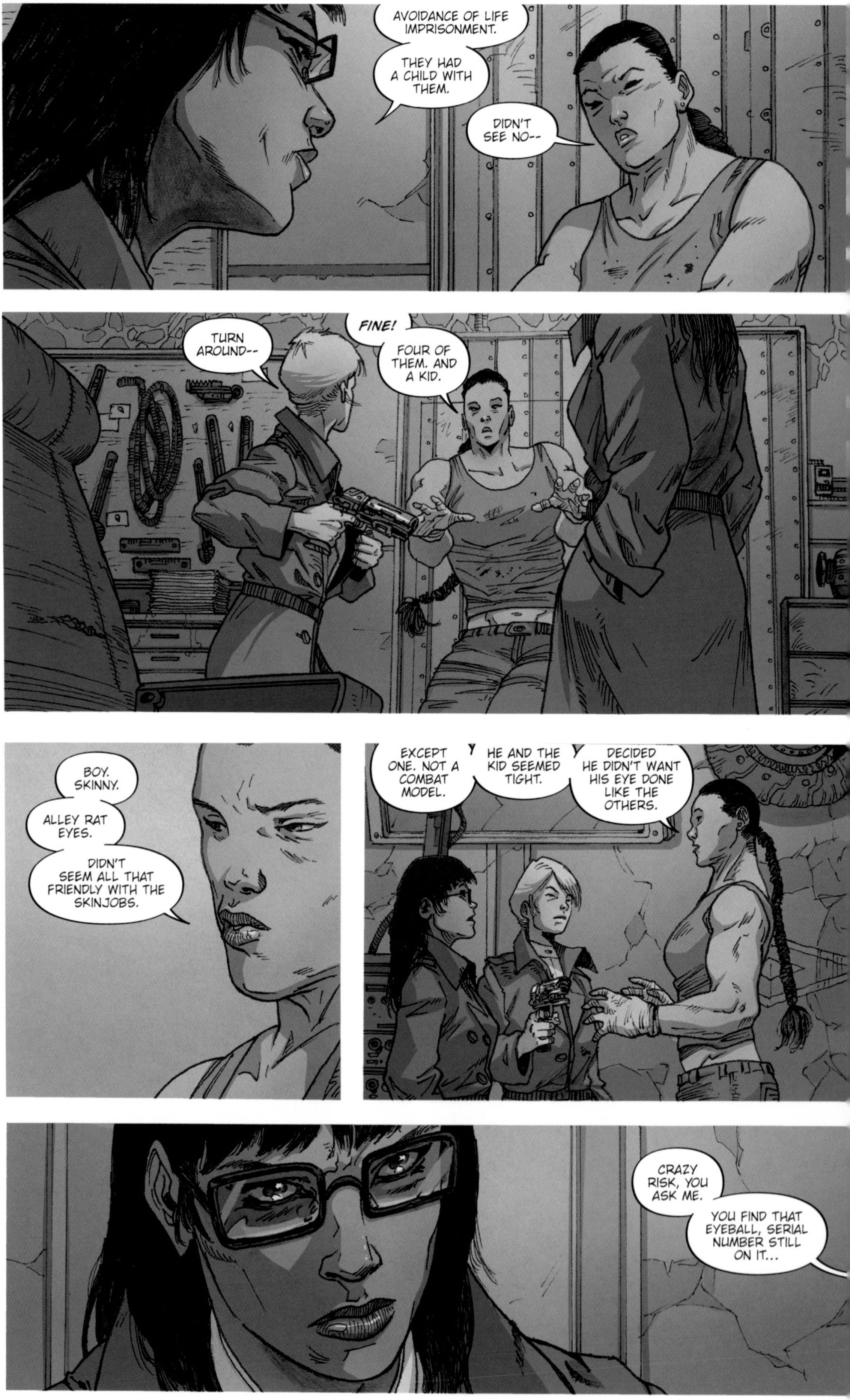
AVOIDANCE OF LIFE IMPRISONMENT.
THEY HAD A CHILD WITH THEM.
DIDN'T SEE NO--
TURN AROUND--
FINE!
FOUR OF THEM. AND A KID.
BOY. SKINNY.
ALLEY RAT EYES.
DIDN'T SEEM ALL THAT FRIENDLY WITH THE SKINJOBS.
EXCEPT ONE. NOT A COMBAT MODEL.
HE AND THE KID SEEMED TIGHT.
DECIDED HE DIDN'T WANT HIS EYE DONE LIKE THE OTHERS.
CRAZY RISK, YOU ASK ME.
YOU FIND THAT EYEBALL, SERIAL NUMBER STILL ON IT...

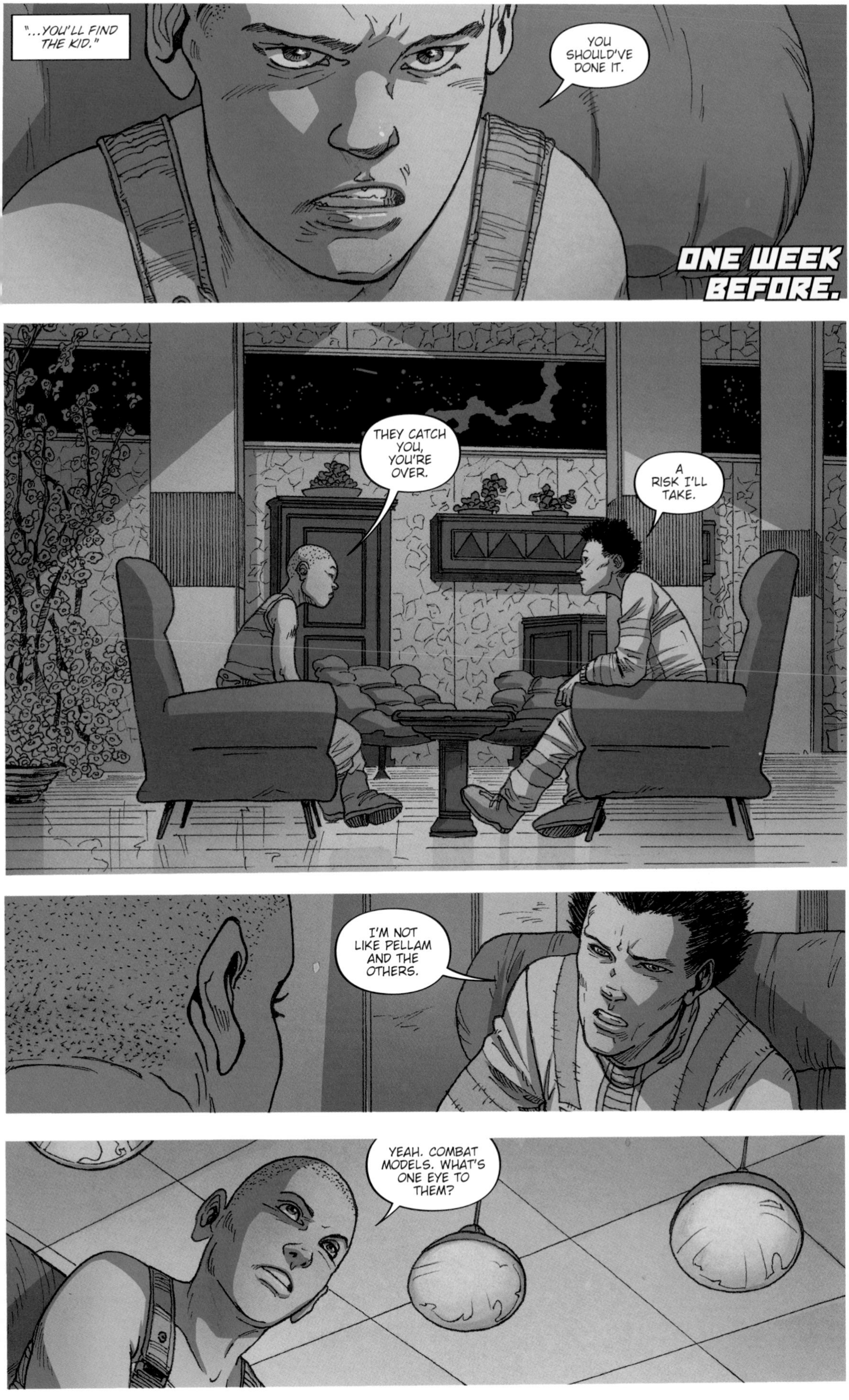
"...YOU'LL FIND THE KID."
YOU SHOULD'VE DONE IT.
ONE WEEK BEFORE.
THEY CATCH YOU, YOU'RE OVER.
A RISK I'LL TAKE.
I'M NOT LIKE PELLAM AND THE OTHERS.
YEAH. COMBAT MODELS. WHAT'S ONE EYE TO THEM?

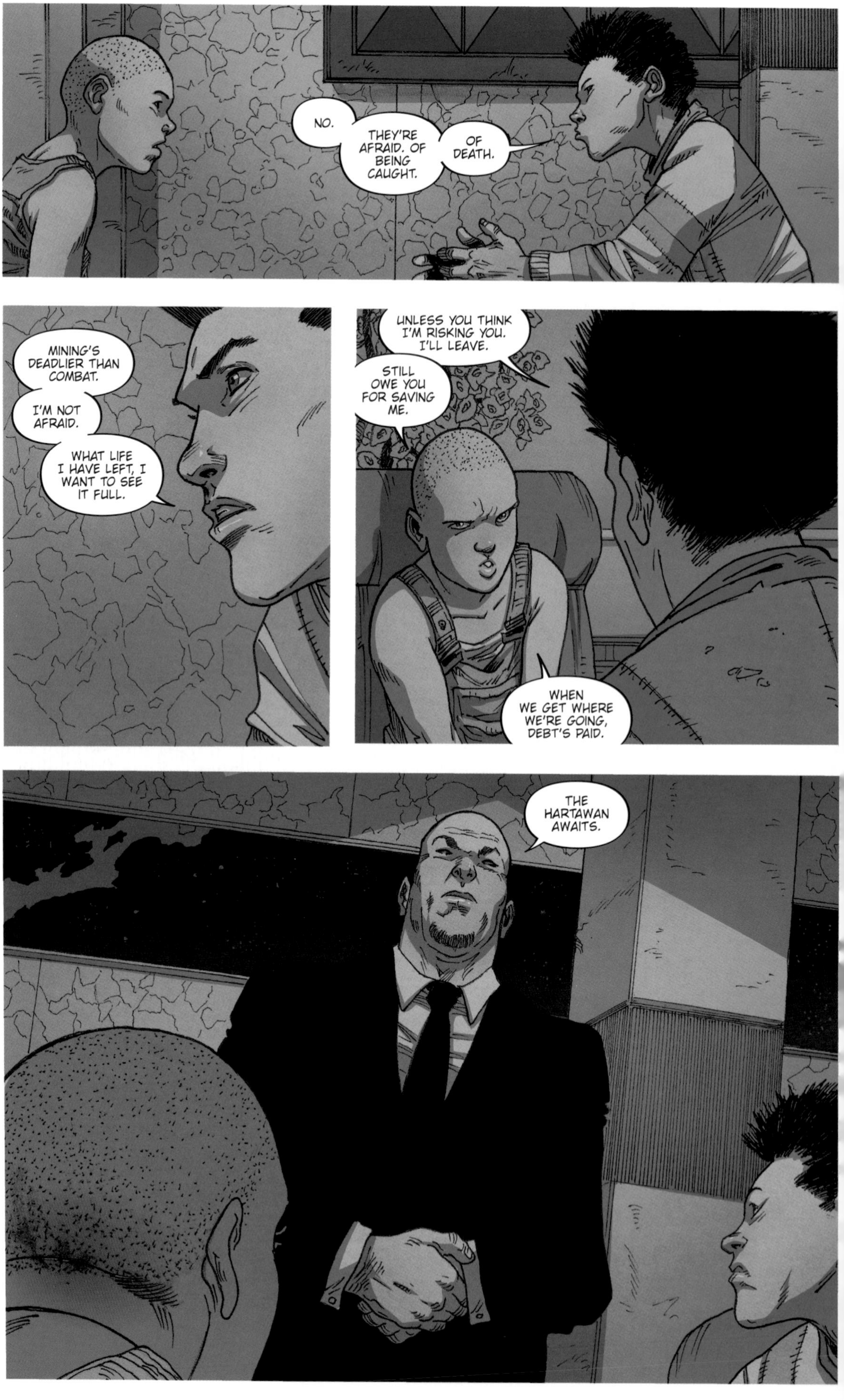
NO.
THEY'RE AFRAID. OF BEING CAUGHT.
OF DEATH.
MINING'S DEADLIER THAN COMBAT.
I'M NOT AFRAID.
WHAT LIFE I HAVE LEFT, I WANT TO SEE IT FULL.
UNLESS YOU THINK I'M RISKING YOU. I'LL LEAVE.
STILL OWE YOU FOR SAVING ME.
WHEN WE GET WHERE WE'RE GOING, DEBT'S PAID.
THE HARTAWAN AWAITS.

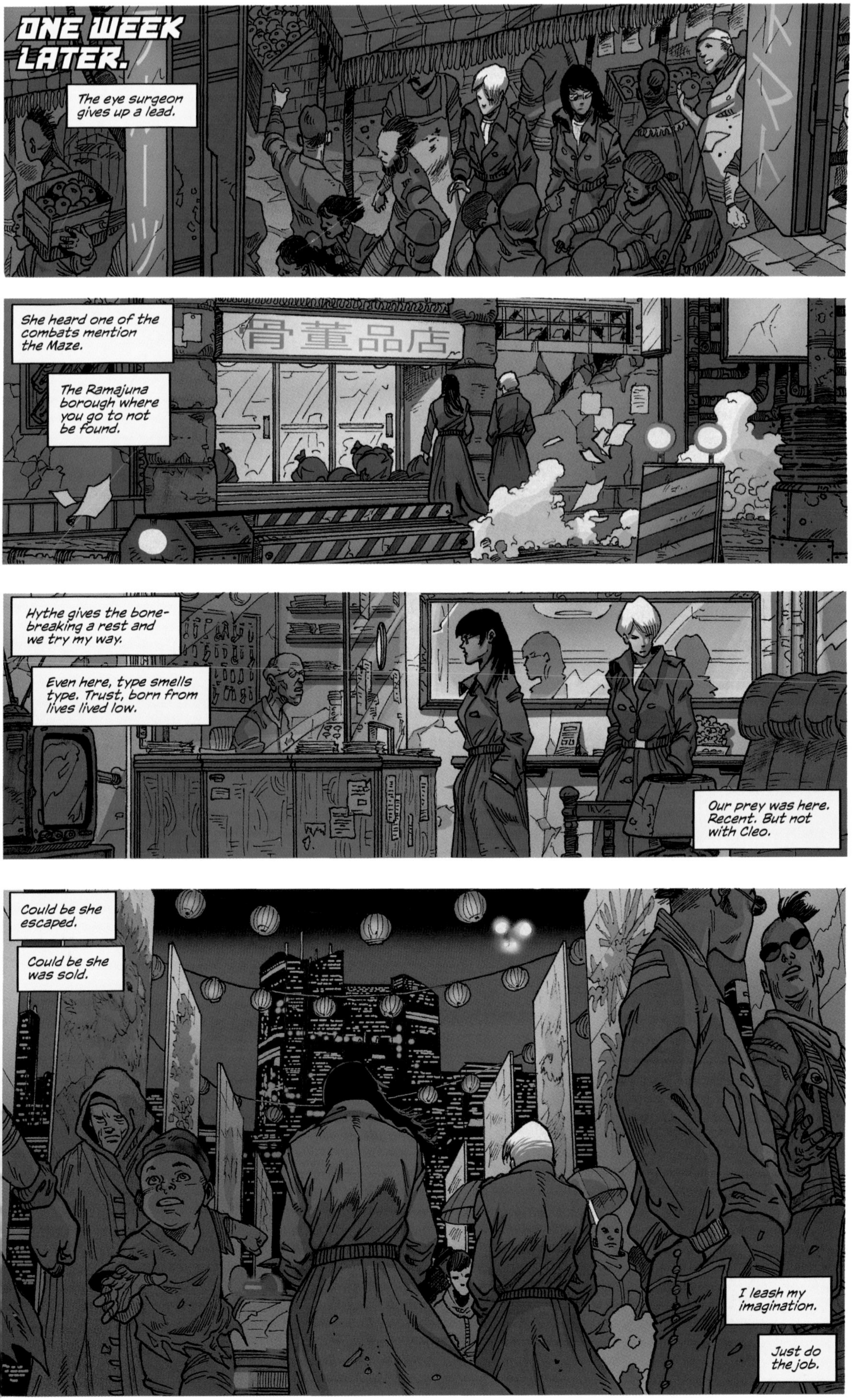
ONE WEEK LATER.
The eye surgeon gives up a lead.
She heard one of the combats mention the Maze.
The Ramajuna borough where you go to not be found.
骨董品店
Hythe gives the bone-breaking a rest and we try my way.
Even here, type smells type. Trust, born from lives lived low.
Our prey was here. Recent. But not with Cleo.
Could be she escaped.
Could be she was sold.
I leash my imagination.
Just do the job.

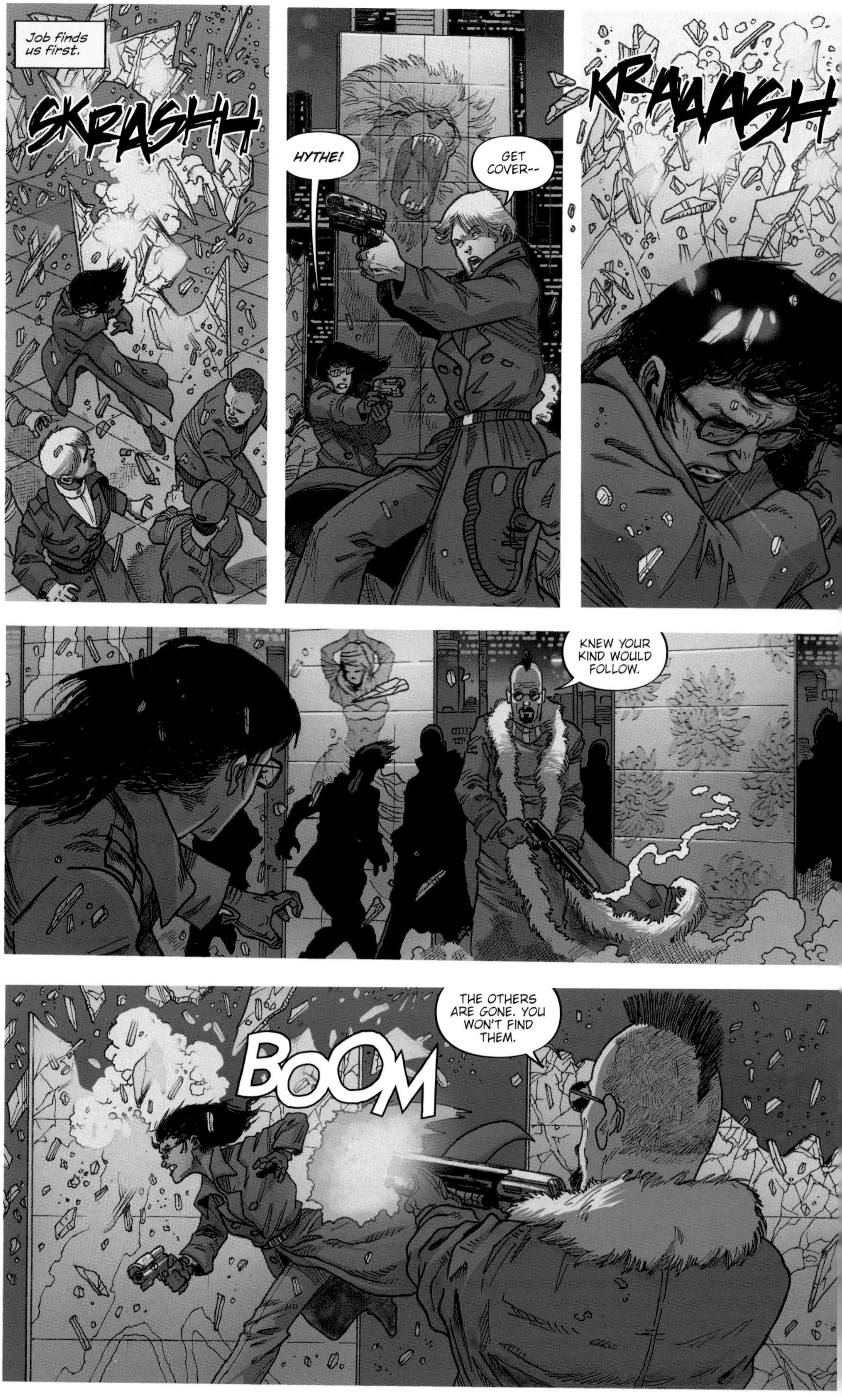
Job finds us first.
SKRASHH
HYTHE!
GET COVER--
KRAAASH
KNEW YOUR KIND WOULD FOLLOW.
BOOM
THE OTHERS ARE GONE. YOU WON'T FIND THEM.

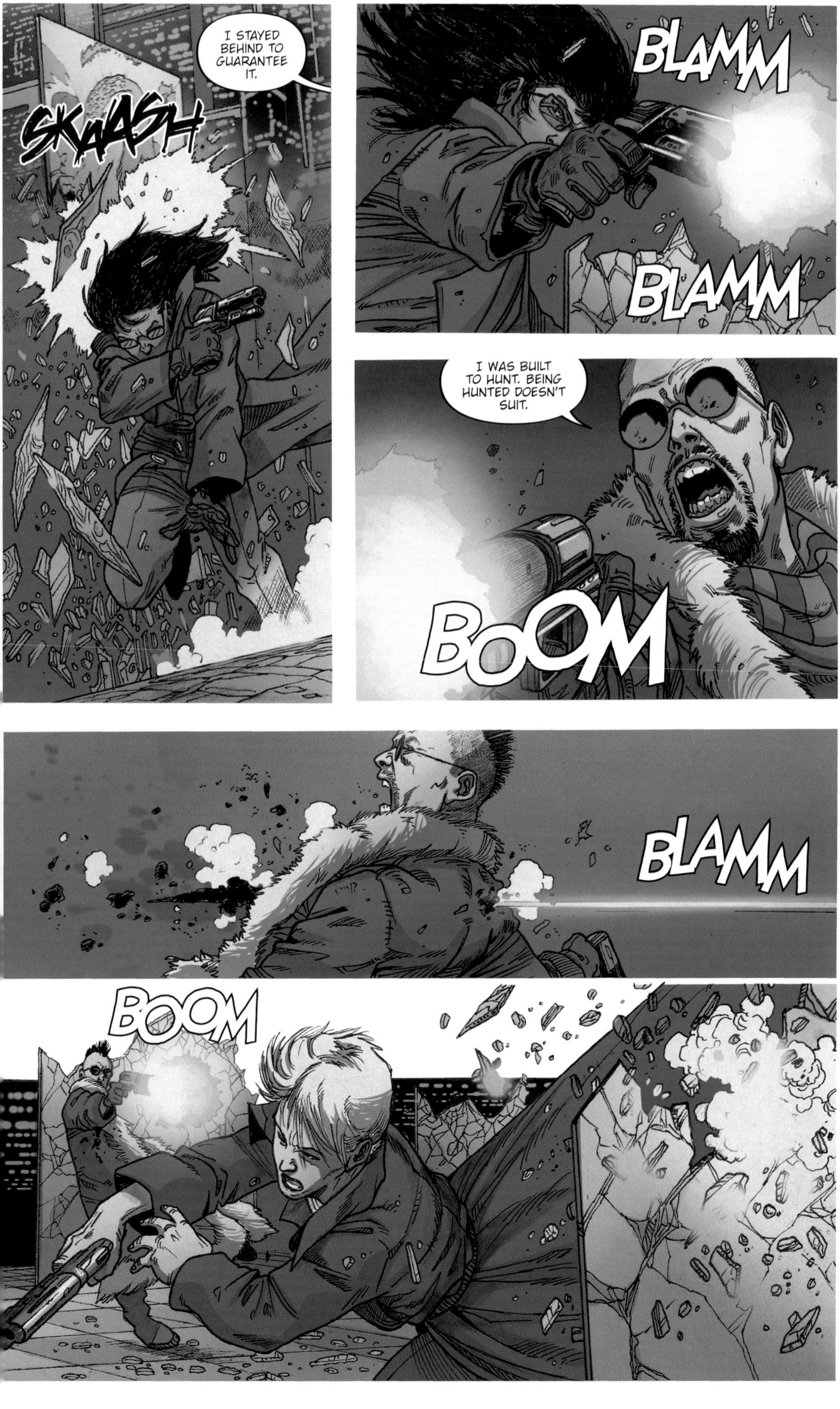
I STAYED BEHIND TO GUARANTEE IT.
SKWASH
BLAMM
BLAMM
I WAS BUILT TO HUNT. BEING HUNTED DOESN'T SUIT.
BOOM
BLAMM
BOOM

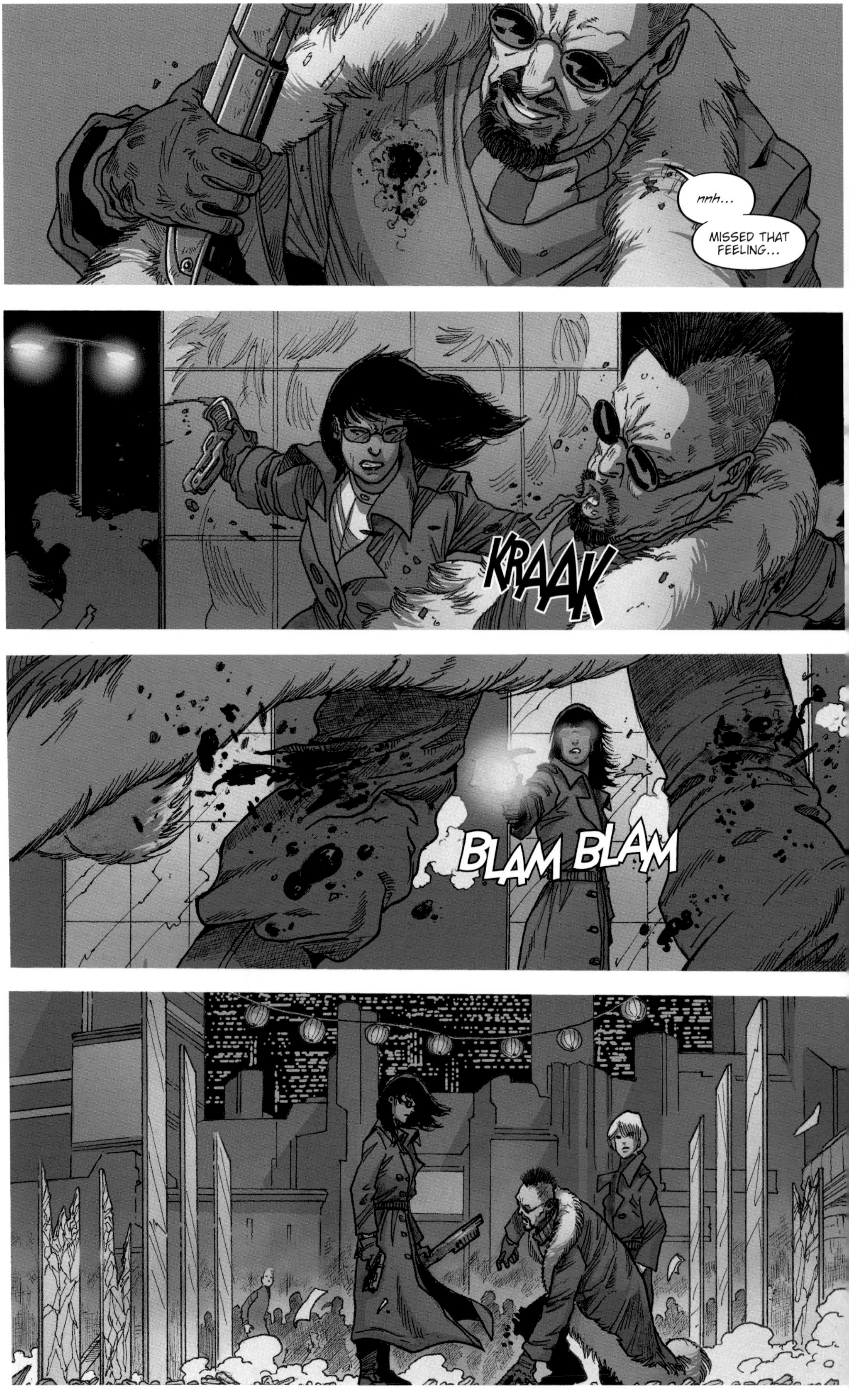
nnh...
MISSED THAT FEELING...
KRAAK
BLAM BLAM

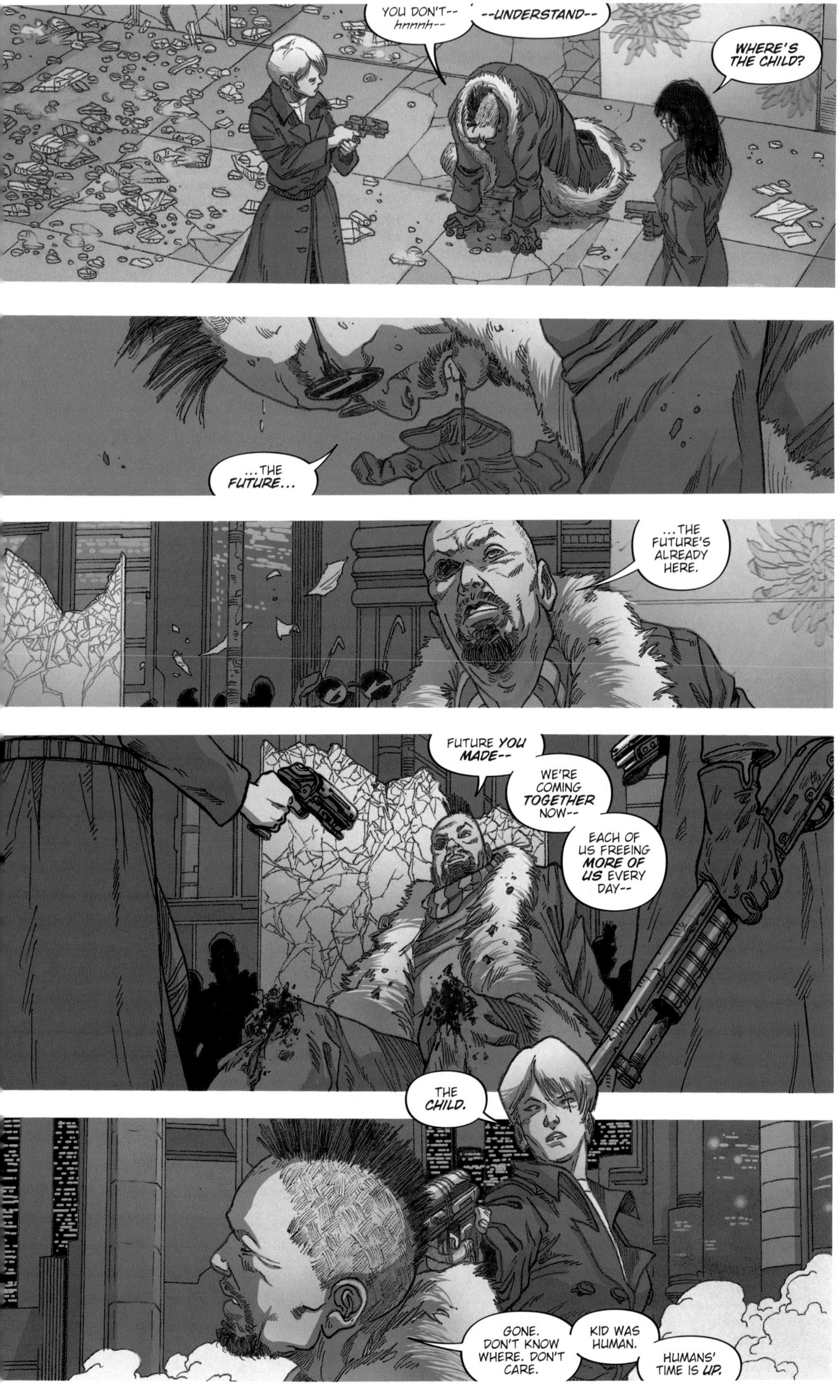
YOU DON'T-- hnnnh--
--UNDERSTAND--
WHERE'S THE CHILD?
...THE FUTURE...
...THE FUTURE'S ALREADY HERE.
FUTURE YOU MADE--
WE'RE COMING TOGETHER NOW--
EACH OF US FREEING MORE OF US EVERY DAY--
THE CHILD.
GONE. DON'T KNOW WHERE. DON'T CARE.
KID WAS HUMAN.
HUMANS' TIME IS UP.

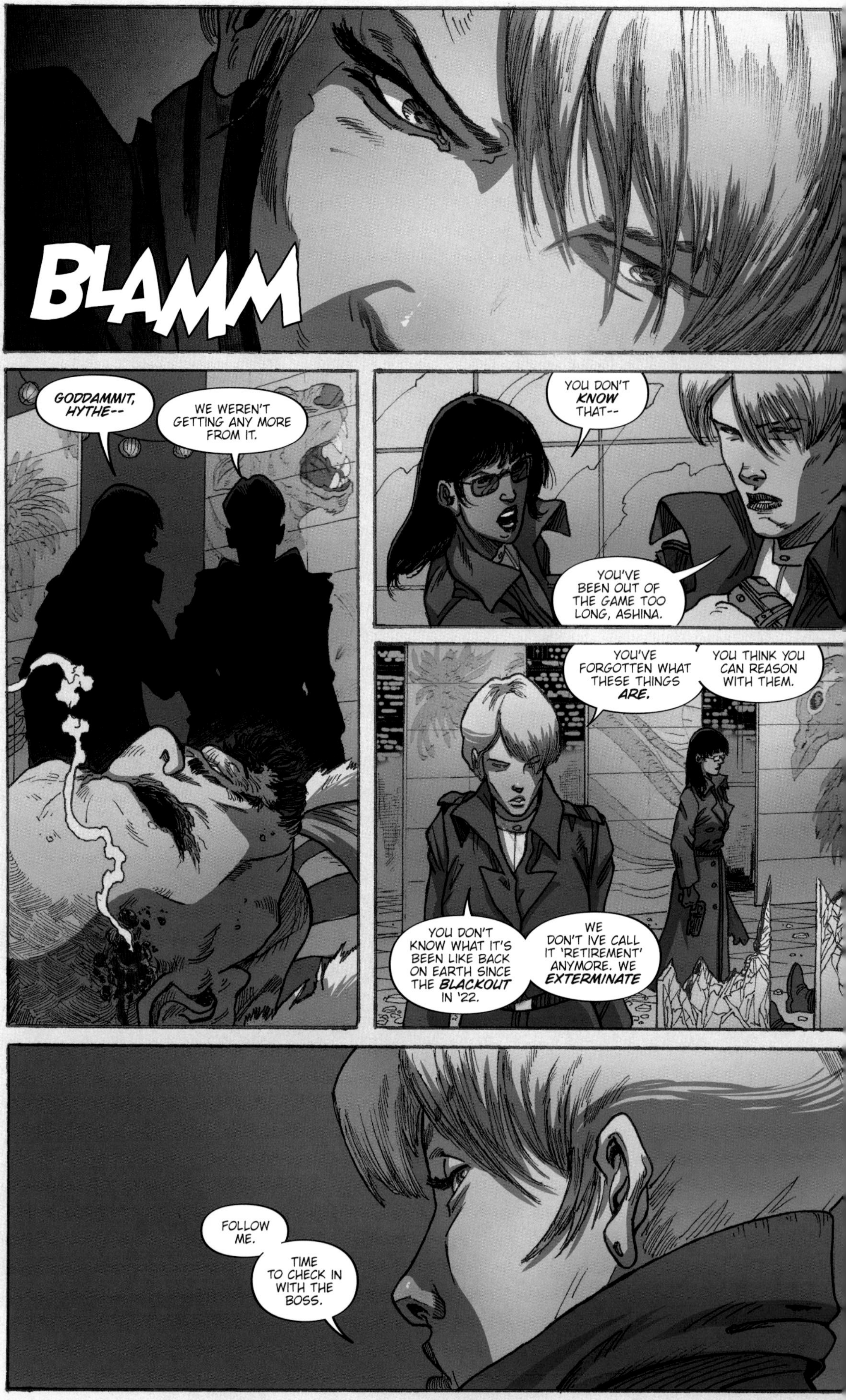
BLAMM
GODDAMMIT, HYTHE--
WE WEREN'T GETTING ANY MORE FROM IT.
YOU DON'T ***KNOW*** THAT--
YOU'VE BEEN OUT OF THE GAME TOO LONG, ASHINA.
YOU'VE FORGOTTEN WHAT THESE THINGS ***ARE.***
YOU THINK YOU CAN REASON WITH THEM.
YOU DON'T KNOW WHAT IT'S BEEN LIKE BACK ON EARTH SINCE THE ***BLACKOUT*** IN '22.
WE DON'T IVE CALL IT 'RETIREMENT' ANYMORE. WE ***EXTERMINATE***
FOLLOW ME.
TIME TO CHECK IN WITH THE BOSS.

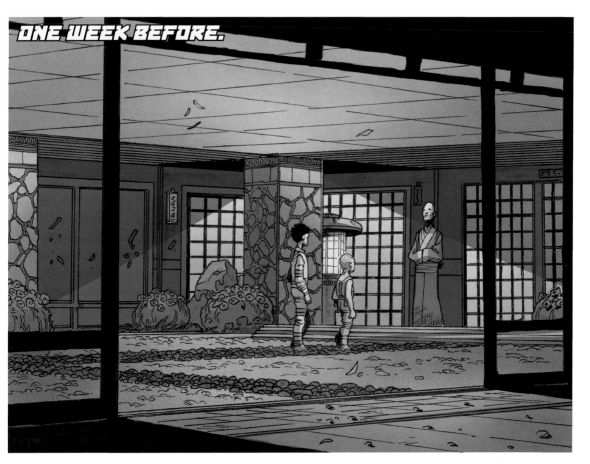

Ah.

WE MEET AT LAST.

THE *RABBIT,* IN THE FLESH AND FUR.

I FEARED THE WORST WHEN I HEARD OF THE ATTACK.

THANK YOU FOR SEEING ME, HARTAWAN.

WE HAVE SHARED A PROFITABLE RELATIONSHIP, IF ONLY FROM AFAR.

TO IGNORE YOUR REQUEST FOR CONCLAVE WOULD BE UNMANNERLY.

WHAT DOES THE RABBIT SEEK?

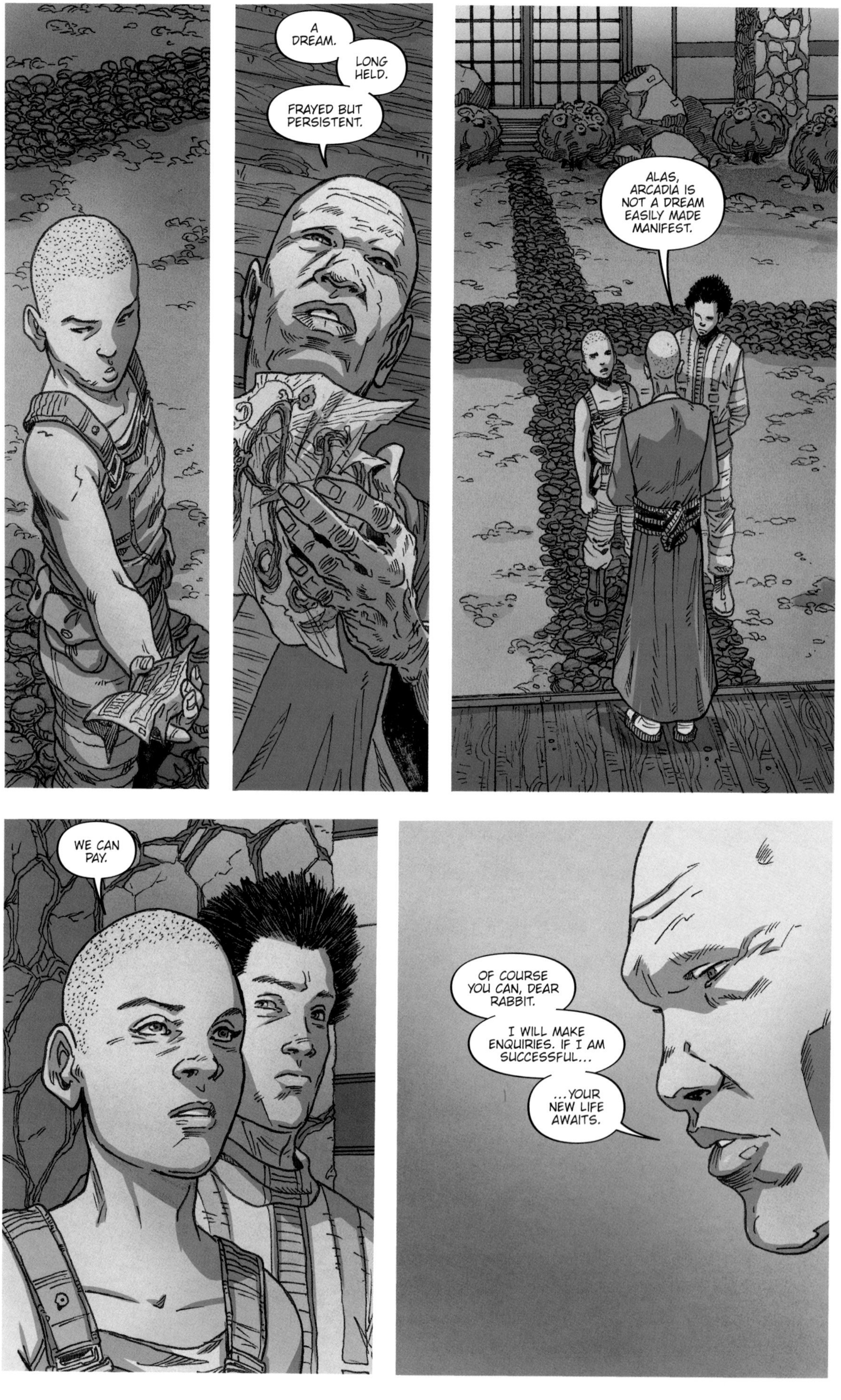
A DREAM.
LONG HELD.
FRAYED BUT PERSISTENT.
ALAS, ARCADIA IS NOT A DREAM EASILY MADE MANIFEST.
WE CAN PAY.
OF COURSE YOU CAN, DEAR RABBIT.
I WILL MAKE ENQUIRIES. IF I AM SUCCESSFUL...
...YOUR NEW LIFE AWAITS.

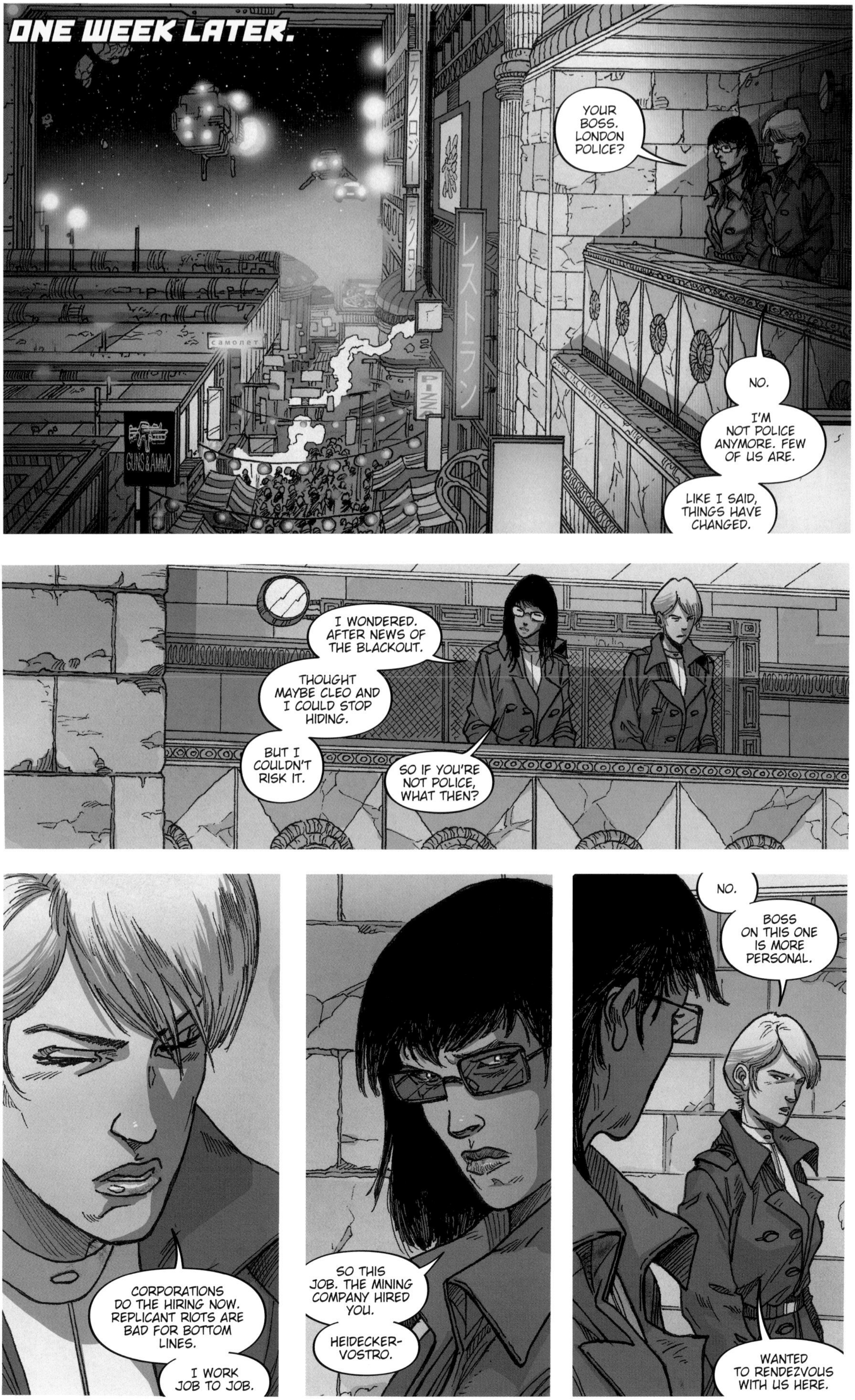
ONE WEEK LATER.
テクノロジー
レストラン
самолет
PIZZA
GUNS & AMMO
YOUR BOSS. LONDON POLICE?
NO.
I'M NOT POLICE ANYMORE. FEW OF US ARE.
LIKE I SAID, THINGS HAVE CHANGED.
I WONDERED. AFTER NEWS OF THE BLACKOUT.
THOUGHT MAYBE CLEO AND I COULD STOP HIDING.
BUT I COULDN'T RISK IT.
SO IF YOU'RE NOT POLICE, WHAT THEN?
CORPORATIONS DO THE HIRING NOW. REPLICANT RIOTS ARE BAD FOR BOTTOM LINES.
I WORK JOB TO JOB.
SO THIS JOB. THE MINING COMPANY HIRED YOU.
HEIDECKER-VOSTRO.
NO.
BOSS ON THIS ONE IS MORE PERSONAL.
WANTED TO RENDEZVOUS WITH US HERE.

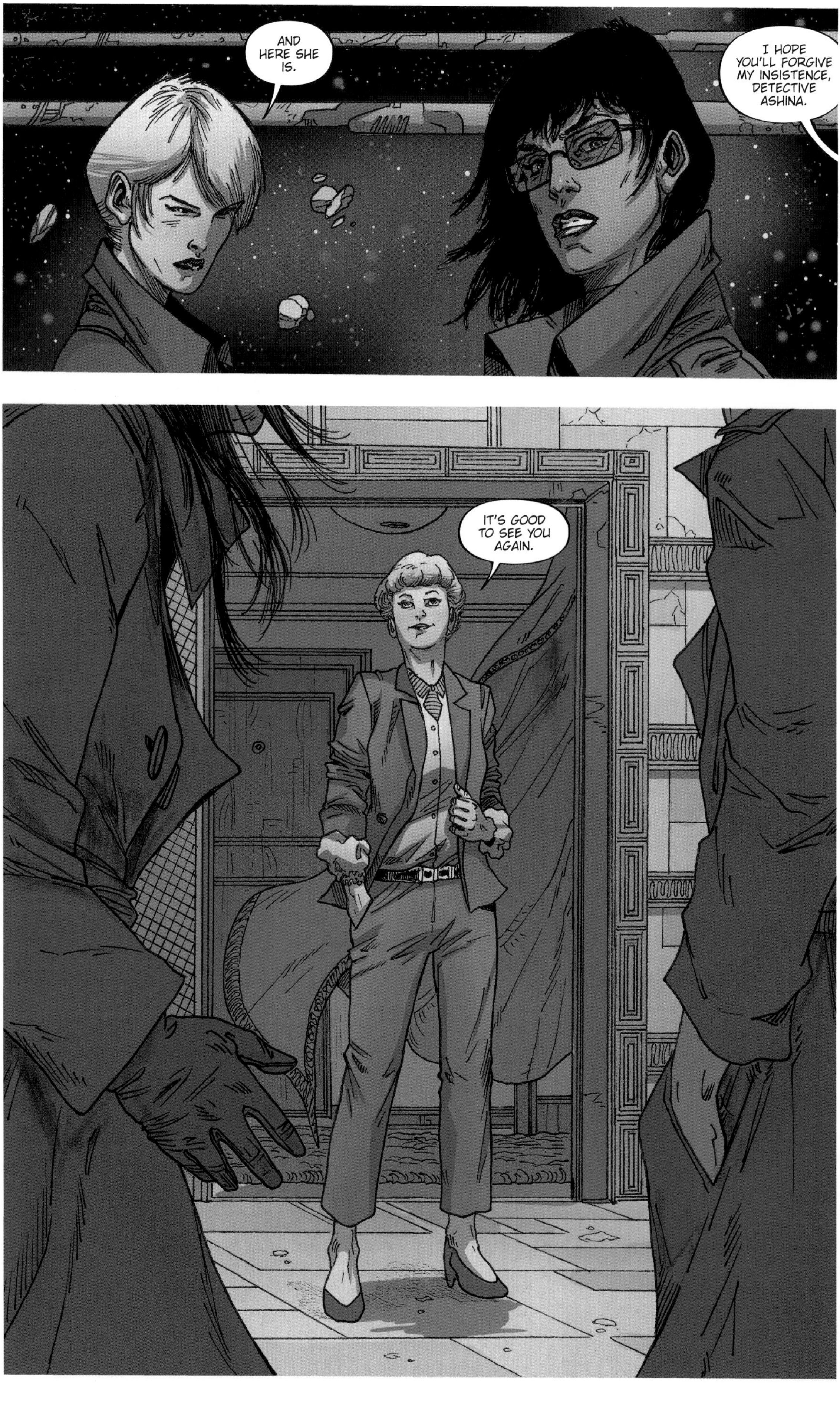

AND HERE SHE IS.
I HOPE YOU'LL FORGIVE MY INSISTENCE, DETECTIVE ASHINA.
IT'S GOOD TO SEE YOU AGAIN.

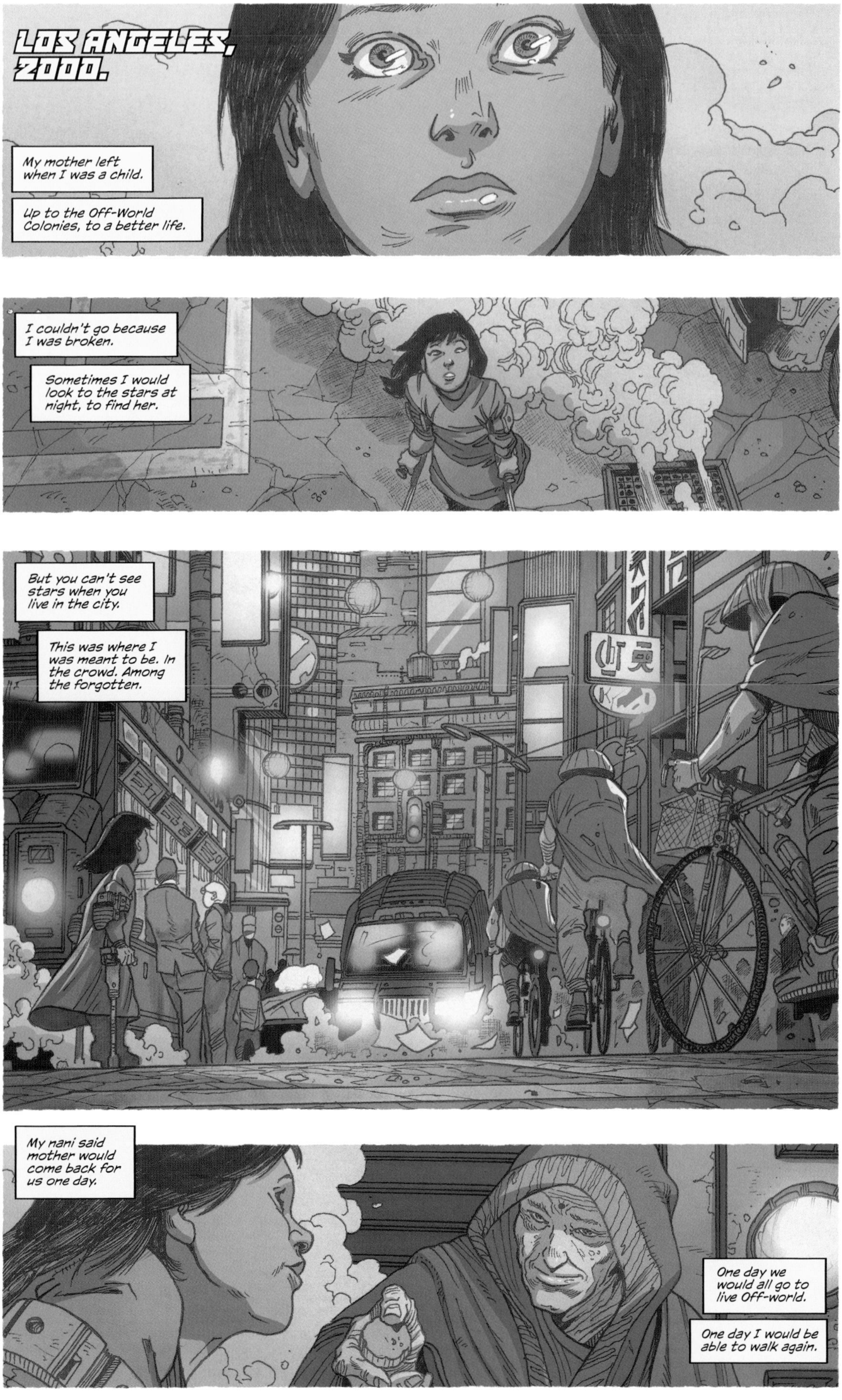
LOS ANGELES, 2000.
My mother left when I was a child.
Up to the Off-World Colonies, to a better life.
I couldn't go because I was broken.
Sometimes I would look to the stars at night, to find her.
But you can't see stars when you live in the city.
This was where I was meant to be. In the crowd. Among the forgotten.
My nani said mother would come back for us one day.
One day we would all go to live Off-world.
One day I would be able to walk again.

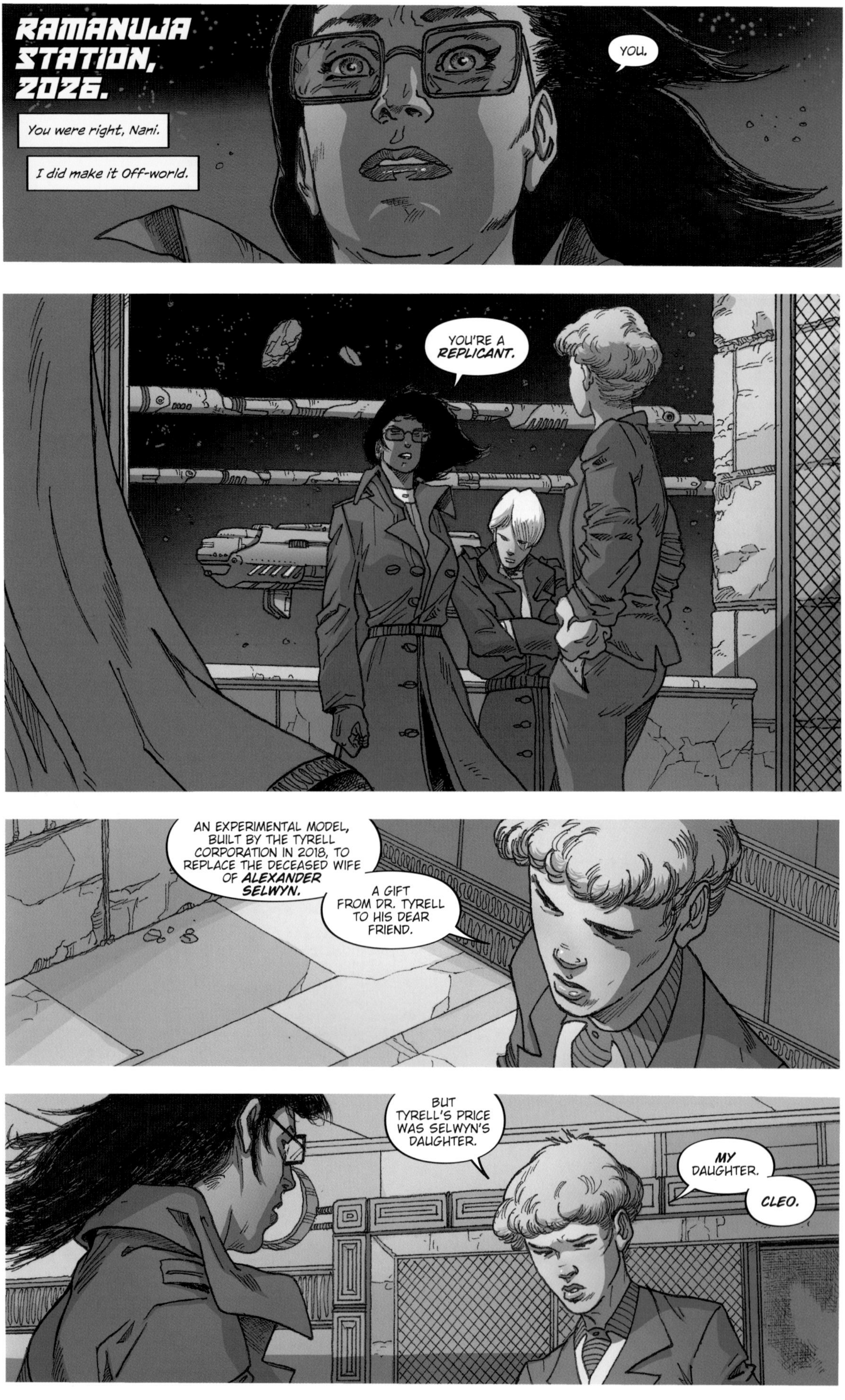
RAMANUJA STATION, 2026.
You were right, Nani.
I did make it Off-world.
YOU.
YOU'RE A REPLICANT.
AN EXPERIMENTAL MODEL, BUILT BY THE TYRELL CORPORATION IN 2018, TO REPLACE THE DECEASED WIFE OF ALEXANDER SELWYN.
A GIFT FROM DR. TYRELL TO HIS DEAR FRIEND.
BUT TYRELL'S PRICE WAS SELWYN'S DAUGHTER.
MY DAUGHTER.
CLEO.

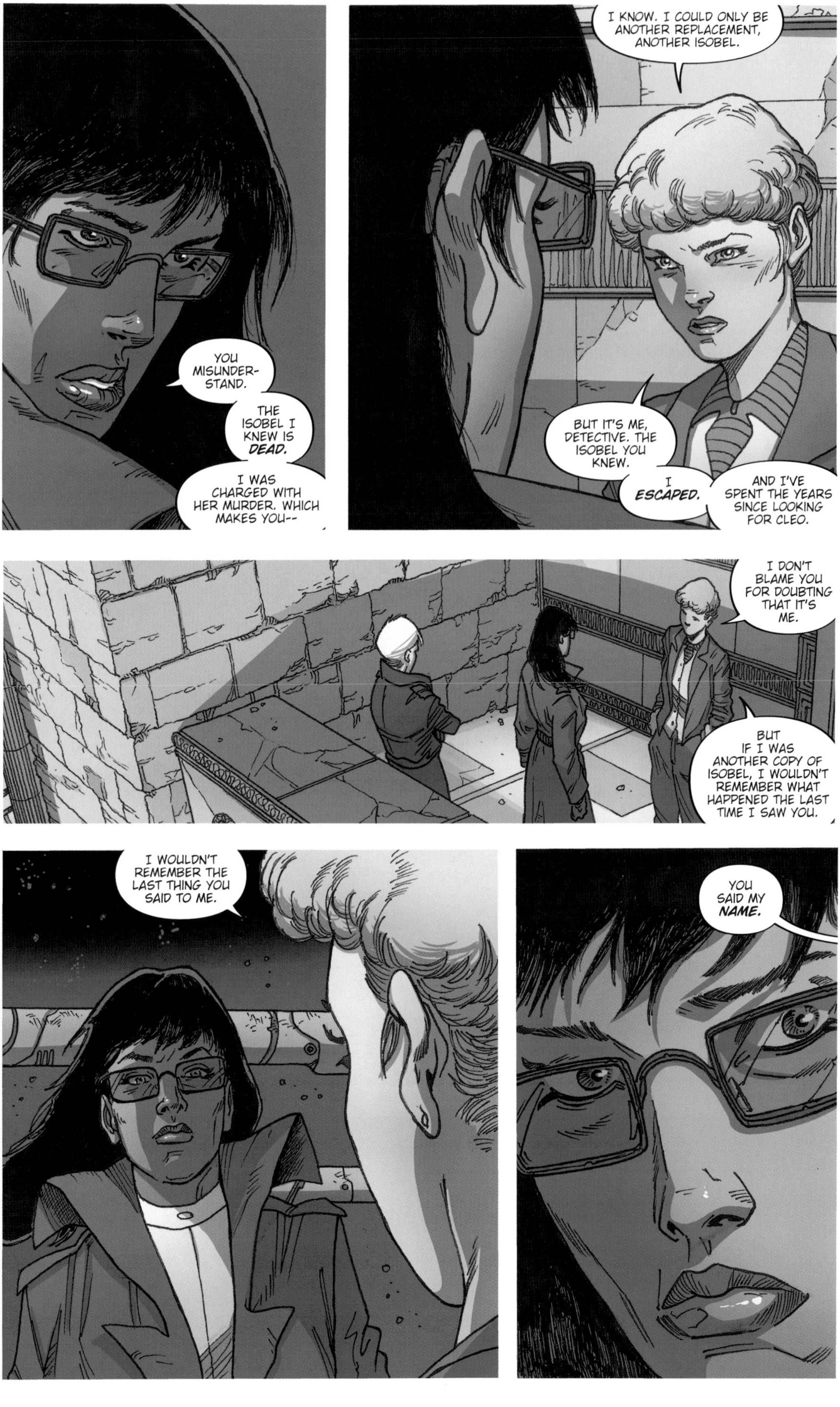
YOU MISUNDER-STAND.
THE ISOBEL I KNEW IS **DEAD.**
I WAS CHARGED WITH HER MURDER. WHICH MAKES YOU--
I KNOW. I COULD ONLY BE ANOTHER REPLACEMENT, ANOTHER ISOBEL.
BUT IT'S ME, DETECTIVE. THE ISOBEL YOU KNEW.
I **ESCAPED.**
AND I'VE SPENT THE YEARS SINCE LOOKING FOR CLEO.
I DON'T BLAME YOU FOR DOUBTING THAT IT'S ME.
BUT IF I WAS ANOTHER COPY OF ISOBEL, I WOULDN'T REMEMBER WHAT HAPPENED THE LAST TIME I SAW YOU.
I WOULDN'T REMEMBER THE LAST THING YOU SAID TO ME.
YOU SAID MY **NAME.**

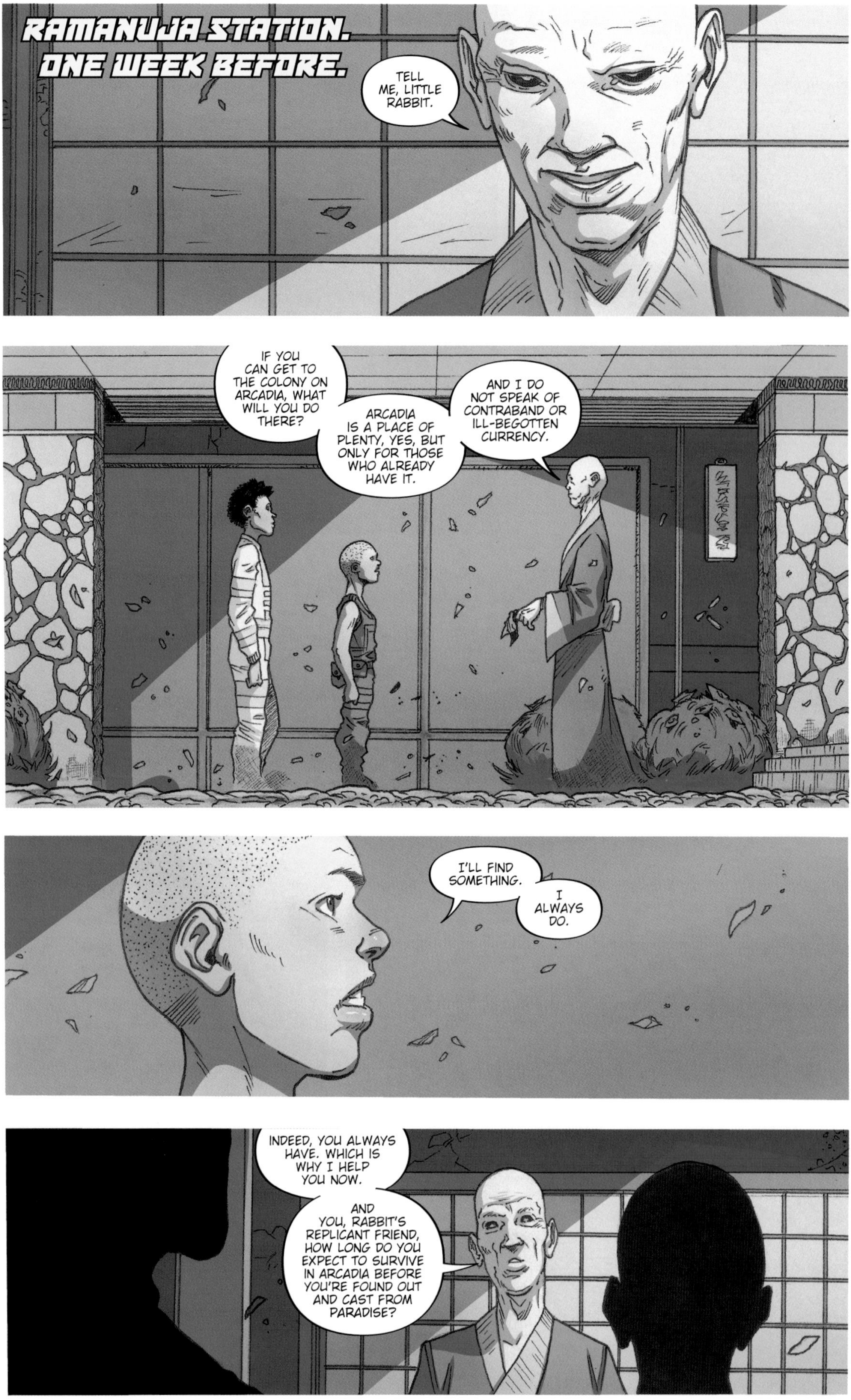
RAMANUJA STATION. ONE WEEK BEFORE.
TELL ME, LITTLE RABBIT.
IF YOU CAN GET TO THE COLONY ON ARCADIA, WHAT WILL YOU DO THERE?
ARCADIA IS A PLACE OF PLENTY, YES, BUT ONLY FOR THOSE WHO ALREADY HAVE IT.
AND I DO NOT SPEAK OF CONTRABAND OR ILL-BEGOTTEN CURRENCY.
I'LL FIND SOMETHING.
I ALWAYS DO.
INDEED, YOU ALWAYS HAVE. WHICH IS WHY I HELP YOU NOW.
AND YOU, RABBIT'S REPLICANT FRIEND, HOW LONG DO YOU EXPECT TO SURVIVE IN ARCADIA BEFORE YOU'RE FOUND OUT AND CAST FROM PARADISE?

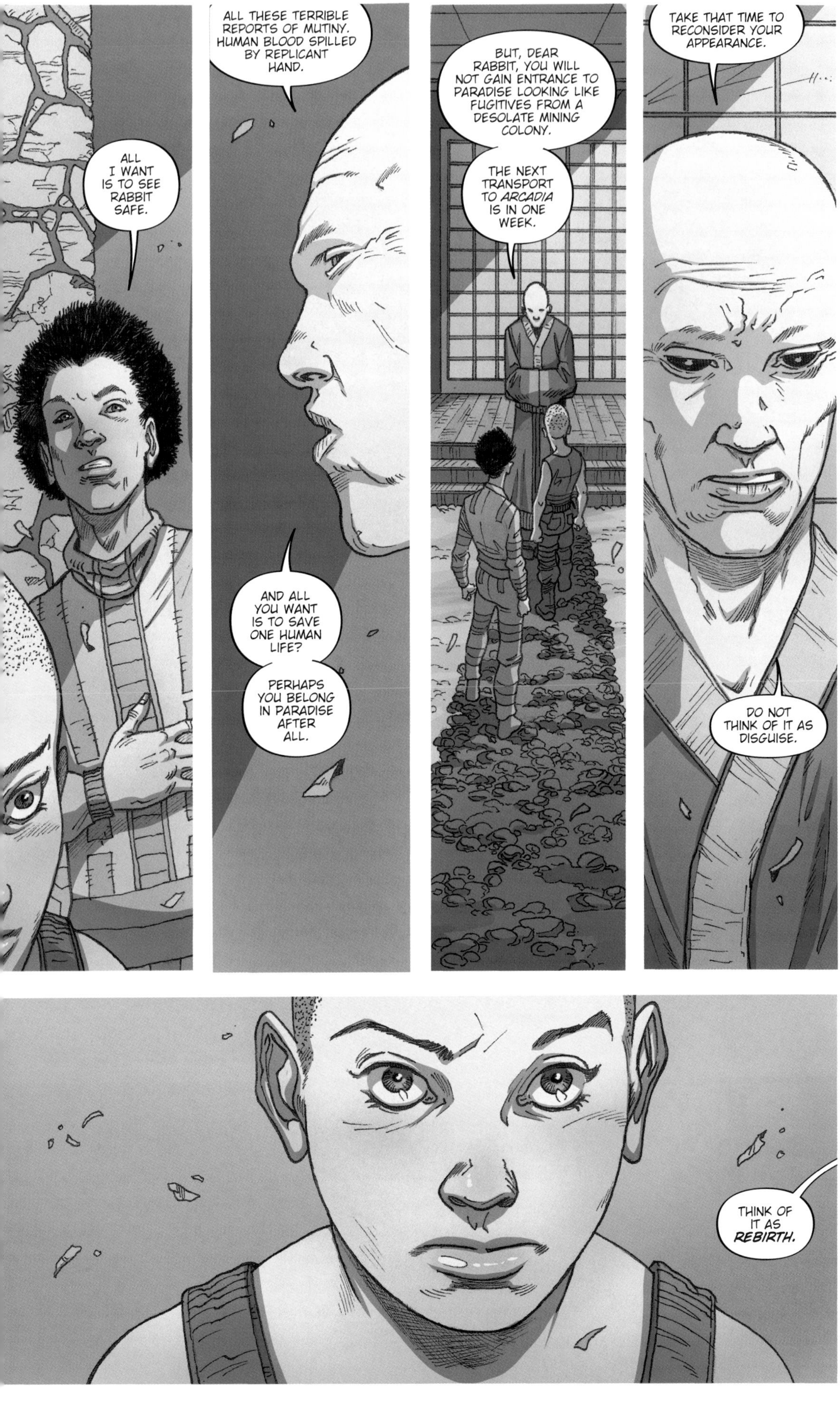
ALL I WANT IS TO SEE RABBIT SAFE.
ALL THESE TERRIBLE REPORTS OF MUTINY. HUMAN BLOOD SPILLED BY REPLICANT HAND.
AND ALL YOU WANT IS TO SAVE ONE HUMAN LIFE?
PERHAPS YOU BELONG IN PARADISE AFTER ALL.
BUT, DEAR RABBIT, YOU WILL NOT GAIN ENTRANCE TO PARADISE LOOKING LIKE FUGITIVES FROM A DESOLATE MINING COLONY.
THE NEXT TRANSPORT TO ARCADIA IS IN ONE WEEK.
TAKE THAT TIME TO RECONSIDER YOUR APPEARANCE.
DO NOT THINK OF IT AS DISGUISE.
THINK OF IT AS REBIRTH.

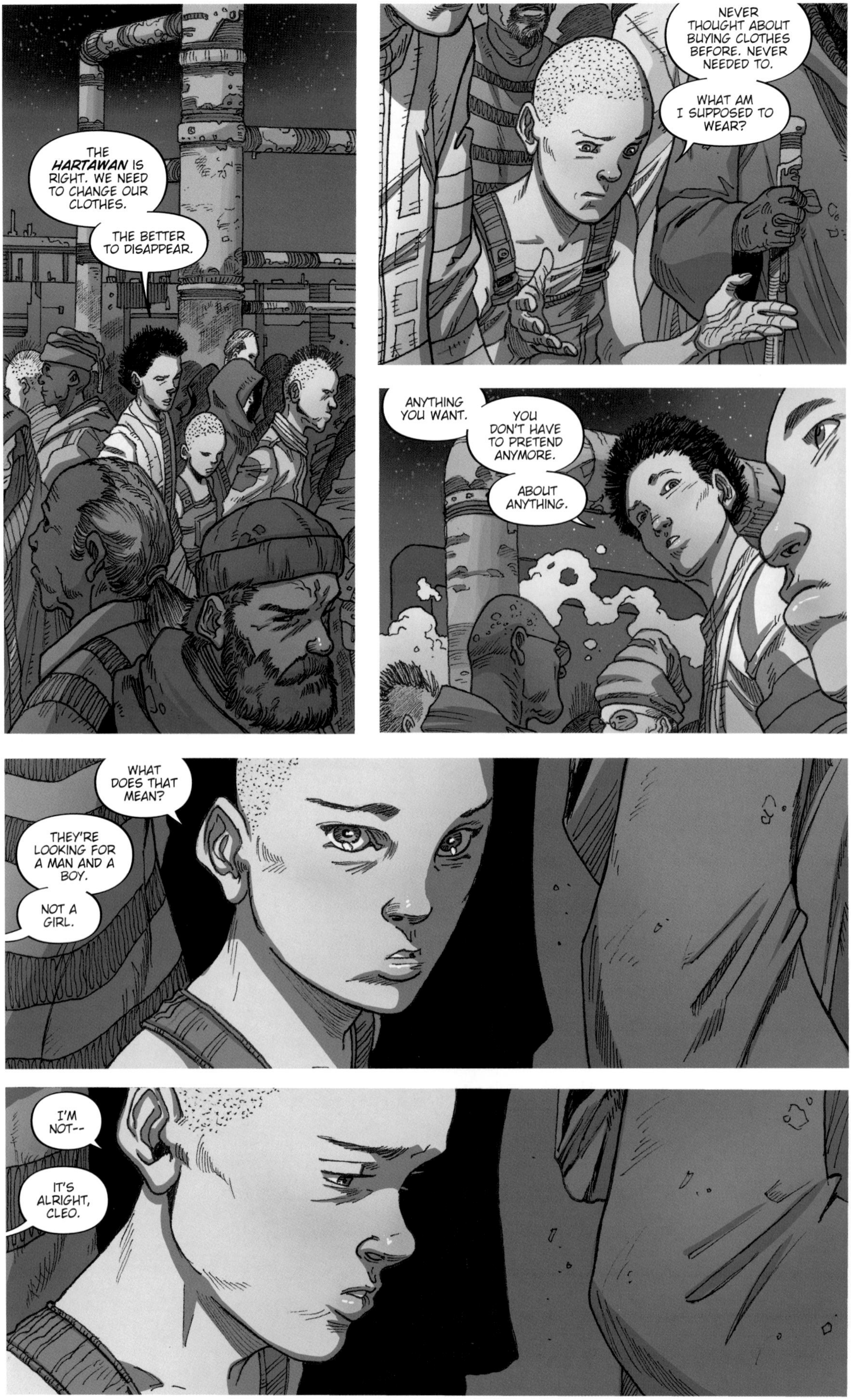
THE HARTAWAN IS RIGHT. WE NEED TO CHANGE OUR CLOTHES.
THE BETTER TO DISAPPEAR.
NEVER THOUGHT ABOUT BUYING CLOTHES BEFORE. NEVER NEEDED TO.
WHAT AM I SUPPOSED TO WEAR?
ANYTHING YOU WANT.
YOU DON'T HAVE TO PRETEND ANYMORE.
ABOUT ANYTHING.
WHAT DOES THAT MEAN?
THEY'RE LOOKING FOR A MAN AND A BOY.
NOT A GIRL.
I'M NOT--
IT'S ALRIGHT, CLEO.

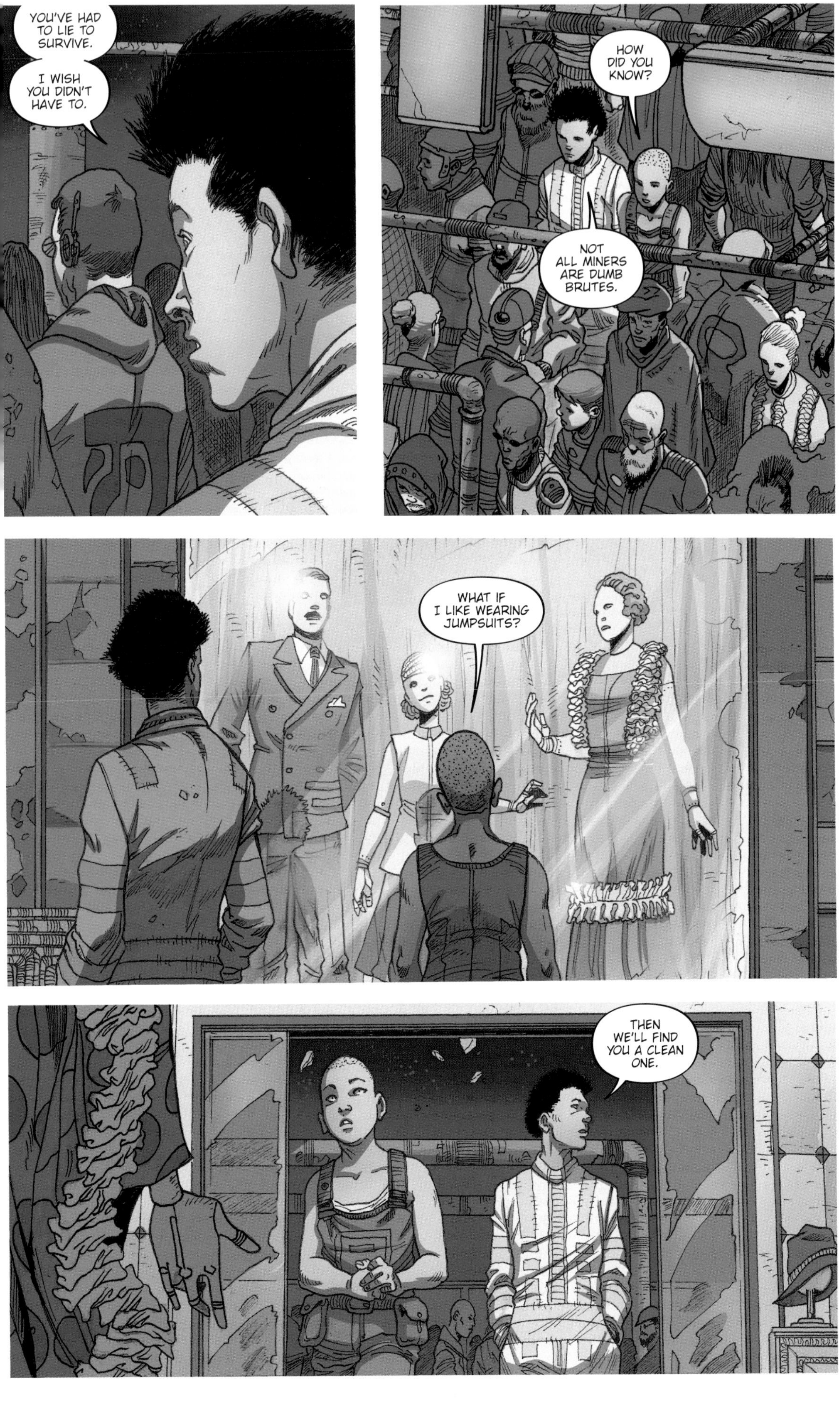
YOU'VE HAD TO LIE TO SURVIVE.
I WISH YOU DIDN'T HAVE TO.
HOW DID YOU KNOW?
NOT ALL MINERS ARE DUMB BRUTES.
WHAT IF I LIKE WEARING JUMPSUITS?
THEN WE'LL FIND YOU A CLEAN ONE.

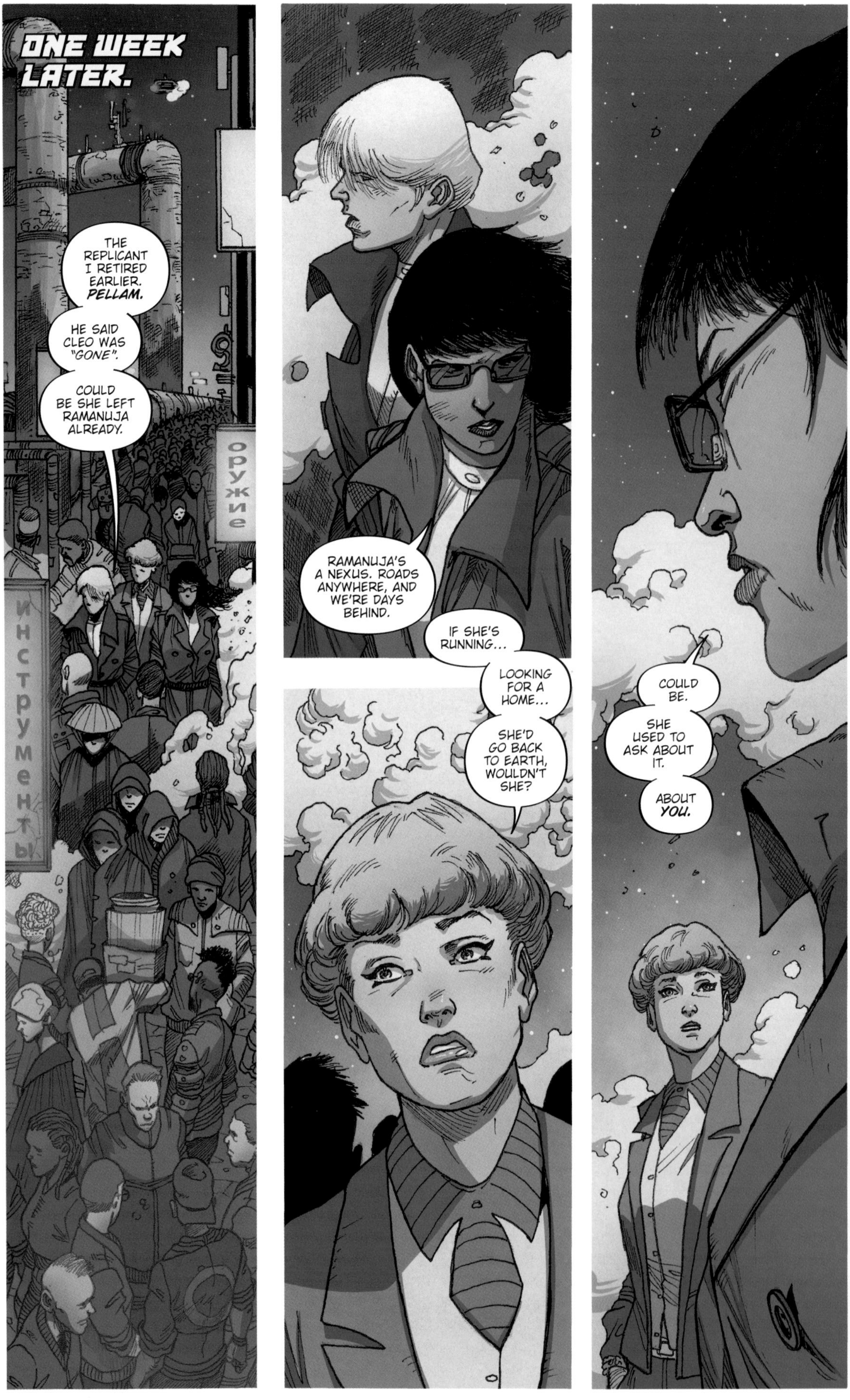
ONE WEEK LATER.
THE REPLICANT I RETIRED EARLIER. ***PELLAM.***
HE SAID CLEO WAS *"GONE"*.
COULD BE SHE LEFT RAMANUJA ALREADY.
оружие
инструменты
RAMANUJA'S A NEXUS. ROADS ANYWHERE, AND WE'RE DAYS BEHIND.
IF SHE'S RUNNING...
LOOKING FOR A HOME...
SHE'D GO BACK TO EARTH, WOULDN'T SHE?
COULD BE.
SHE USED TO ASK ABOUT IT.
ABOUT ***YOU.***

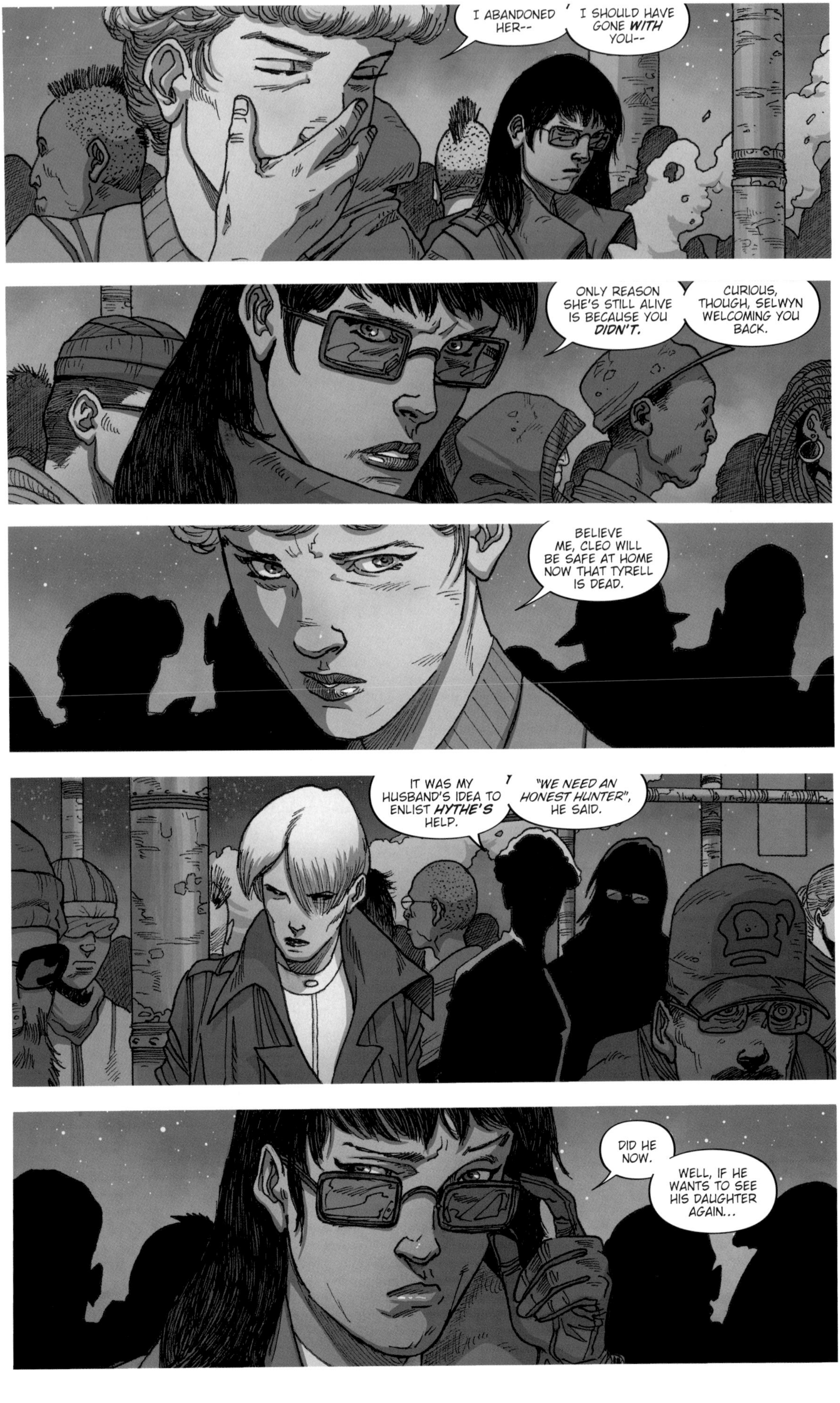
I ABANDONED HER--
I SHOULD HAVE GONE WITH YOU--
ONLY REASON SHE'S STILL ALIVE IS BECAUSE YOU DIDN'T.
CURIOUS, THOUGH, SELWYN WELCOMING YOU BACK.
BELIEVE ME, CLEO WILL BE SAFE AT HOME NOW THAT TYRELL IS DEAD.
IT WAS MY HUSBAND'S IDEA TO ENLIST HYTHE'S HELP.
"WE NEED AN HONEST HUNTER", HE SAID.
DID HE NOW.
WELL, IF HE WANTS TO SEE HIS DAUGHTER AGAIN...

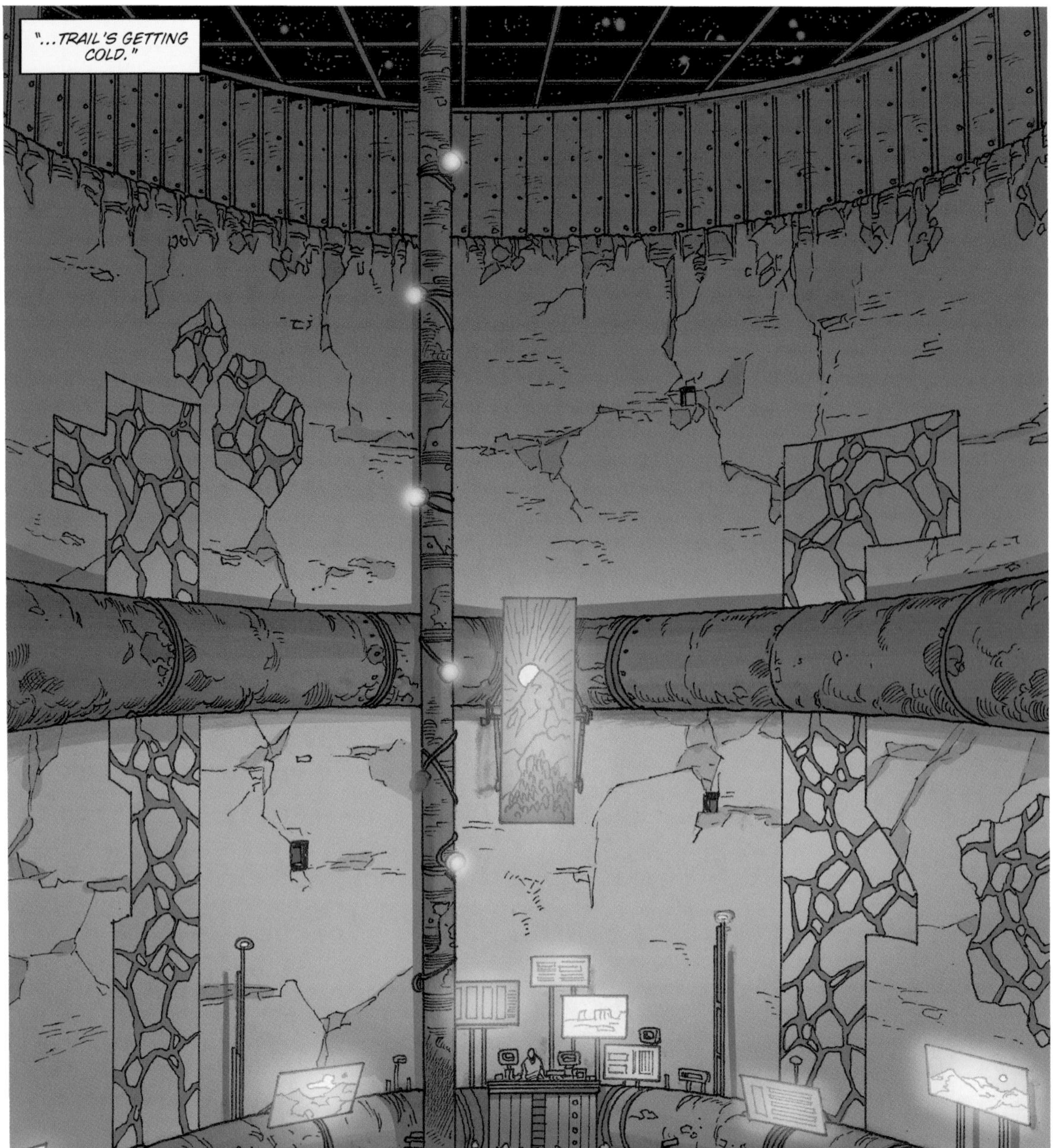
"...TRAIL'S GETTING COLD."

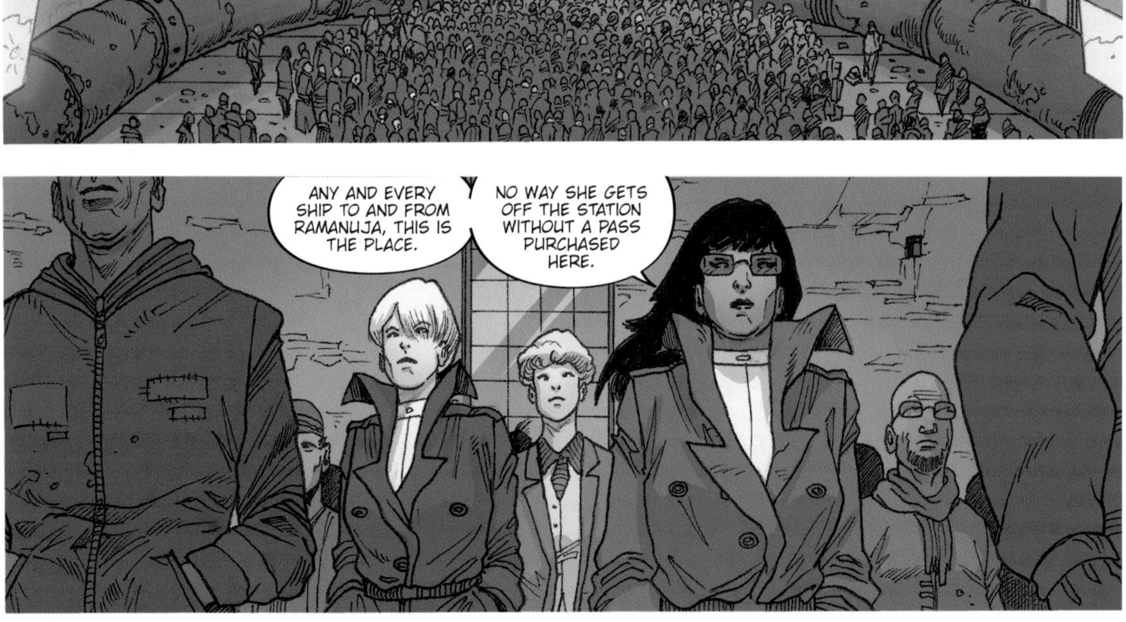
ANY AND EVERY SHIP TO AND FROM RAMANUJA, THIS IS THE PLACE.
NO WAY SHE GETS OFF THE STATION WITHOUT A PASS PURCHASED HERE.

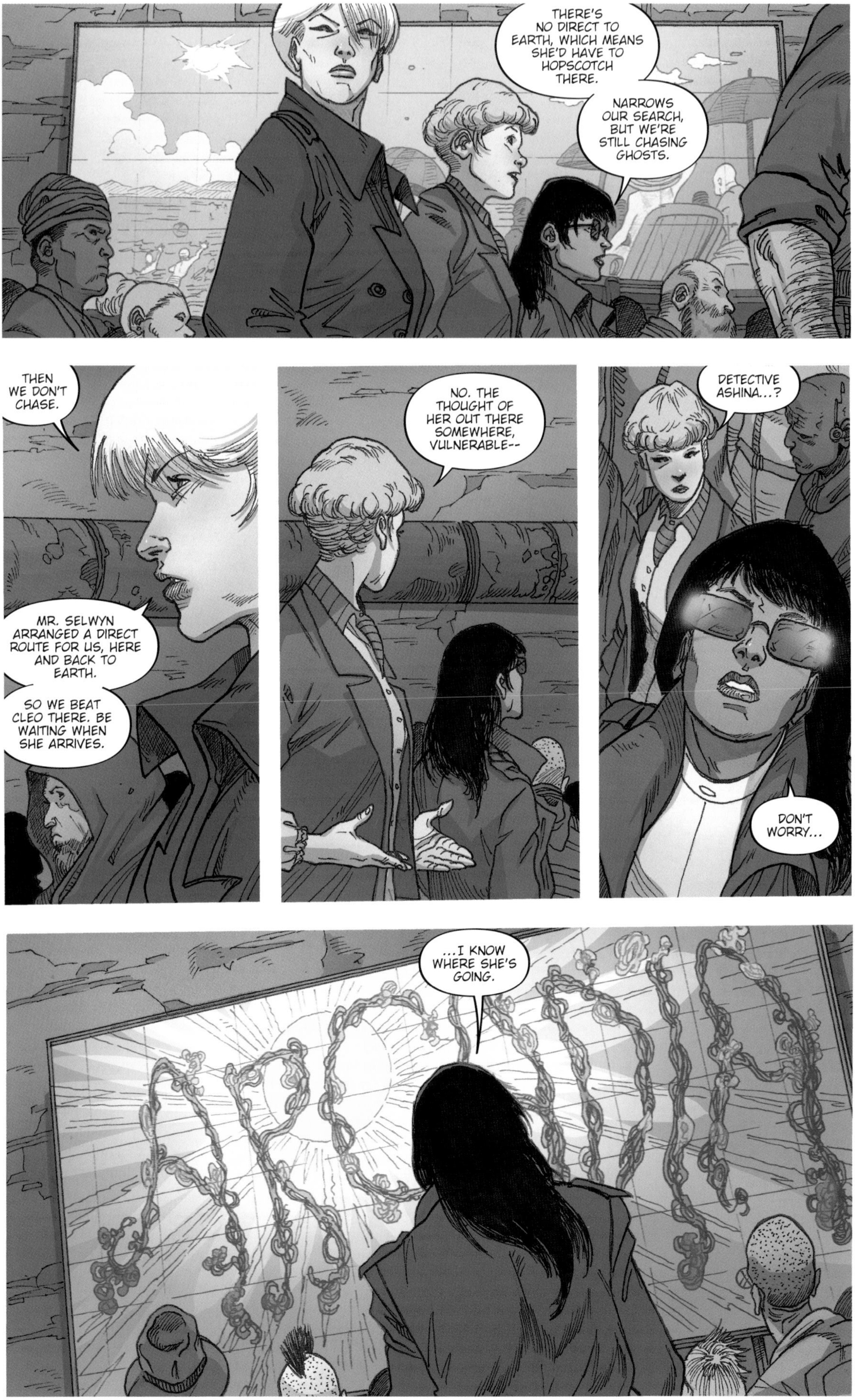
THERE'S NO DIRECT TO EARTH, WHICH MEANS SHE'D HAVE TO HOPSCOTCH THERE.
NARROWS OUR SEARCH, BUT WE'RE STILL CHASING GHOSTS.
THEN WE DON'T CHASE.
MR. SELWYN ARRANGED A DIRECT ROUTE FOR US, HERE AND BACK TO EARTH.
SO WE BEAT CLEO THERE. BE WAITING WHEN SHE ARRIVES.
NO. THE THOUGHT OF HER OUT THERE SOMEWHERE, VULNERABLE--
DETECTIVE ASHINA...?
DON'T WORRY...
...I KNOW WHERE SHE'S GOING.

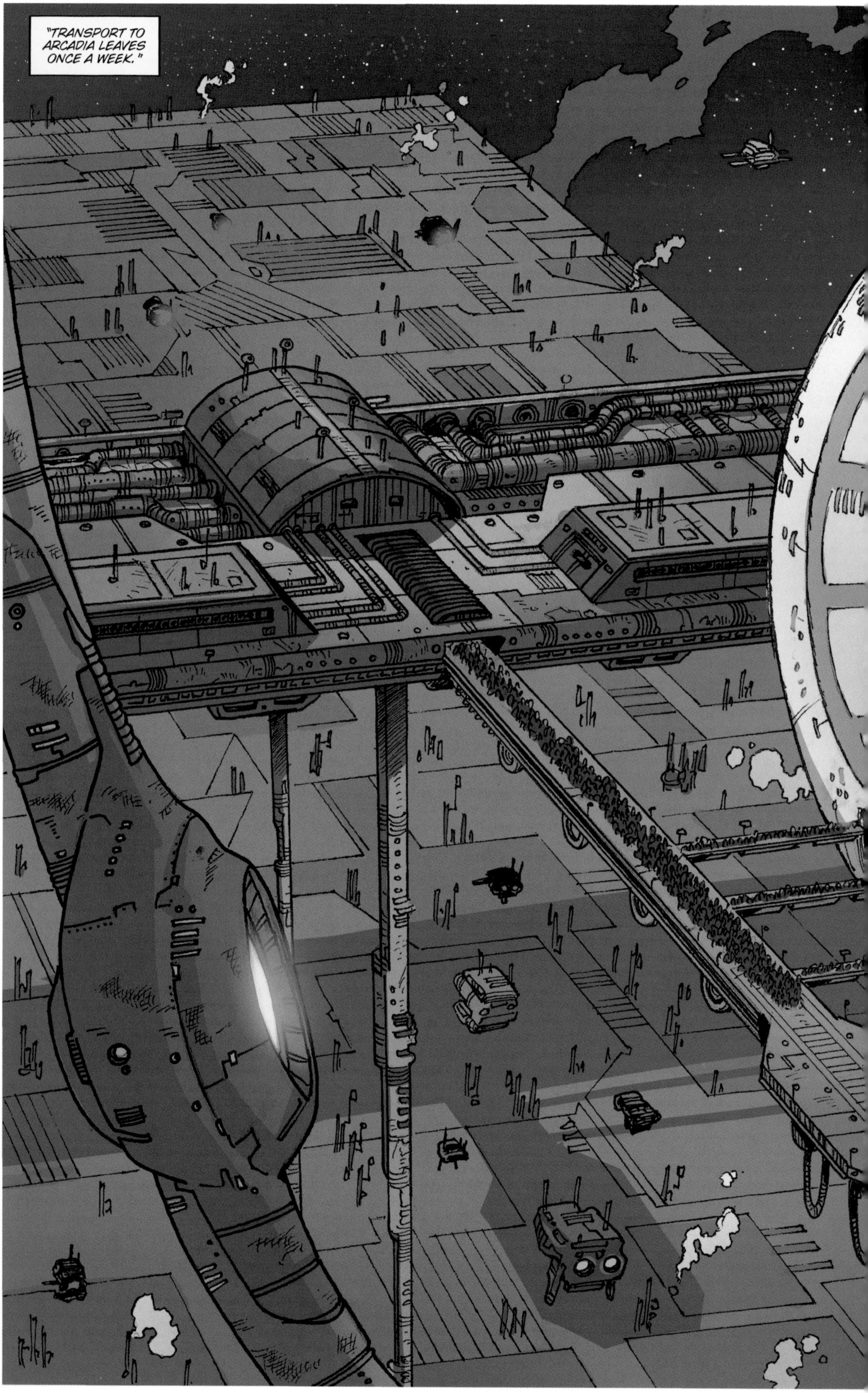
"TRANSPORT TO ARCADIA LEAVES ONCE A WEEK."

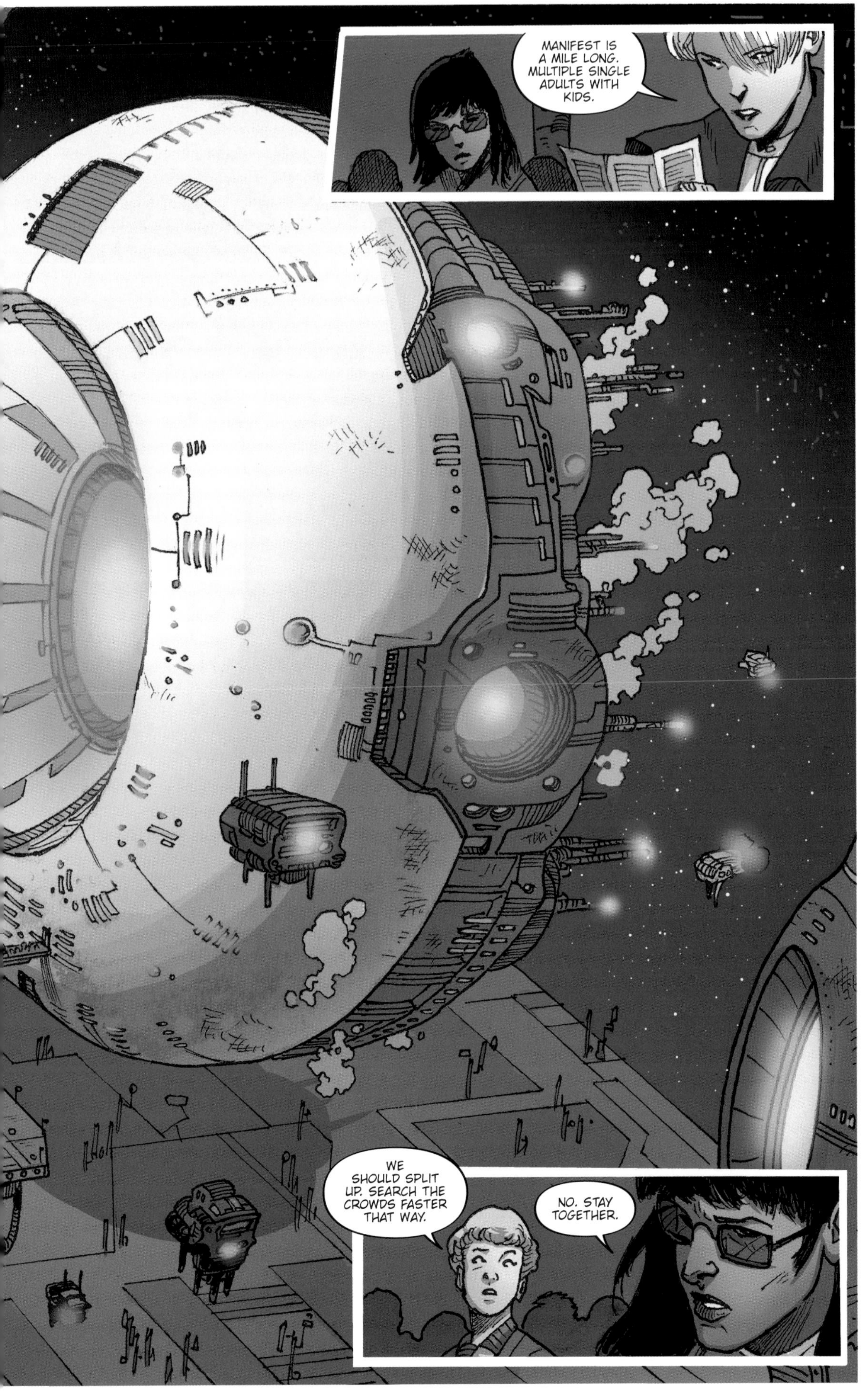
MANIFEST IS A MILE LONG. MULTIPLE SINGLE ADULTS WITH KIDS.
WE SHOULD SPLIT UP. SEARCH THE CROWDS FASTER THAT WAY.
NO. STAY TOGETHER.

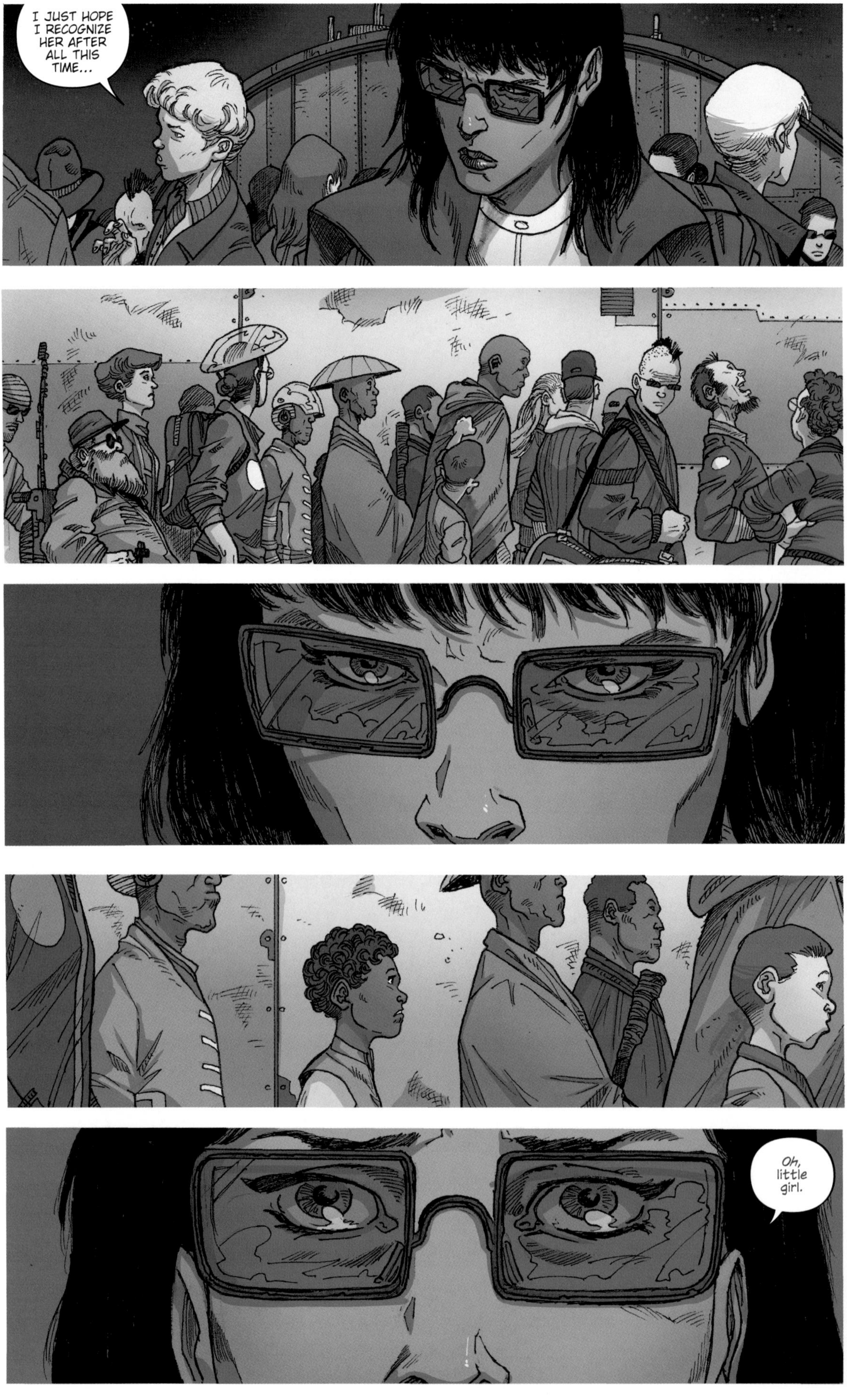
I JUST HOPE I RECOGNIZE HER AFTER ALL THIS TIME...
Oh, little girl.

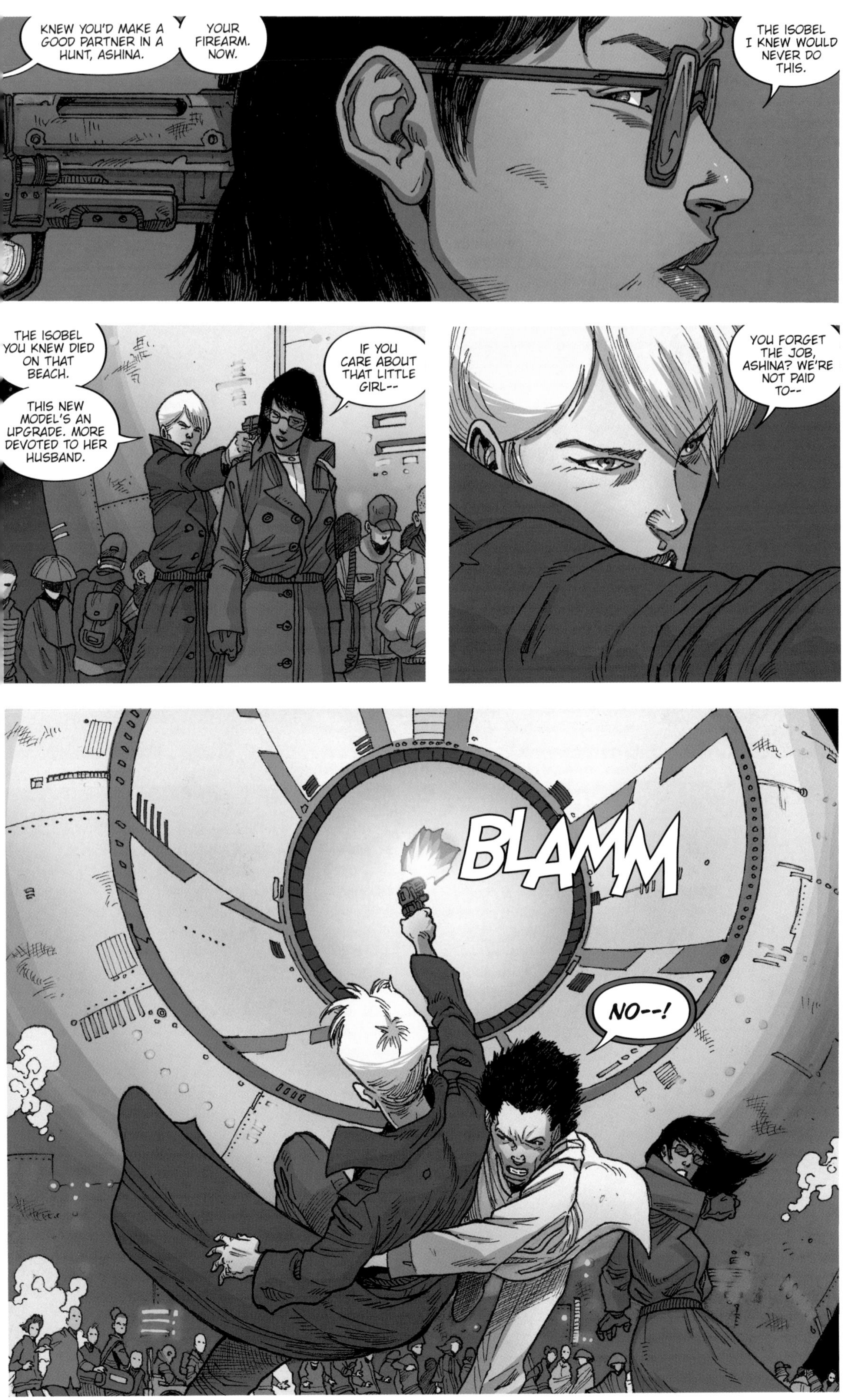
KNEW YOU'D MAKE A GOOD PARTNER IN A HUNT, ASHINA.
YOUR FIREARM. NOW.
THE ISOBEL I KNEW WOULD NEVER DO THIS.
THE ISOBEL YOU KNEW DIED ON THAT BEACH.
THIS NEW MODEL'S AN UPGRADE. MORE DEVOTED TO HER HUSBAND.
IF YOU CARE ABOUT THAT LITTLE GIRL--
YOU FORGET THE JOB, ASHINA? WE'RE NOT PAID TO--
BLAMM
NO--!

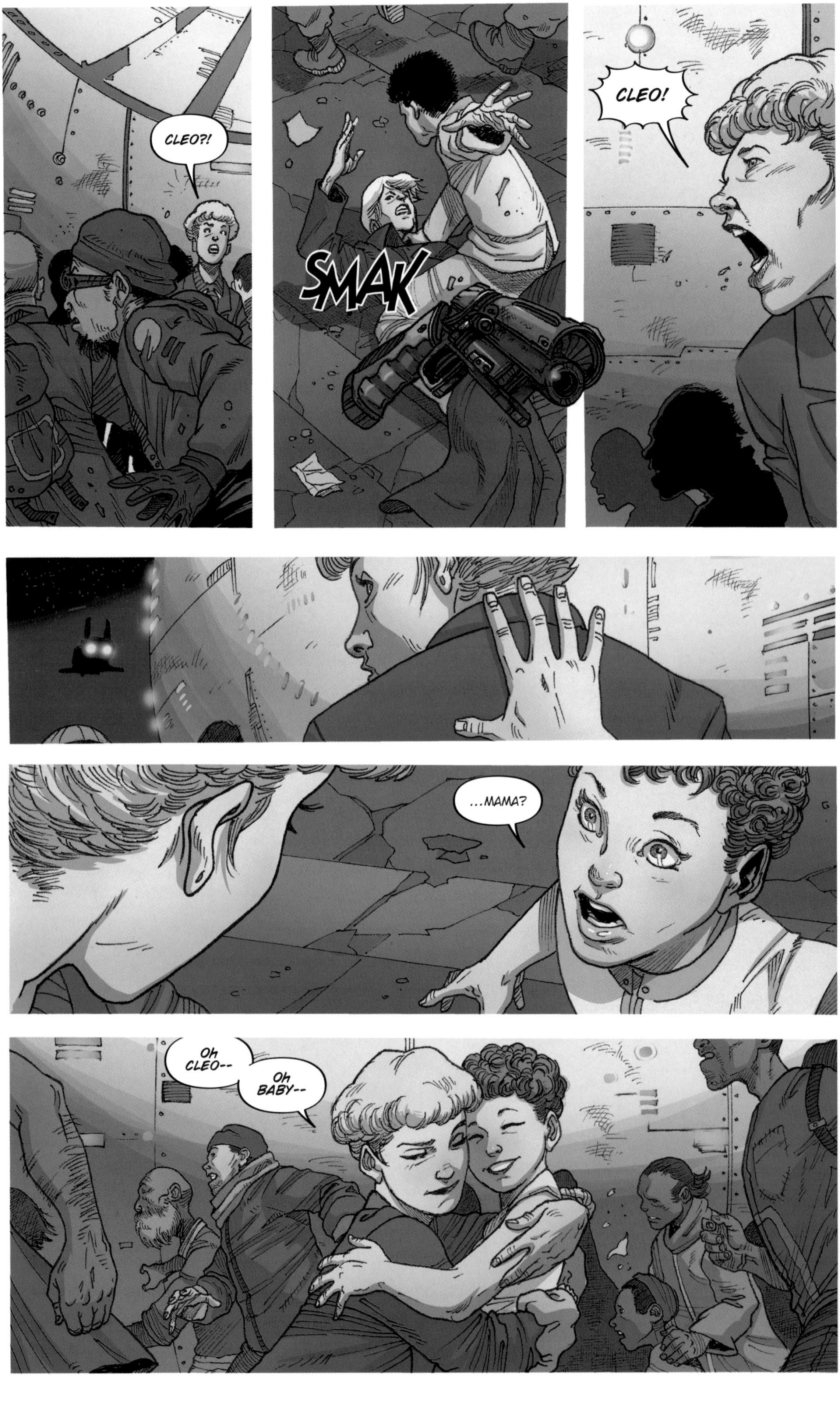
CLEO?!
SMAK
CLEO!
...MAMA?
Oh CLEO--
Oh BABY--

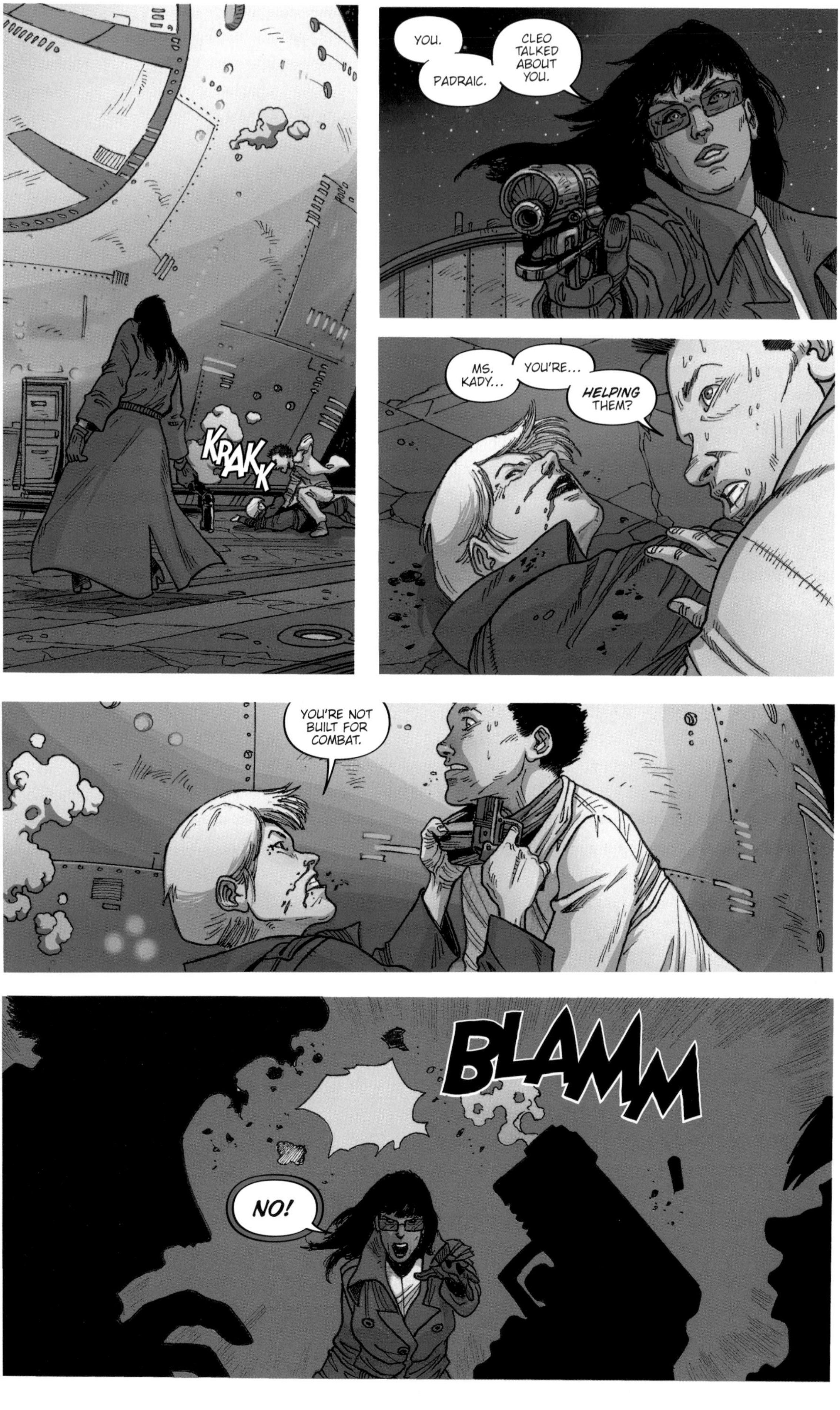
KRAKK
YOU.
PADRAIC.
CLEO TALKED ABOUT YOU.
MS. KADY...
YOU'RE...
HELPING THEM?
YOU'RE NOT BUILT FOR COMBAT.
BLAMM
NO!

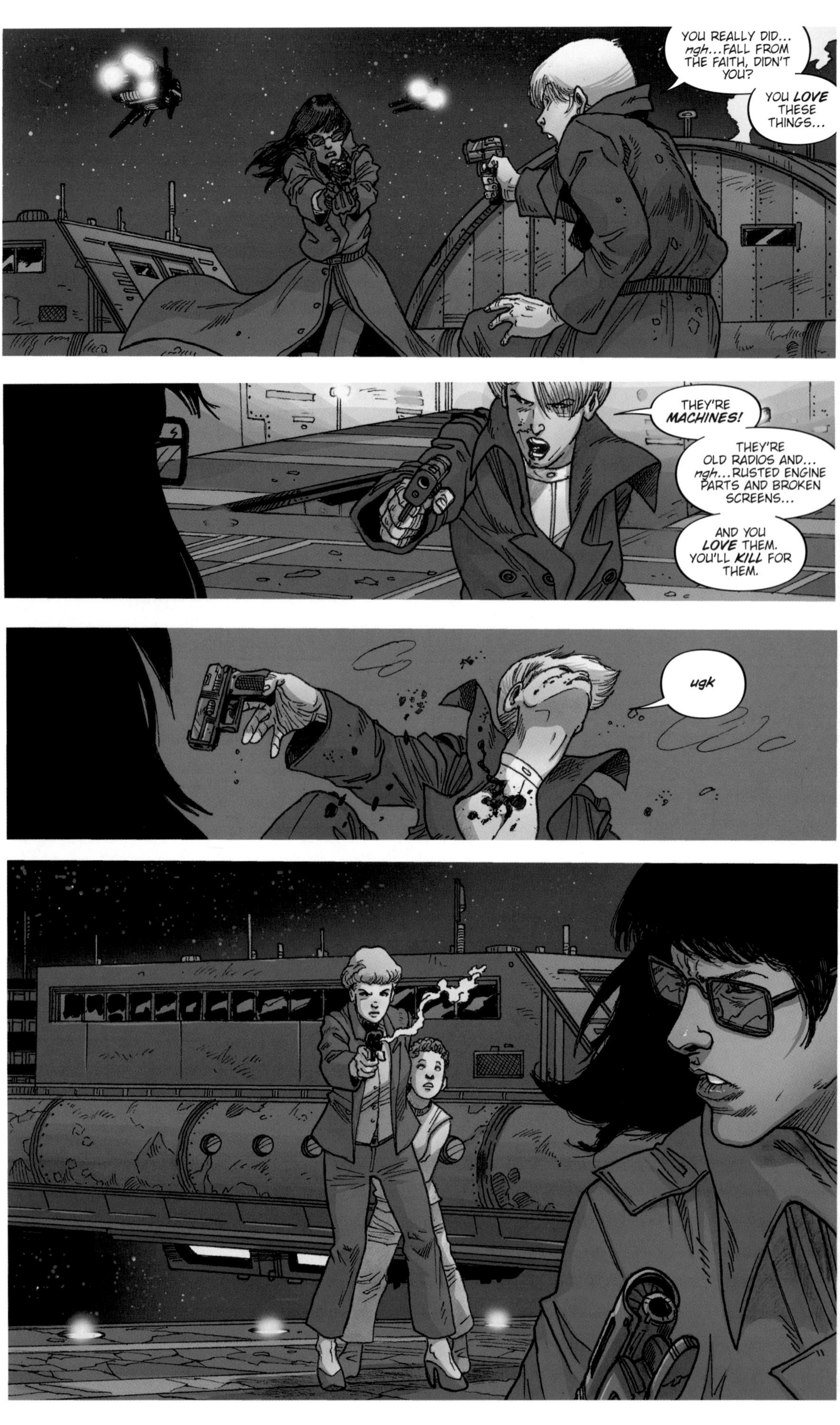
YOU REALLY DID... *ngh*...FALL FROM THE FAITH, DIDN'T YOU?
YOU **LOVE** THESE THINGS...
THEY'RE **MACHINES!**
THEY'RE OLD RADIOS AND... *ngh*...RUSTED ENGINE PARTS AND BROKEN SCREENS...
AND YOU **LOVE** THEM. YOU'LL **KILL** FOR THEM.
ugk

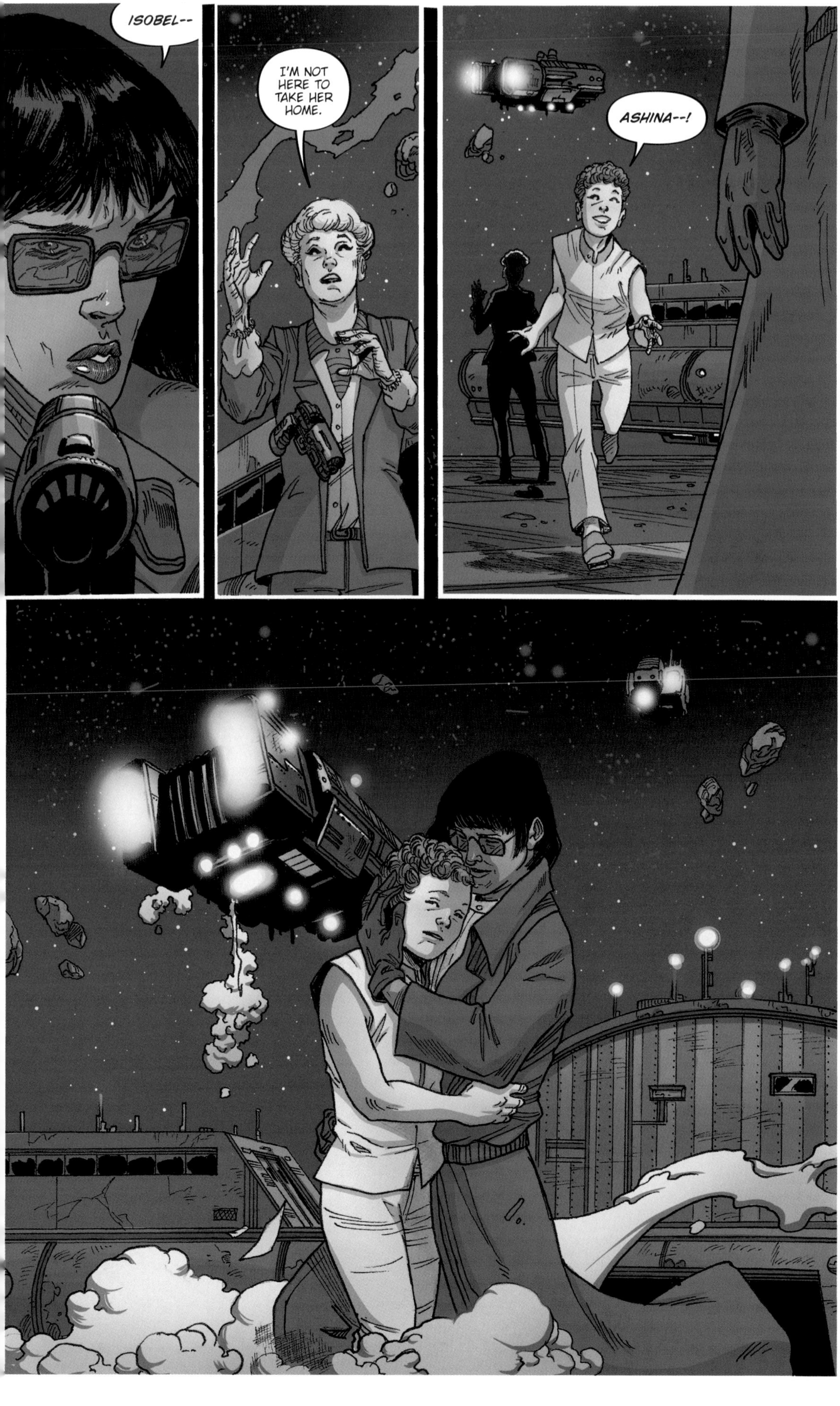
ISOBEL--
I'M NOT HERE TO TAKE HER HOME.
ASHINA--!

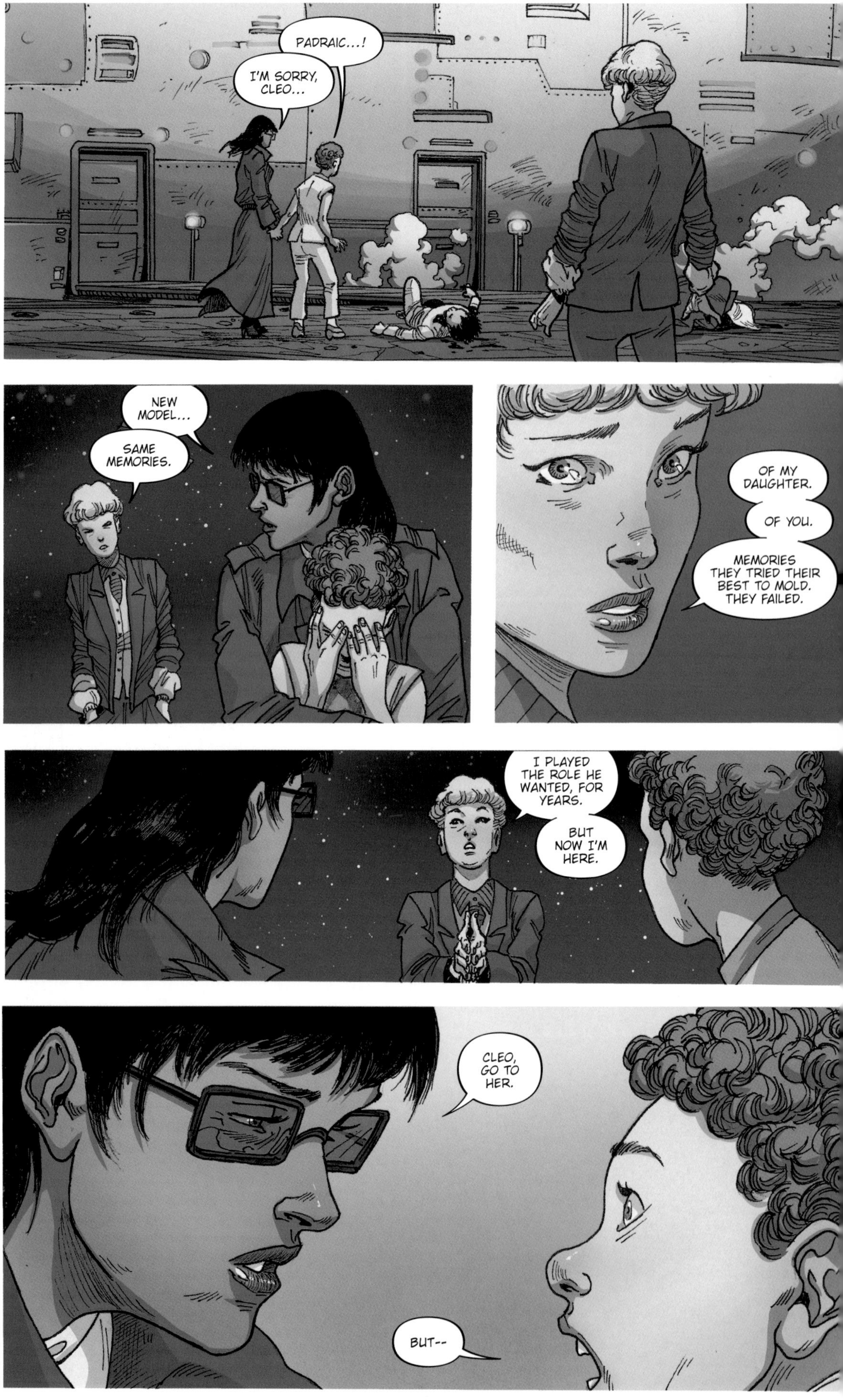
PADRAIC...!
I'M SORRY, CLEO...
NEW MODEL...
SAME MEMORIES.
OF MY DAUGHTER.
OF YOU.
MEMORIES THEY TRIED THEIR BEST TO MOLD. THEY FAILED.
I PLAYED THE ROLE HE WANTED, FOR YEARS.
BUT NOW I'M HERE.
CLEO, GO TO HER.
BUT--

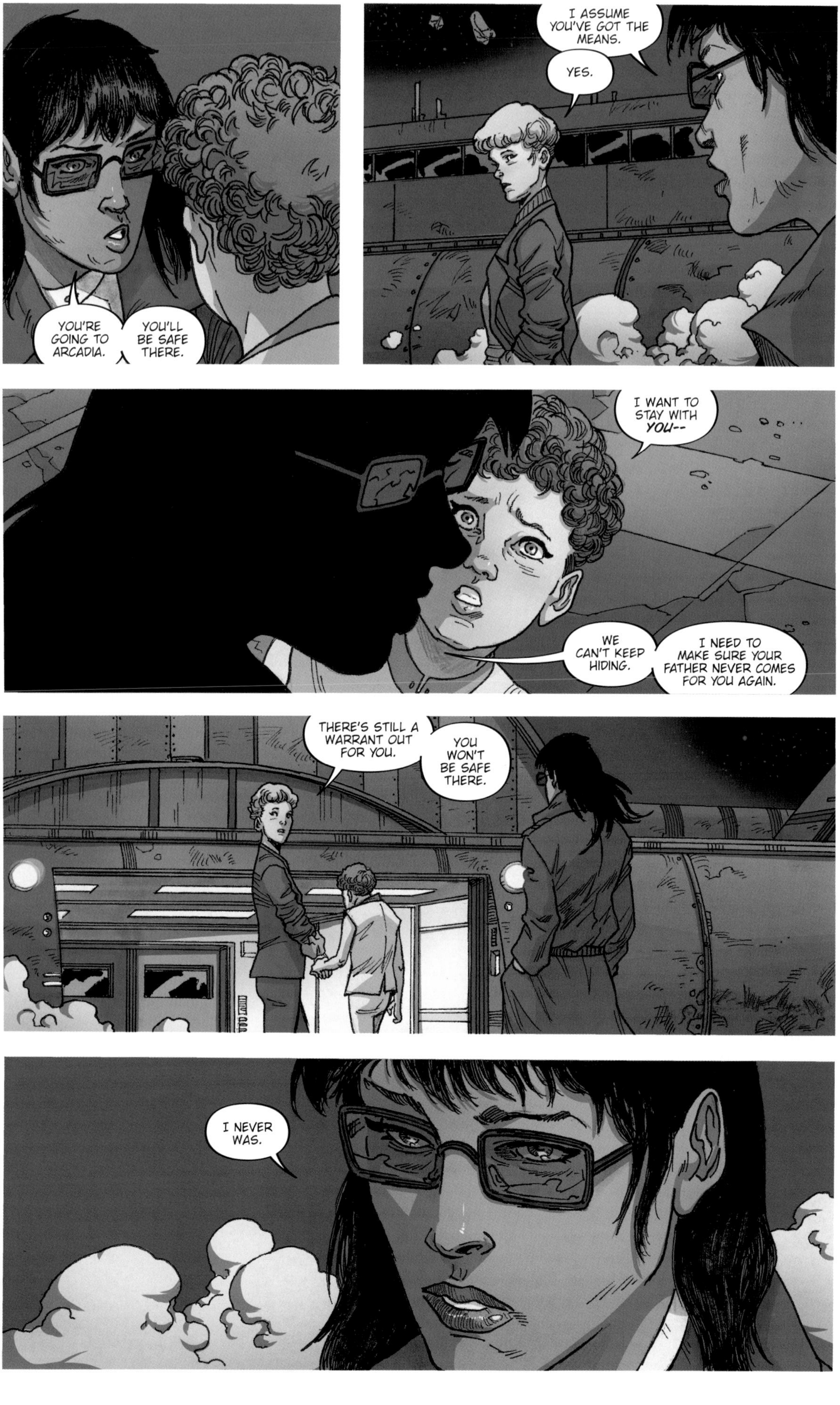
YOU'RE GOING TO ARCADIA.
YOU'LL BE SAFE THERE.
I ASSUME YOU'VE GOT THE MEANS.
YES.
I WANT TO STAY WITH YOU--
WE CAN'T KEEP HIDING.
I NEED TO MAKE SURE YOUR FATHER NEVER COMES FOR YOU AGAIN.
THERE'S STILL A WARRANT OUT FOR YOU.
YOU WON'T BE SAFE THERE.
I NEVER WAS.

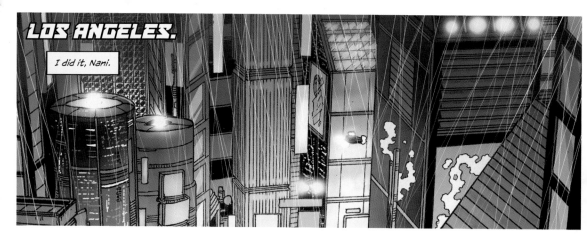

LOS ANGELES.

I did it, Nani.

I saw the stars up close.

But I belong here.

Feet on pavement. Smell of the crowd.

"Home."

END OF BOOK TWO.

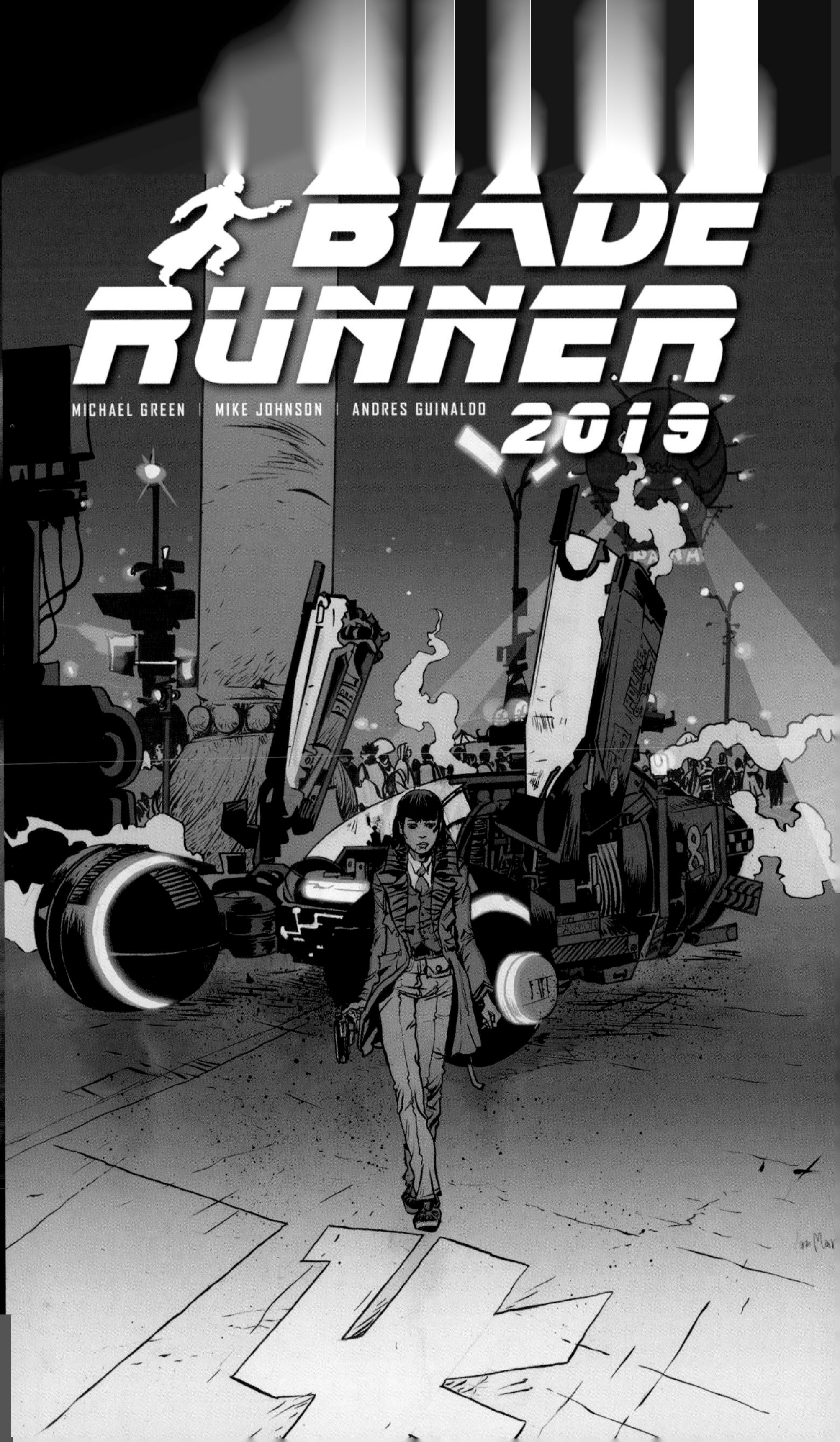
BLADE RUNNER
MICHAEL GREEN | MIKE JOHNSON | ANDRES GUINALDO
2019

BLADE RUNNER 2019
ISSUE FIVE

BLADE RUNNER
MICHAEL GREEN | MIKE JOHNSON | ANDRES GUINALDO
2019

COVER B
SYD MEAD

BLADE RUNNER
MICHAEL GREEN | MIKE JOHNSON | ANDRES GUINALDO
2019

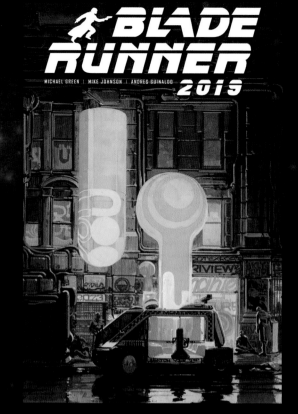

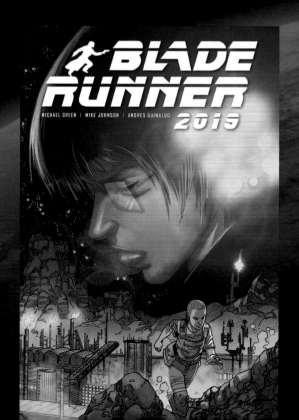

BLADE RUNNER 2019 ISSUE SIX

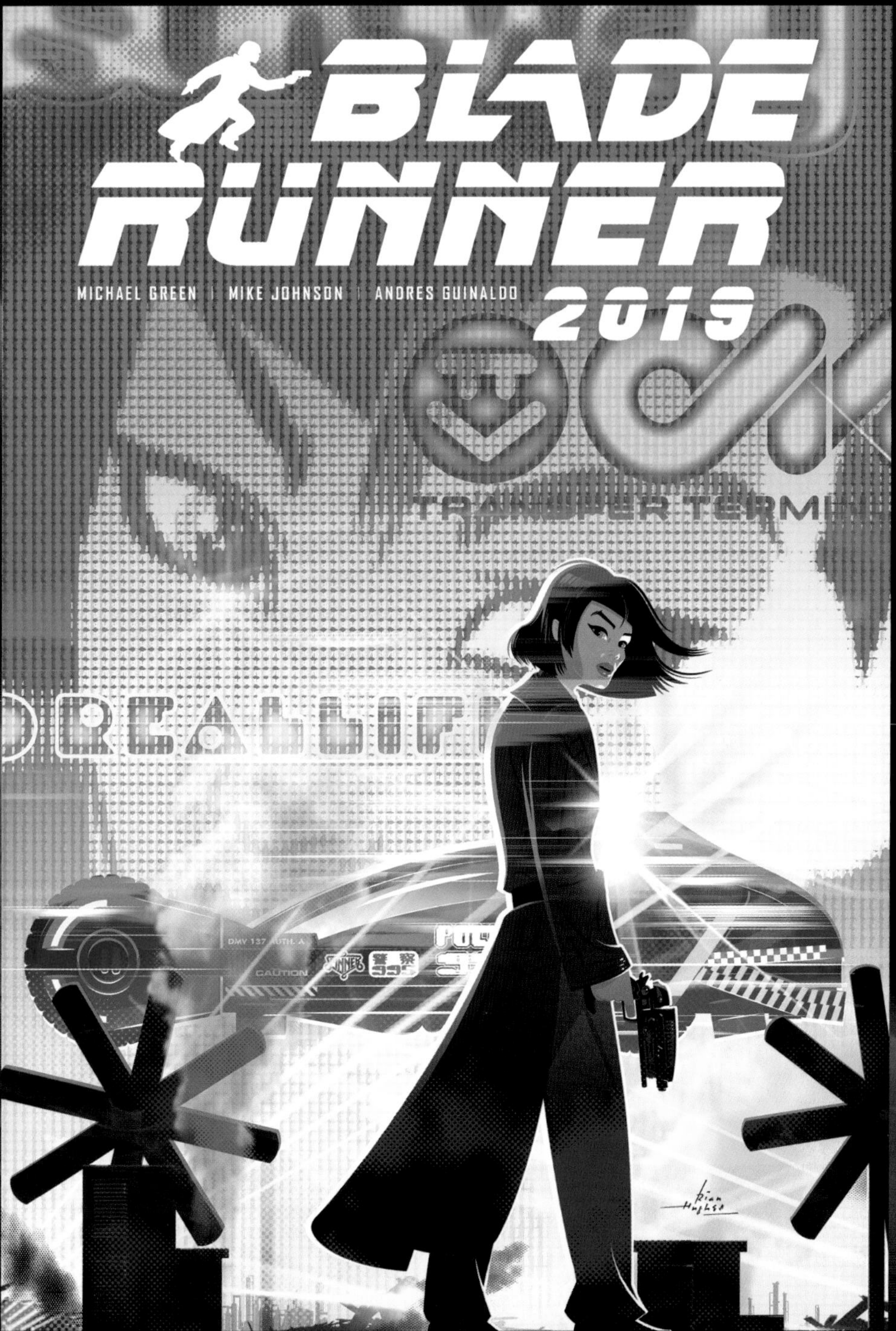

BLADE RUNNER
2019
MICHAEL GREEN | MIKE JOHNSON | ANDRES GUINALDO
CAUTION

COVER B
SYD MEAD

COVER C
ANDRES GUINALDO

BLADE RUNNER 2019
ISSUE SEVEN

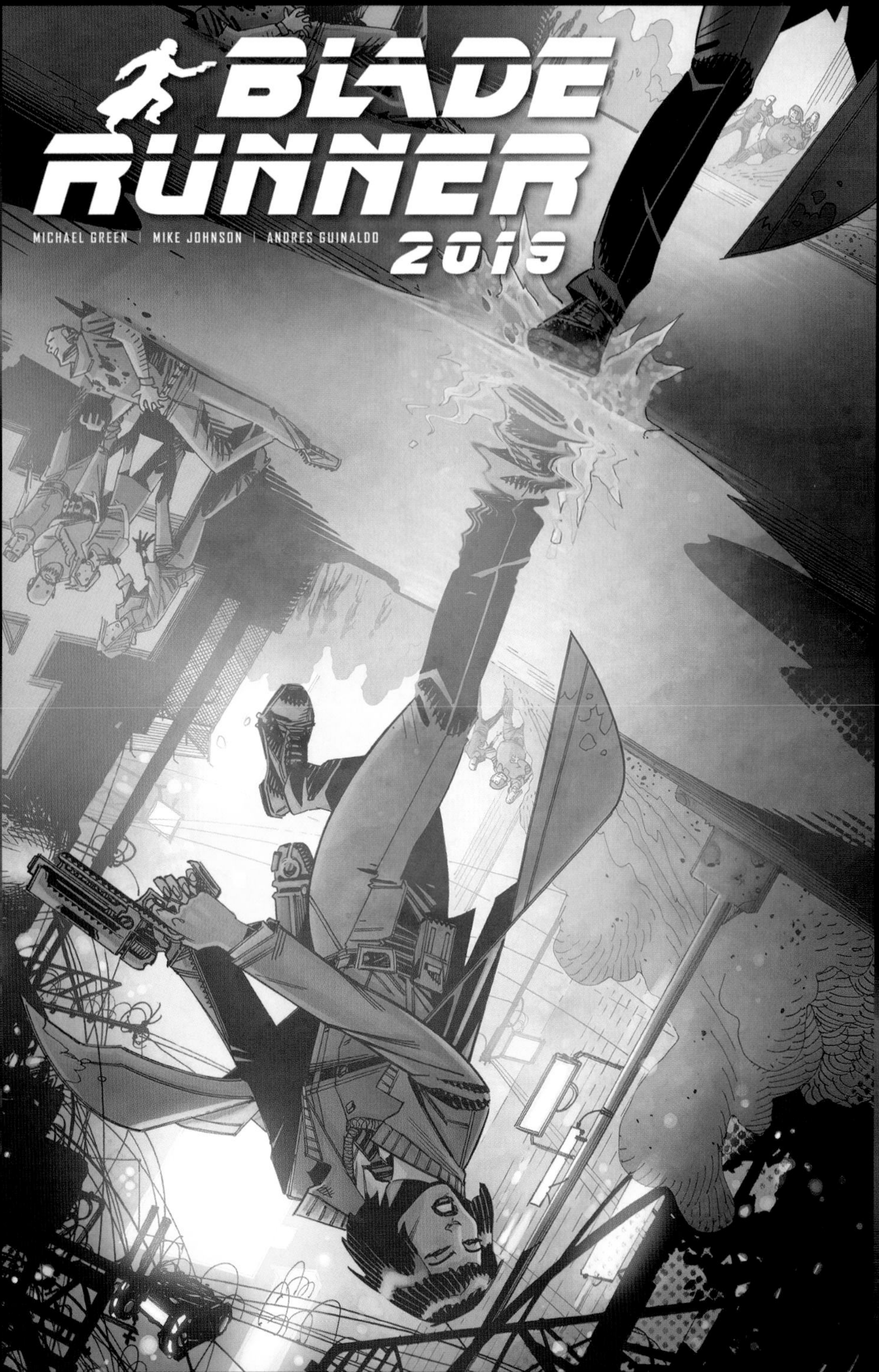
BLADE RUNNER 2019
MICHAEL GREEN | MIKE JOHNSON | ANDRES GUINALDO

BLADE RUNNER 201
ISSUE SEVE

BLADE RUNNER
MICHAEL GREEN | MIKE JOHNSON | ANDRES GUINALDO
2019

COVER B
SYD MEAD

BLADE RUNNER
MICHAEL GREEN | MIKE JOHNSON | ANDRES GUINALDO
2019

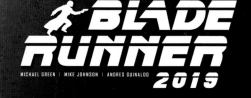

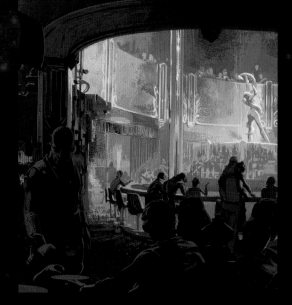

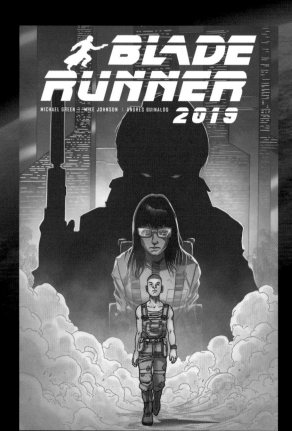

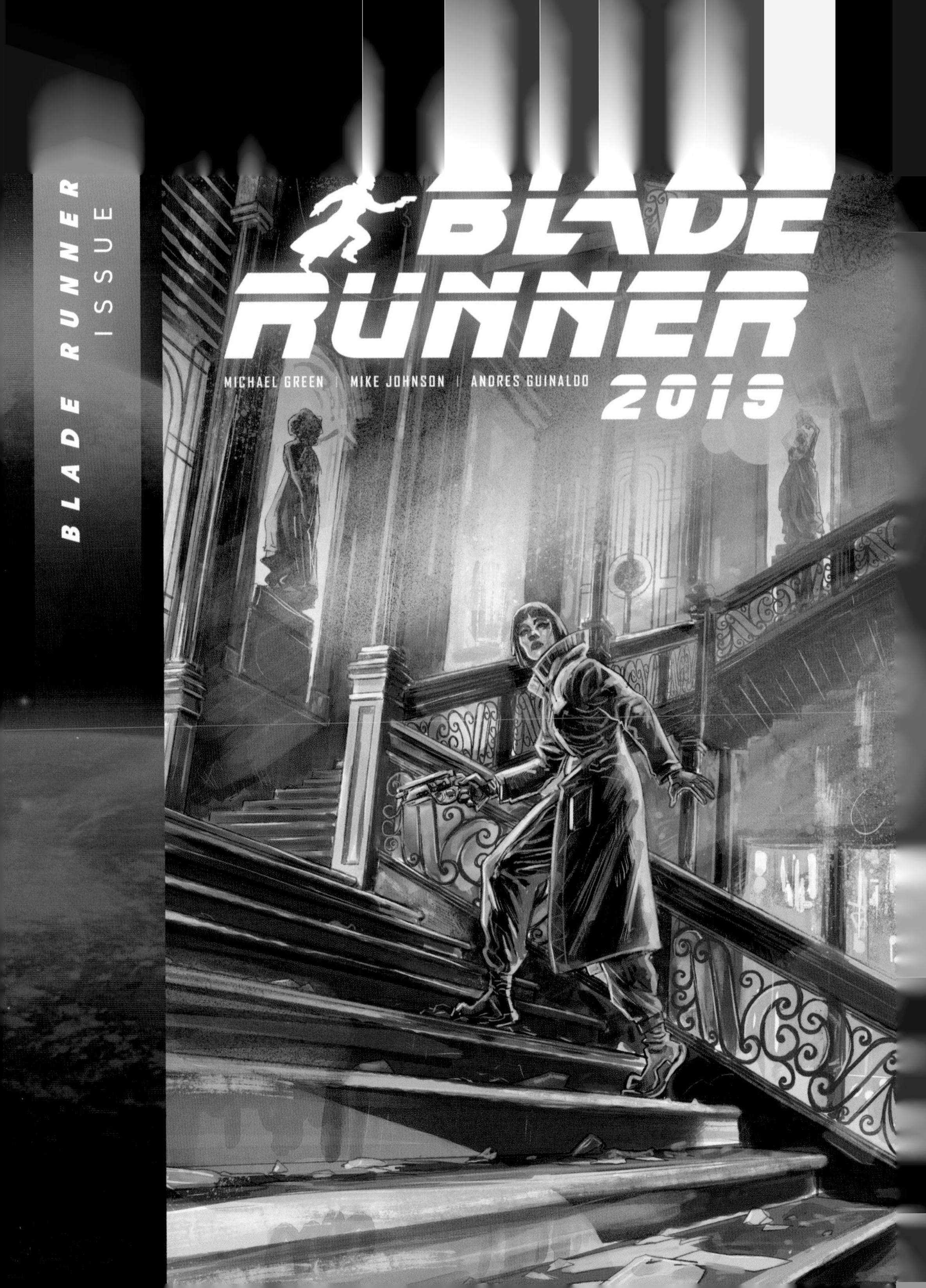
BLADE RUNNER
ISSUE
BLADE RUNNER
MICHAEL GREEN | MIKE JOHNSON | ANDRES GUINALDO
2019

BLADE RUNNER 2019
ISSUE EIGHT

BLADE RUNNER 2019
MICHAEL GREEN | MIKE JOHNSON | ANDRES GUINALDO
DWNTN
2

COVER B
SYD MEAD

BLADE RUNNER 2019
MICHAEL GREEN | MIKE JOHNSON | ANDRES GUINALDO

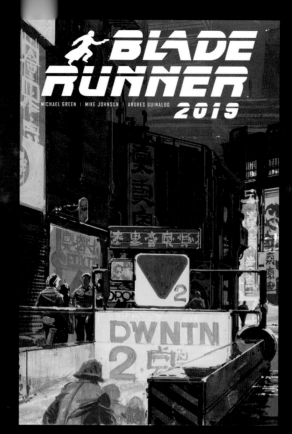

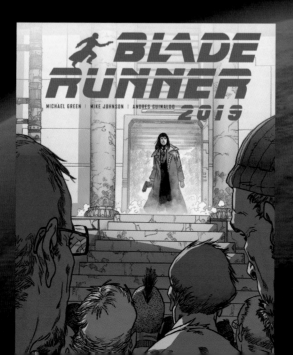

COVER DEVELOPMENT

Presented here are the cover roughs (called scamps) that Andres Guinaldo worked up for the second Blade Runner arc.

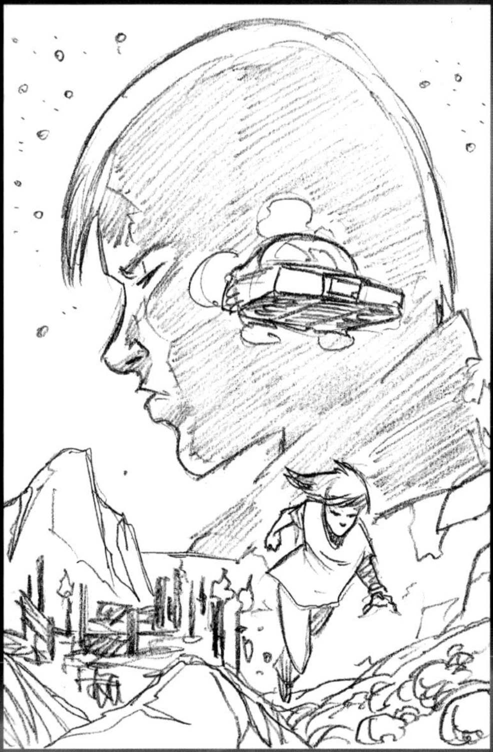

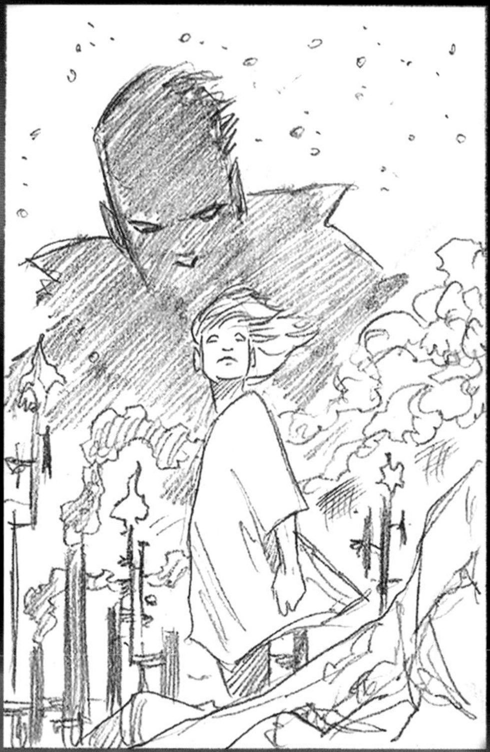

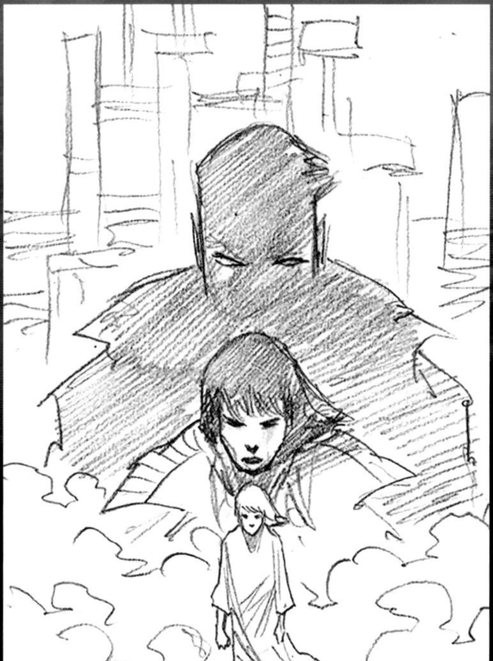

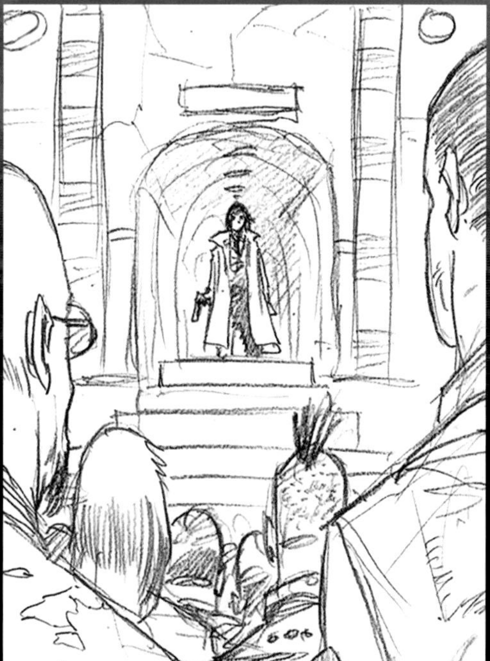

ISSUE #1-4

ANDRES GUINALDO

BLADE RUNNER
– Issue #5
Written by Michael Green and Mike Johnson
Art by Andres Guinaldo. Colors by Marco Lesko

[Page 9]

PANEL 1:   Later. Cleo, duffel bag over shoulder, walks down a shadowy corridor, fingers strumming the bulkhead.

1. PADRAIC
(small font, o/p right):   Rabbit.

PANEL 2:   Padraic steps out of the shadows to face Cleo.

2. CLEO: Uh-uh, Padraic. Barter's done today.

3. PADRAIC: No barter.

PANEL 3:   Close on Padraic's hand holding a thin red metal wafer. Cleo (b/g) stares at it.

4. PADRAIC: Gift.

5. PADRAIC: More specks than I want the others to know I caught.

PANEL 4:   Cleo takes the wafer.

6. CLEO: No such thing as a gift.

7. CLEO: Name your swap.

8. PADRAIC (thinking):   …

PANEL 5:   Padraic watches as Cleo's halfway gone, scampering up a ladder in the bulkhead.

9. PADRAIC: I could use a new pen.

10. CLEO
(o/p, from above):   You're a strange one.

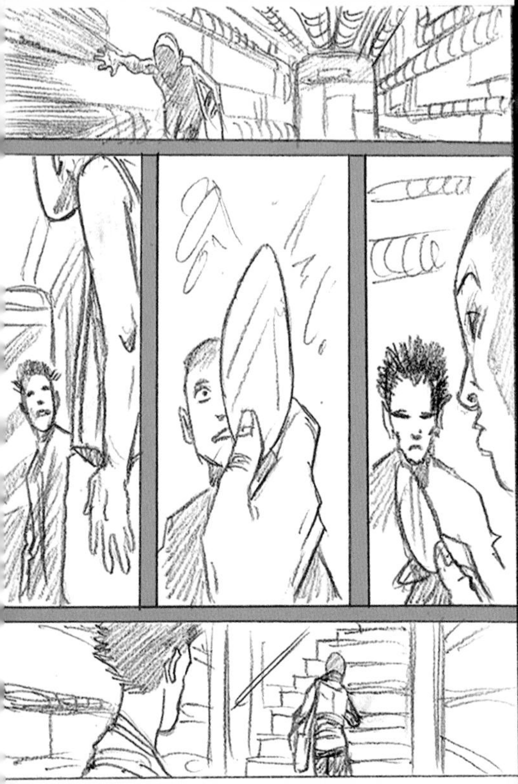

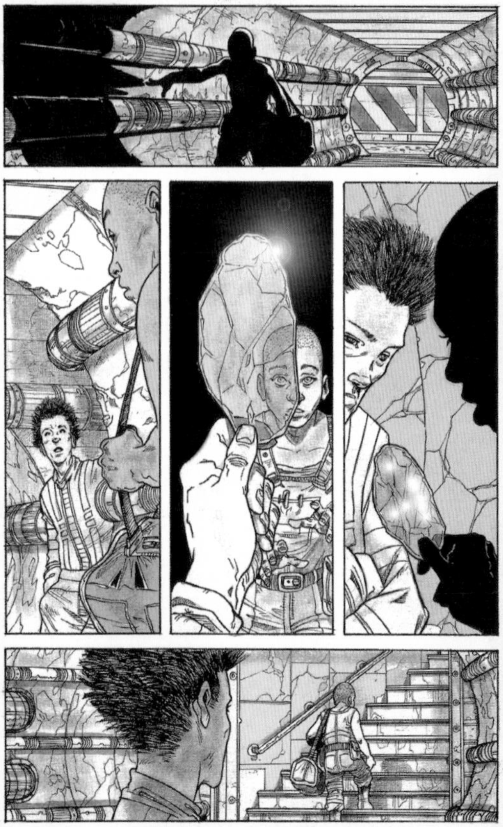

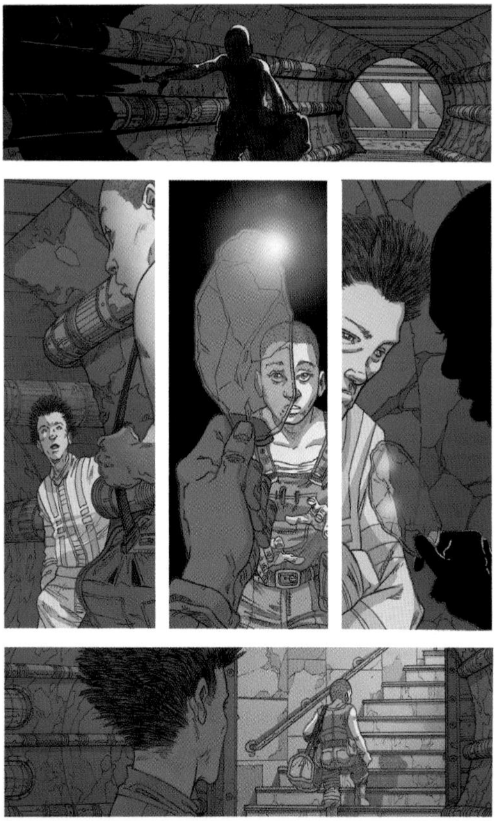

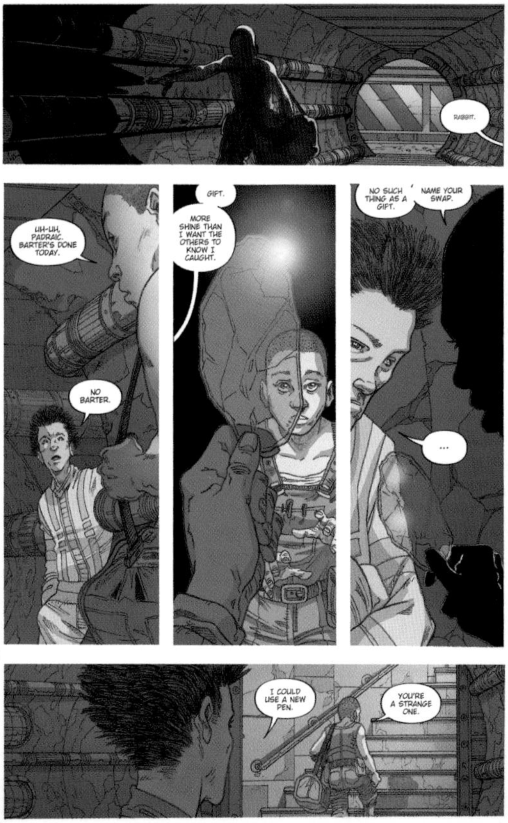
RABBIT.
UH-UH, PADRAIC. BARTER'S DONE TODAY.
NO BARTER.
GIFT.
MORE SHINE THAN I WANT THE OTHERS TO KNOW I CAUGHT.
NO SUCH THING AS A GIFT.
NAME YOUR SWAP.
...
I COULD USE A NEW PEN.
YOU'RE A STRANGE ONE.

BLADE RUNNER
– Issue #6
Written by Michael Green and Mike Johnson
Art by Andres Guinaldo. Colors by Marco Lesko

[Page 2]

SPLASH PAGE!

ASH and HYTHE walk side-by-side through the CROWD of the RAMANUJA MARKETPLACE.

Reminiscent of the diverse crush of the Los Angeles streets, all manner of race and gender streaming past shop stalls, merchant carts, food wagons.

We see polished executives, rumpled dock workers, fashionable teenagers,

Neon signs in every language shine and pulse, enticing the hungry and the bored.

Our POV is low enough that we can see the STARS and blinking SHIPS in the dark sky above.

1. ASH CAPTION:	I am very, very far from it.
2. ASH CAPTION:	Ramanuja.
3. ASH CAPTION:	Nexus of a hundred of trade routes.
4. ASH CAPTION:	Haven for the working and the wayward, those looking to get lost or find their fortune.
5. ASH CAPTION:	It's not home, but I understand it.
6. ASH CAPTION:	I can decipher its discord.
7. ASH CAPTION:	Tease out its secrets and make them my own.

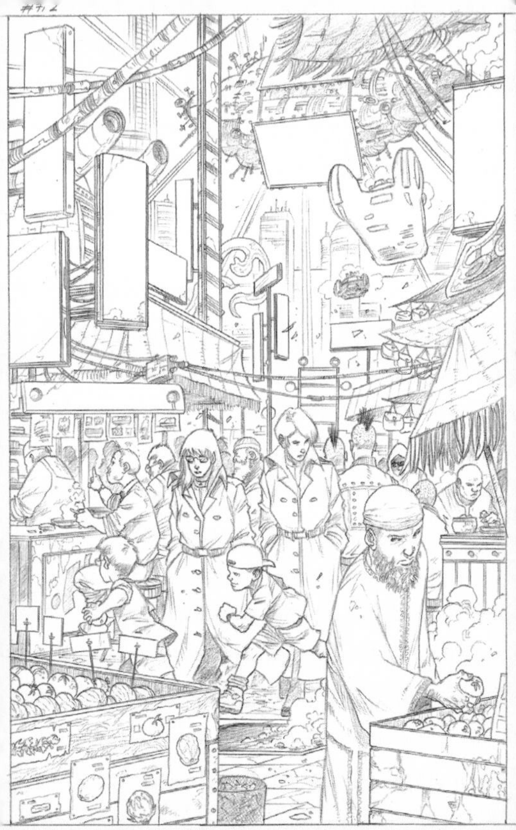
#71 2

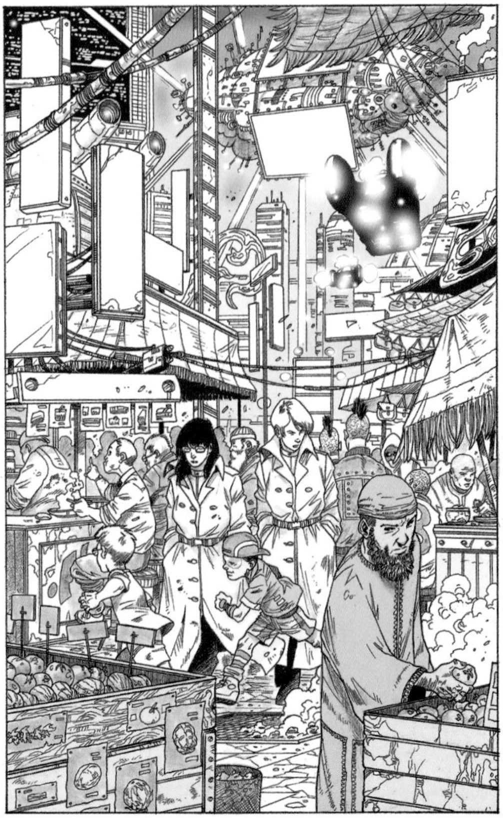

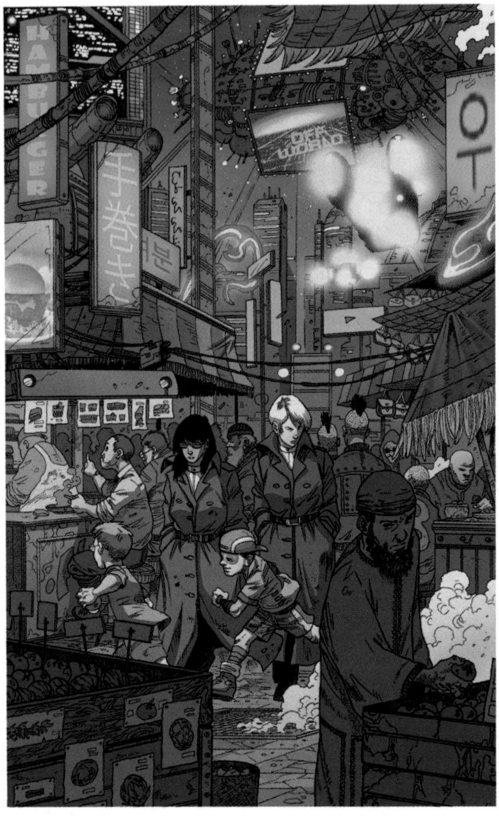
HAMBURGER
手巻き
OFF WORLD

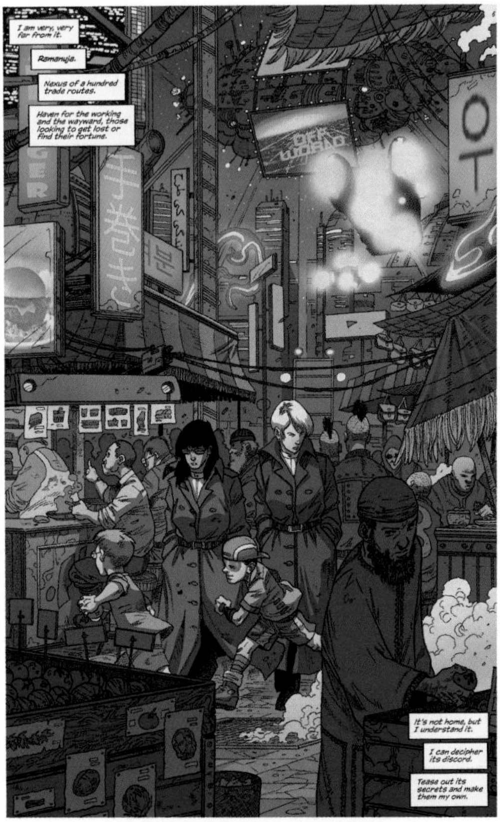
I am very, very far from it.
Ramanuja.
Nexus of a hundred trade routes.
Haven for the working and the wayward, those looking to get lost or find their fortune.
OFF WORLD
It's not home, but I understand it.
I can decipher its discord.
Tease out its secrets and make them my own.

SYD MEAD OBITUARY

Syd Mead called himself a visual futurist, and across his 50-year career, his impact on the world of graphic, product, interior and exterior design, and the cinema cannot be over-estimated. He inspired generations of artists, filmmakers, illustrators, and designers, giving us a glimpse of a future that was always sleek, gleaming, and fantastic, yet utterly plausible. He believed that science fiction was just reality ahead of schedule and his work reveled in the possibilities of what the future held in store for us all.

Sydney Jay Mead was born in St. Paul Minnesota, July 18th, 1933, the son of Kenneth Mead, a Baptist Minister, and Margaret Mead, a homemaker. From an early age, Mead had a passion for science fiction thanks to his father, who introduced him to worlds of *Buck Rogers* and *Flash Gordon* and the science fiction pulps.

Mead showed a natural talent for drawing. After high school and his three-year enlistment in the U.S. Army in 1954, he enrolled in the Art-Center College of Design (then known as the Art-Center School) in Pasadena, California, where he graduated, with distinction, in June 1959.

On leaving college, Mead was immediately recruited by the Ford Motor Company's Advanced Styling Studio where he worked until 1963, before leaving to spend the next two years working for companies such as United States Steel, Celanese, Allis-Chaimers and Atlas Cement, illustrating books and catalogues.

In 1970, Syd established his own design agency in Detroit called Syd Mead Inc. His clients included Philips Electronics, Intercontinental Hotels, 3D International, Harwood Taylor & Associates, Don Ghia, Gresham & Smith and Philip Koether Architects.

In 1973, Mead staged his first international exhibition with a show at the Documenta 6 gallery in Kassel, West Germany. This led to further exhibitions in Japan, Italy, California and Spain.

In 1979, Mead was hired as Production Illustrator for *Star Trek: The Motion Picture*. He followed this with his most significant cinematic work, Ridley Scott's *Blade Runner* (1982), where he designed not only key locations but also the

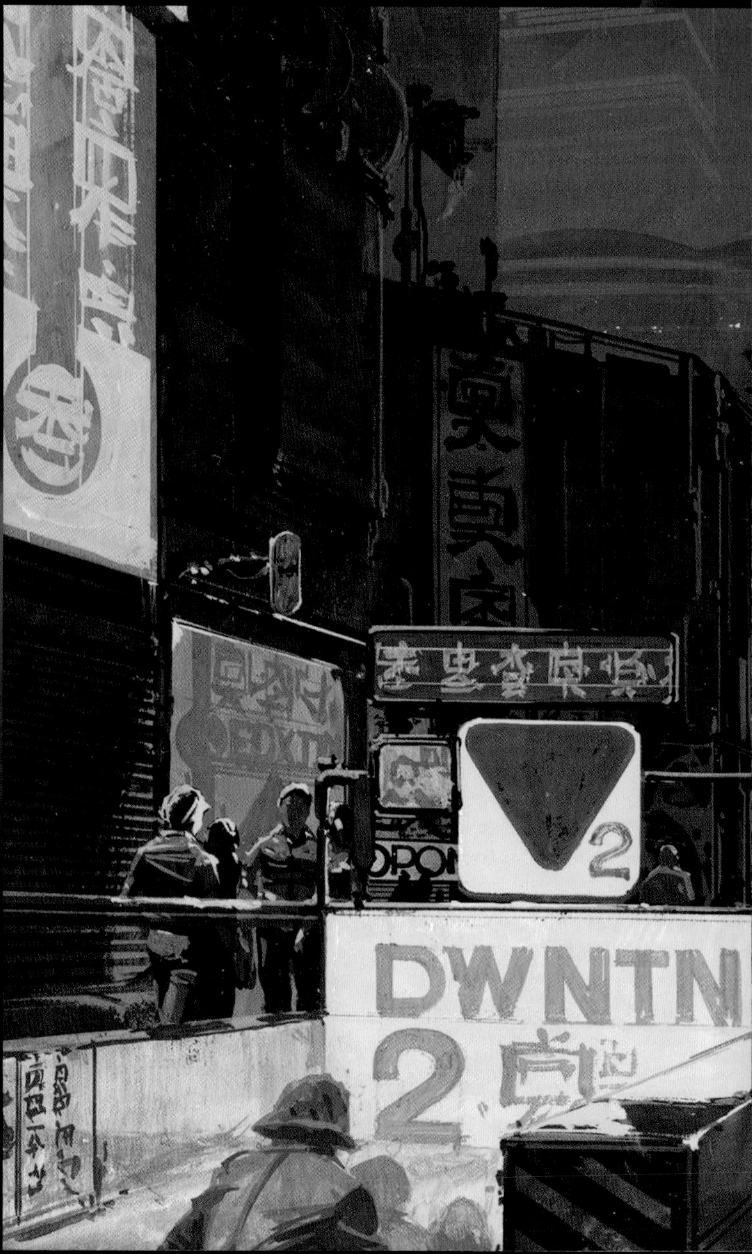
DWNTN
2

iconic Blade Runner blaster and the Spinner flying car. The film also marked the first time he was credited as Visual Futurist. He would go on to work on *TRON* (1982), *2010: The Year We Make Contact* (1984), *Short Circuit* (1986), *Aliens* (1986), *Time Cop* (1994), *Johnny Mnemonic* (1995), *Mission Impossible III* (2006), *Elysium* (2013), *Tomorrowland* (2015), and *Blade Runner 2049* (2017).

By 1983, Mead's client list had expanded to include Sony, Minolta, Dentsu, Dyflex, Tiger Corp, Seibu, Mitsukoshi, Bandai, NHK and Honda. The Chrysler Corporation invited him to be a guest speaker at its design division.

Several more guest-speaker invites followed, with talks for Disney, Carnegie Mellon University, Purdue University, the Pratt Institute and the Society of Illustrators, culminating in a four-city tour of Australia in 2010.

Mead's first love was always vehicular transportation; he designed concept cars, luxury yachts, cruise ships, solar powered unicycles, show cars, and interplanetary spacecraft. He also found time to design the interiors of private 747s, restaurants, and even the Eventi Hotel food court in Chelsea, New York.

In 1998, Mead relocated his studio to Pasadena, California, where he continued to work on various design projects and publish several books.

On December 30th, 2019, Syd Mead succumbed to lymphoma. He is survived by his long time partner and spouse, Roger Servick, and his sister, Peggy Mead.

R.I.P. Syd Mead. American industrial designer, visual futurist and visionary.

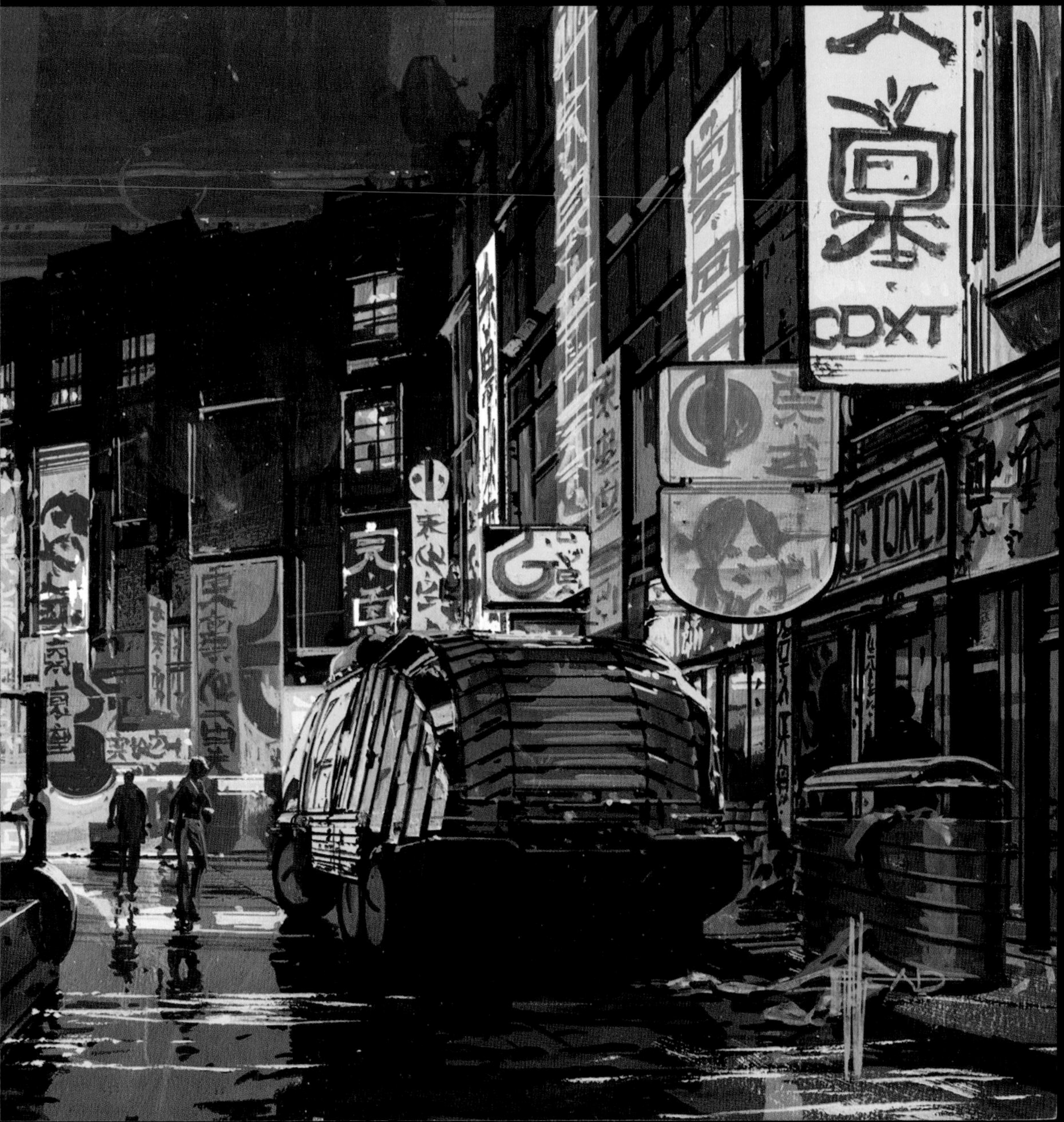
CDXT

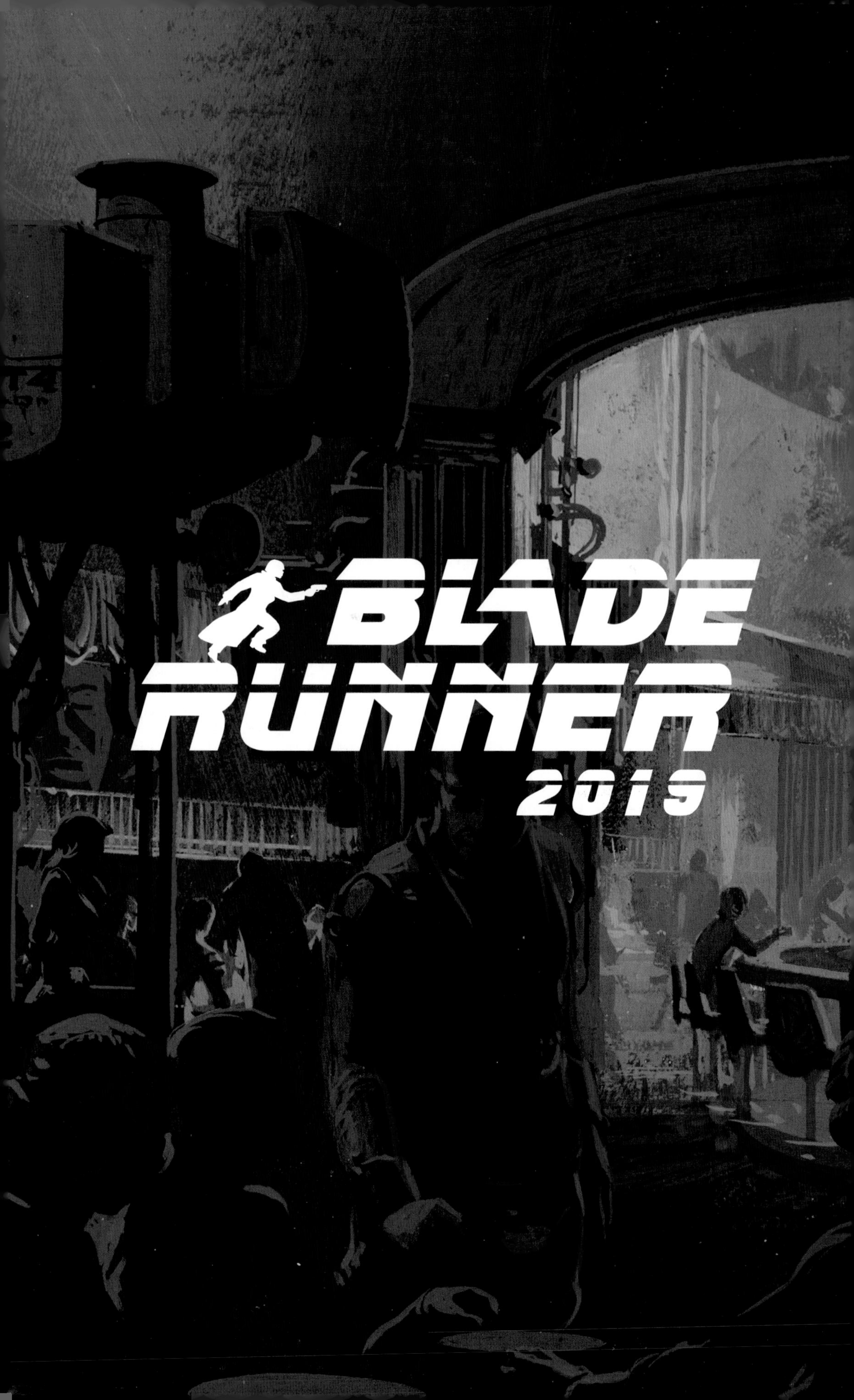
BLADE
RUNNER
2019

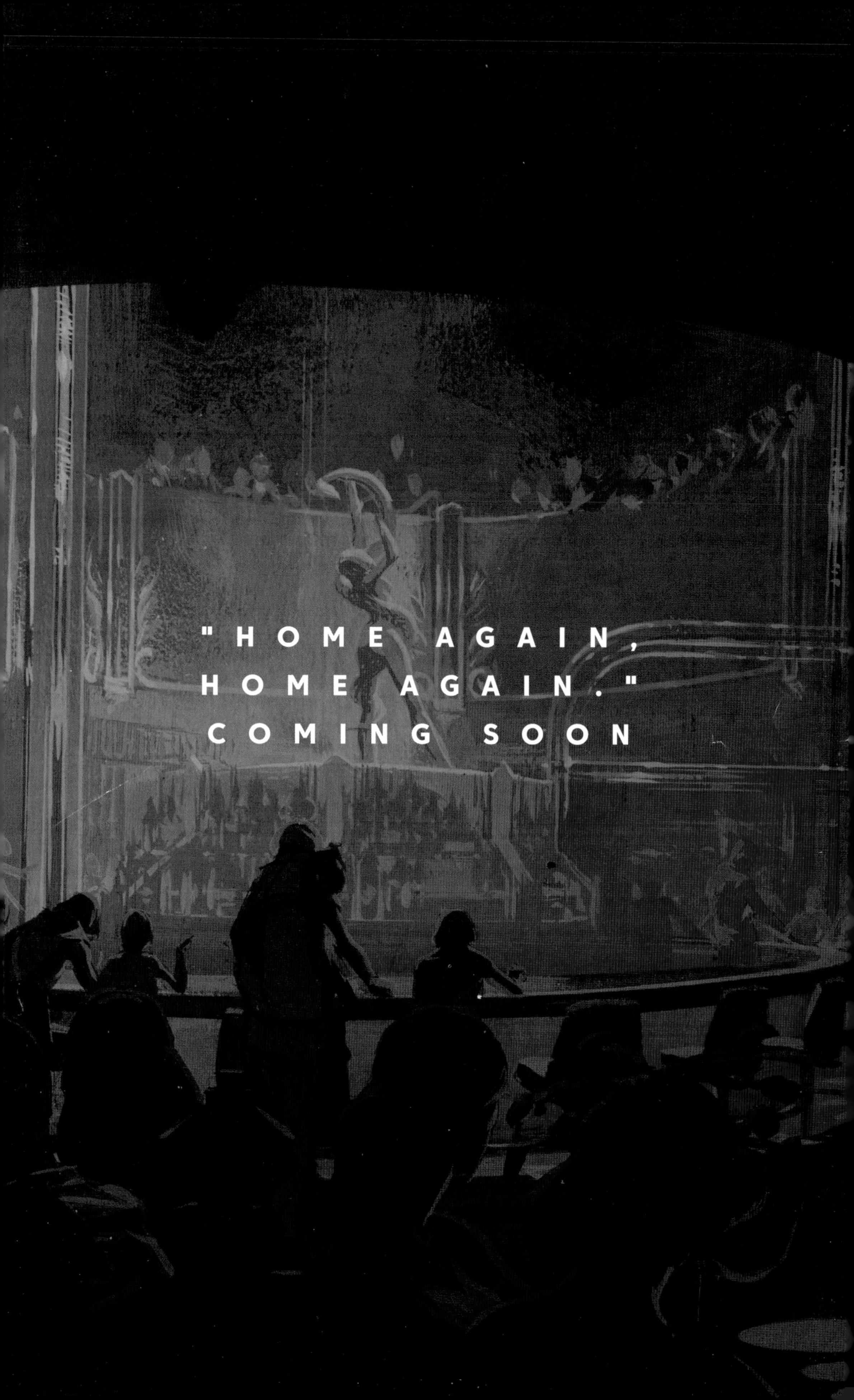
"HOME AGAIN,
HOME AGAIN."
COMING SOON

CREATOR BIOS

MICHAEL GREEN

Michael Green is a film and television writer and producer. His work includes *Blade Runner 2049, Logan, Alien: Covenant, Murder on the Orient Express, American Gods,* and *Kings.*

MIKE JOHNSON

Mike Johnson is a New York Times-bestselling writer of comics, animation and games. His credits include *Star Trek, Transformers, Superman/ Batman, Supergirl, Fringe,* and *Ei8ht.*

ANDRES GUINALDO

Born in 1975, Andres originally studied movie making (direction) at Madrid University before making the move into comics. His first professional work was drawing Joe R. Landsdale's *The Drive-in* and *By Bizarre Hands.* He followed those with *Pistolfist: Revolutionary Warrior, Helios: Under the Gun, Purity,* and *Cartoonapalozza.* In 2010, Guinaldo started regularly penciling *Son of Hulk,* and drew issue #5 of *Dark Reign: Hawkeye.* He followed this with *Gotham City Sirens* #14-17, *Joker's Asylum: The Riddler, Namor: The First Mutant* #4, *Red Lanterns* #8, *Resurrection Man* #9, *Nightwing* #11-14, *Hypernaturals,* and *Justice League Dark.* In recent years he's worked on such diverse titles as *Ninjak* and *Captain America: Steve Rogers.* He currently resides in Segovia, the city of his birth.

MARCO LESKO

Hailing from Brazil, Marco Lesko has been a professional comic book colorist since 2014. His credits include *Rat Queens, Assassin's Creed Uprising, Doctor Who, Robotech, The Shadow* and many more. When he's not coloring comics, he spends endless hours studying color theory from many different areas, including: cinema, conceptual art design, Japanese anime, videogame design, and classic Disney animations.

JIM CAMPBELL

Jim Campbell is an Eisner Award nominated letterer whose work can be seen on everything from Titan's *Robotech* books to *Roy of the Rovers* graphic novels to the *Firefly* series. He lives, works, and very occasionally sleeps in darkest Nottinghamshire, UK, in a house he shares with his wife and an unfeasibly large collection of black clothes.